IT'S NOT JUST CRICKET

To. Barbra (and her
minder Paul!)

Very best wishes and
memories of a lovely
trip "down under"

[signature]

IT'S NOT JUST CRICKET

Peter Walker

FAIRFIELD BOOKS

To my late parents Oliver and Freda

who deserved better all those years ago
when their support never wavered

Fairfield Books

17 George's Road, Fairfield Park, Bath BA1 6EY
Tel 01225-335813

Copyright © Peter Walker

First published 2006
ISBN 0 9544886 4 4

Page design by Niall Allsop

Printed and bound in Great Britain by Bath Press Ltd, Bath

CONTENTS

PREFACE

"I should write a book" is an over-worked cliché. In my case the book has also been a mighty long time in its gestation.

A half-completed manuscript, last looked at in 1961, would have lain where it perhaps belonged, in a trunk in the garage of my home in Cardiff, had it not been for a series of prods from my pal Derek Ingham, with whom I had chewed over our separate youthful experiences of life in the merchant navy.

On the eve of the third Test at Newlands, Cape Town between South Africa and England, Derek and I chatted on the verandah of our hotel room looking up at the magnificence of a floodlit Table Mountain. He was a client of Gullivers Sports Travel, I an ex-Glamorgan and England cricketer, a 'hired gun' employed to jolly things along and discuss cricket matters with the group.

As each new memory surfaced, I wrote down a bullet-point reminder. Over the course of the next three weeks there were literally dozens of these. Fortunately I retain a good recall of off-beat experiences, but later I needed Andrew Hignell, the Glamorgan archivist and scorer, to source many of the photographs from the club's picture library, and professional photographer Colin Sykes, to make some fading old black-and-white stills come alive again. To them both and to the original providers, especially the *Western Mail* and the *South Wales Evening Post*, many, many thanks. My next door neighbour, Grahame Lloyd, himself a published author, then added trenchant criticisms of my text, which sometimes tested our friendship but never broke it.

This book of reminiscences would never have got beyond the hard drive on my PC without the commitment of publishers Stephen Chalke and Susanna Kendall. We've been aided by the laser-eyes of David Smith and Douglas Miller, who have both pulled me up on the occasions when memories of cricketing events, while in essence true, were not altogether factually accurate!

Stand easy in your traps. This is most definitely NOT a book just about cricket – although almost two decades playing the professional game keelhauled me through a gamut of emotional ups and downs. I'm grateful to it too, for its taking me to all parts of the globe where cricket is played, allowing me to live like a millionaire, albeit without the money.

If in patches this book reads like the lifestyle of a pampered playboy, it is. But there are two fundamental differences from this being a memoir of a without-a-care-in-the-world playboy drone. I came to the party without any family financial backing, and I only survived in a tough professional sport because, when it mattered, I had the inner resolve and sufficient talent to, as they say in modern sporting parlance, 'put my hand up and be counted.'

My time at the crease is nearly over; but before the great skipper in the sky finally declares my innings closed, this last task has been principally driven by a desire to let my three children, Sarah, Justin and Daniel, know that their 'idiosyncratic old man' was once young – and very footloose and fancy free.

Peter Walker, July 2006

Chapter 1
AN UNLIKELY BEGINNING ...

Across the deck flew a potato. Back and forth, revolving in small, irregular circles until it disappeared over the ship's side and down into the blue depths of the Pacific Ocean. It was immediately replaced by another from the vast potato lockers on the top deck of an ancient Finnish oil tanker, the M/V *Aruba*.

Potatoes come in all shapes and sizes, demanding flexibility and sure hands on the part of thrower as well as catcher. On the other side of the deck from me stood Bennie Laros, a man who was to play a key role in shaping my attitude to life as well as shaping my professional catching ability.

I'm certain that the fielding records I set in an 18-year cricketing career with Glamorgan, Transvaal, Western Province and England date back to this daily fielding practice done to relieve the boredom of the 80-day journey from the Persian Gulf to the tiny oil port of El Segundo, just south of Los Angeles.

Cricket was later to become my life, my food, my need, a part of my soul and a barometer of my moods. It provided moments of unparalleled joy, bitter disappointment, long-lasting friendships and poorly concealed frustrations. But my start along this rocky road was still two years away.

My love of the game began with an old, dirty white, floppy hat, now one of my most treasured cricketing mementos. It had been on the head of Glamorgan's Allan Watkins, one of the finest close fielders of all time, when in December 1948, during the first Test at Kingsmead in Durban, off the bowling of leg-spinner Doug Wright, he made a brilliant one-handed diving catch to his right at short square leg to remove South African captain and principal batsman, Dudley Nourse.

Dudley Nourse, caught Allan Watkins bowled Doug Wright, 37.
The catch that won a Test match in Durban 1948 and my inspiration.

Allan had given me this memento when, later during the MCC tour, he had come to dinner at the family home in Highlands North – after following up a suggestion from Les Spence, the Honorary Secretary, that when in Johannesburg he should contact an old Canton High School pal of his, Oliver Walker, my father. When five years later I tentatively opened the door to the Glamorgan County Cricket Club offices on the second floor of 6 High Street, Cardiff, in pursuit of cricketing fame, facing me was a photograph of Allan's Kingsmead catch. The die had been cast.

Home and school life was idyllic, with parents both loving and encouraging. School was of no great importance, other than to act as the vehicle for playing as much sport as I could. My father, Birmingham-born but Cardiff-bred, came from good journalistic stock. His father James had been a founder member of the National Union of Journalists and of the Fabian Society, even now an important Labour think-tank. His contemporaries included H.G. Wells, George Bernard Shaw and the Sackville-Wests. Yorkshire-born James and his family migrated from Fleet Street in London to Birmingham and eventually to Cardiff, where he became a legendary figure as a pungent leader-writer columnist for the *Western Mail*, the national morning newspaper of Wales.

At Canton High School my father, tall for his age and wearing glasses from a very early age, was apparently never short of views or words on any issue. As a medium-slow left-arm bowler, cricket was his forte but he was secretly quite proud of being banned, sine die, for vigorously objecting to a referee's decision in a needle football match against his school's main rivals! He also became an accomplished violinist playing in a dance band which, he told me years later, used to wow them in docklands Cardiff in the 1920s.

He emigrated to South Africa in 1938 to escape a smog-ridden Britain which had given him TB and six months in Talgarth Hospital in mid-Wales. My mother and I, then aged two, joined him in Durban later that year. By then he had started 'The Idler' gossip column in the *Natal Mercury* newspaper which is still running 68 years later. During the war we moved north to Pretoria where he'd landed a job with the State-controlled 'Institute of Race Relations'. This gave him an insider's view of the government's separate development policy, known as apartheid, which entrenched racial inequalities in law.

In all but name, post-war South Africa rapidly evolved into a police state where, if you were white and agreed with the government's policies, you could do little wrong. However, being born black gave you no rights and certainly no privileges.

What Oliver Walker learnt and experienced, from living in such a society, dramatically shaped his future political beliefs and writings. By British standards he would have been considered a slightly left-of-centre liberal. But the whites-only government of South Africa regarded people of his persuasion as Communists. Here was a potentially dangerous man and certainly not one to be trusted. They were right, for he became a highly critical published author on the evils and idiocies of the apartheid system. Unsurprisingly it wasn't long before he was asked to leave the Institute. Books such as *White Man Boss*,

Kaffirs are Lively (Kaffir is very much a pejorative word for blacks) and *Kaffirs are Livelier* followed; all had to be written under a nom de plume and printed in Britain. They were inevitably banned by the South African censors.

A biography of John Dunn, a 19th century white adventurer who had 'gone native' by living with and marrying nearly 40 Zulu maidens and fathering over 100 children, had to undergo a title change as the original *White Zulu* was too strong a mix for the South African authorities to allow into the country. In order to circumvent the censors and much to my father's chagrin, its descriptively accurate title had to metamorphose into *Proud Zulu*. Oliver Walker was in good company for that same department also banned the children's classic *Black Beauty* for the same reason! In post-war South Africa, black was most certainly NOT beautiful.

The Afrikaner government passed legislation which enabled them to slap 90-day house arrests on dissidents who, they believed, were not toeing the party line but against whom they did not have enough firm evidence to convict in the courts. My father twice received official notification that he was under surveillance. Plain-clothes policemen watching him became familiar figures at concerts and theatres he attended in his capacity as the Music & Literary Editor of *The Star, Johannesburg*, Africa's largest-selling evening newspaper. Neither warning actually led to his being put under house arrest, but the suspicion – and the threat – hung over him until his death.

Despite this, soon-to-be-banned African National Congress members including Nelson Mandela and Walter Sisulu were occasionally smuggled under cover of darkness into our house. This enabled my father to be kept abreast of African thinking. There was a passing parade, too, of visiting international musicians, painters, sculptors and authors as well as fellow white political activists. All this meant life in the Walker household was never dull and, as a juvenile eavesdropper, their discussions certainly widened my perspective and made me question life in what was even then advertised as 'sunny South Africa'.

By the time he died aged 59, playing golf on Christmas Day 1965, my father had become recognised as the most influential theatre and music critic in South Africa. His trenchant comments on the poor standards of artistic life in that country won him many admirers but an almost equal number of cultural enemies, too. As a boy, when I accompanied him to concerts given by the Johannesburg Symphony Orchestra, he instilled in me a love of classical music. Thanks to a large number of talented European musicians who had fled the early stages of the Nazi march across Europe, the orchestra was a highly skilled, professional outfit who drew large audiences to their concerts.

There are always regrets which linger. Mine is that I never really knew or was able to talk to my father on a man-to-man basis until the last time I saw him alive. In November '65 we had dinner together in a very ordinary restaurant in Newport, Gwent, before he flew back to South Africa and his appointment with his maker a month later when he suffered a massive heart attack on the fifth hole at Kyalami golf course near Johannesburg.

My mother had met Oliver when he was working as motoring correspondent on the now defunct *Bristol Evening World*. Faded sepia photographs from the 1930s show her as a typically clean-cut young lady of her time, he more like a member of Al Capone's bodyguard in double breasted pin-striped suit, trilby hat, cigar and slicked-down, centrally parted hair. Freda Miller was a far more accomplished all-round sports person than her husband, who had played for the Cardiff Cricket Club. She was of Somerset County standard in both tennis and golf and a very capable pianist to boot. However, in her early twenties, a heavy fall down a steep, wet, grassy bank at Knowle golf club in Bristol set off the development of rheumatoid arthritis in her left hip. By mid-life this had led to a marked shortening of that leg and ever-present pain. The tumble ended her sporting career, but not her love of music or her family. She was everything a mother should be: uncomplaining, supportive and never failing to put others before herself.

Oliver Walker and Freda Miller's wedding, Bristol 1935.

My brother Tim, seven years my junior, had sporting talent, too. To this day he maintains that, excluding Geoffrey Boycott, he had the finest forward defensive shot in cricket. But tennis, up to Transvaal Junior squad level, and eventually table tennis were his forte.

On the domestic culture front the family taped a wholly improvised soap opera we called 'The Shooting of Bunkhouse Boris'. Brother Tim, then aged four, played the monosyllabic lead role of Boris. His main contribution was to provide some very terminal-sounding strangulated grunts. This production came about after my father had acquired one of the first domestic tape recorders imported into South Africa, and the end product rivalled in awfulness any of Ernie Wise's 'a play what I wrote'. I have the Boris master tape to this day – hidden safely away.

Tim developed a teenage passion and talent for playing, and eventually teaching, the guitar. It quickly came to dominate his life. Initially inspired by rock'n'roll guitarist Tommy Steele, Tim soon gravitated to the more musically highbrow climate within our home at number 74, 5th Avenue, Highlands North, Johannesburg. I have vivid memories of his endless, mind-blowingly boring, repetitive scale and arpeggio practice sessions; they nearly drove me and the rest of the household to strong drink. While still at High School, Tim eagerly accepted an invitation to decamp to Spain where he studied under the tutelage of renowned concert guitarist Narcisso Yepès and had several master classes with Andrés Segovia.

Oliver Walker, music critic of the *Johannesburg Star* newspaper, with younger son Tim and his new Ramirez guitar.

Later, as a concert performer in his own right, Tim went on to tour the world, becoming in the process a guitarist and composer, consulted by high-profile practitioners like John Williams on fiendishly difficult pieces written by modern composers such as Peter Maxwell Davies and David Bedford. For more than a decade he has tutored the guitar at the Royal Academy of Music in London.

Off duty my brother has concentrated on building two small, soundproofed wooden sheds in his back garden, perfect for those still-ongoing scale and arpeggio sessions, and a couple of shallow pools into which he puts goldfish won at various fairs. The fish rarely survive the shock or his tender ministrations. He's a Bohemian in the truest sense – somewhat different from his older brother.

He is a living reminder of our parents and in particular our father, for – to my ear – Tim's vocal pitch and manner of speaking are almost identical.

My own early ambition, aged eight, was to become a circus performer – then, as a teenager, a TT motorcyclist. A Johannesburg high school pal Clive Jacobs and I thought that we'd build our own underground repair workshop. It was of truly massive proportions; an eight-foot deep hole which took up most of our back garden at the then family home, 43 Dunvegan Street in Sydenham, a middle-class suburb of Johannesburg. After two months of Herculean digging and on the point of roofing it with some corrugated sheeting 'borrowed' from a nearby building site, we stood aghast and watched as the arrival of unseasonal torrential rains caused the four earth walls to collapse inwards.

When his time was up, I had to bury my favourite mongrel dog Pluto in the ruins of our collapsed workshop to end a relationship, but not the memory of a very close and special pal.

During this period I listened in wonderment to the first long-playing records to arrive in South Africa. As music critic of *The Star* my father had been given two discs of the Italian/American violin virtuoso Ruggerio Ricci, playing the incredibly difficult 24 Paganini caprices. It was an electrifying experience and helped to confirm my growing love of classical music.

At school, while academically speaking I batted in the middle order, I did achieve a rudimentary but, in those days essential, knowledge of Afrikaans, thanks to two holidays with the van Zyl family who spoke that language – but no English! The first, on their farm in the northern Cape, the other in the far north of the country near Louis Trichardt, a frontier town named after a Boer leader on the Great Trek. Even then, in the early 1950s, in the evenings you could still hear lions roar on the plains at the foot of the nearby Zoutpansberg mountains. I hero-worshipped the van Zyl's eldest son, 16-year-old Pierre, and through dense bush I followed in his footsteps in the ultimately successful pursuit of a wounded kudu bull.

They were free and open days, uncomplicated by any concern about what might lie ahead.

CHAPTER 2
DREAMS COME TRUE

As a 12-year-old at Orange Grove Primary School in Johannesburg, my left-arm fast bowling put the fear of God into all opposing batsmen – or so I believed. Batting and fielding were very much add-ons.

Two years later, and with me now at Highlands North High School, Allan Watkins was again our guest for dinner. He, in the company of two other Glamorgan stalwarts, Emrys and Dai Davies, who shared a surname but not much else, spent several winters in the 1950s, coaching in numerous Johannesburg secondary schools.

The cricket-biased dinner-table talk changed my perception on the role of fielding. Allan passionately argued for its importance, his theme being that a great catch in the last few minutes of a game could deliver an unlikely victory, while a dropped one could lead to an unexpected defeat.

I became one of a hundred boys selected to receive twice-weekly coaching at Ellis Park, then the Test ground for both cricket and rugby. It must have been pure hell for the three Welshmen for they had to handle a huge variety of skill levels. We were segregated according to height not age. As I was nearly six feet tall at the time and still growing, I found myself fending off bouncers and being hit for miles by lads three years older than myself. Tough though this was, it provided an excellent learning environment. It was there that Allan counselled me to turn to bowling slow left-hand orthodox spin: "You'll last much longer in the game than if you charge in without knowing where it's going. And, in any case, it's too bloody hot to bowl fast out here." It proved sound and lasting advice.

Little did either of us guess that six years later we'd be having the same sort of conversation side by side on the first-class cricket fields of England!

At the end of each mass coaching session Allan, Emrys and Dai thankfully retired to enjoy a few cold Castle lagers. They probably hardly noticed that several balls had gone missing. Two friends and I had hidden these out of sight and, when they'd gone and the coast was clear, we'd spend an hour practising our fielding skills, in our imaginations thinking that we were great cover points. Unfortunately I was the only of us one to make anything of our aspirations. Alan Fieldgate tragically lost an eye in a firework incident, and Graham Tyler developed osteoarthritis in his early twenties. Given average luck I believe that both would have made it, certainly to provincial level.

Cricket had now become my obsession. So much so that I walked two miles each way from my home, three evenings a week, just to stand behind the Old Johannians senior club nets at their beautiful Linksfield ground, now transformed into a housing estate. I learnt so much by watching Springbok batsmen like Bruce Mitchell, Russell Endean and Ronnie Grieveson from close up. Very occasionally, as dusk fell, they allowed me to face a few balls. For a State-educated schoolboy like myself, being granted this privilege by the old boys of one of South Africa's leading public schools, was like being thrown a few crumbs from the table at the Last Supper.

Academic work was a necessary chore relieved, in part, by playing the kettledrum in our school cadet band which regularly finished in the top three in the Annual Band competition for Johannesburg high schools. I was happy to let my school pals get on with minor things like exams and career planning. However, I had followed both my parents and younger brother Tim by learning a musical instrument: not the drums, the clarinet. Through my father's contacts within the Johannesburg Symphony Orchestra, I was tutored by Jaap van Opstal, a Dutch refugee from the Second World War. He was principal clarinettist in the orchestra, and he soon became exasperated by my lack of preparation for his weekly visits to our home.

Highlands North High School, Johannesburg 1952. The clarinettist has a limited musical future.

"Do you want to be the best cricketer among clarinettists or the best clarinet player among the cricketers?" he asked one day. In my mind, there was only one choice.

To achieve this, I had a plan. I ran away to sea!

For around two years Roddy Clarke, a classmate of mine, and I had discussed skipping school to reach our respective goals: he to travel to Moscow to meet Stalin (Roddy was already a highly-committed Communist), I to get a trial with Glamorgan or even Gloucestershire, the county of my birth.

Remember, in 1952 we were two unworldly 16-year-olds whose every dream could come true. Roddy had no interest in sport but was intelligent, mischievous in the classroom and single-minded about matters which interested him. Stalin fitted into this category. During school breaks in the first eight months of 1952, our proposed adventure was the sole topic of conversation. He already had a passport, I needed one. So we decided that I'd tell my parents that, during the October school holidays, Roddy and I wanted to make a camping trip to Lourenço Marques, the capital of Portuguese East Africa, now Maputu in Mozambique. I would have to have a passport and, because I'd been born in Bristol, I asked, "Could it be a British one please?"

Unexpectedly my parents agreed to the passport application and our camping idea. And why not? Home life was loving, interesting and varied. I was doing enough academic work at school to pass exams, and my sporting skills were developing too.

We must have been mad! Consider this as but one example. We'd already decided that, if we couldn't find a ship which would sign us on, then we'd hitch-hike 6,000 miles up Africa, an even darker, dark continent then than now. We were oblivious to the fact that, throughout the continent, there was precious little by way of transport infrastructure while there were plenty of wild animals roaming free, most of them almost certainly in need of a square meal, while the natives were likely to be equally unfriendly.

We clubbed together and, for an outlay of £2, bought ourselves a compass at the Johannesburg Army and Navy store in the belief that this would be enough of an aid to guide us north until we reached the Mediterranean. Right, we thought, that's one possible little difficulty out of the way!

So, in early October 1952, my father pressed two £10 notes in my hand as pocket money and Roddy and I caught the train in Johannesburg, waving goodbye to our respective parents as we set off for what they thought was a 10-day holiday to Lourenço Marques. In my case, it lasted 15 months!

As we got off the train in LM, unsurprisingly we both felt the first chill of cold feet. Across the road from the station we booked into the run-down Hotel Central and went into the bar to consider what to do next. There sat a powerfully built, blonde-haired Swedish sailor. Sensing that we were somewhat 'all at sea', and hearing us speaking English, he introduced himself. "My name's Bengt, do you fancy a beer?" While he was curious to know what had brought two South African schoolboys to LM, as we chatted he told us that his ship was due to sail at noon the next day; their crew was short, as four of them had picked up a dose of the pox in a Korean brothel. He was having his last drink ashore before going back on board. The news about the ship, not the sailors, rekindled our flagging spirit of adventure. Without any sea-going experience we asked Bengt if he thought that his ship would take us on. Before going back to his ship, he said that he'd call into the ship agent's office to see if this was possible and we arranged to meet again after breakfast the next day.

A restless night passed. But, true to his word, early next morning Bengt was back at the Hotel Central. The answer was 'yes!'

The agent must have known he was looking at a couple of runaway kids, but he had to fill the missing places in his ship. In broken English he dutifully asked for letters from our parents to prove that we had their consent. Roddy and I literally ran back to the Central Hotel and, with shaking hands, quickly forged what he wanted.

In a very schoolboy hand, mine said… 'This is to certify that my son, Peter Michael Walker, has my full permission to go to England by sea. Yours faithfully, Mrs. Oliver Walker.'

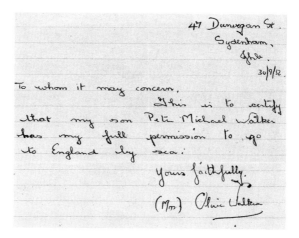

The agent barely looked at our letters before signing us on.

Within 24 hours of arriving in LM, Roddy and I had become crew members of a Swedish tanker, the *Soya Andrea*.

Good luck, be it in civvy street or on the sporting field, is central to realising hopes and ambitions.

The ship left port. Roddy, now a saloon boy, and I, a deck hand, stood amidships being seasick as we watched the African coastline gradually disappear with us both thinking, "what the hell have we done?"

We sent telegrams to our parents, tapped out by the *Soya Andrea*'s radio officer, which briefly explained what had happened and that we were headed to pick up a cargo of crude oil at Mina al Ahmadi in the Persian Gulf. What else could we say? Anxiously we awaited their replies. After our parents' initial shock, their first reaction was to try to get us back. But they soon realised that the reality of the situation made this impossible. So, no doubt with anxious, breaking hearts, mine sent me a telegram with their love, wishing me well and asking me to please keep in regular touch. They had always been caring parents, but this truly was an act of extraordinary forgiveness and support on their part. Their advice and suggestions, in letters which eventually caught up with me wherever I happened to be in the world in the months ahead, were heart-warming, reassuring and invaluable. They helped to keep my resolution firm on the many occasions it wavered.

However, I soon wrote saying that I was homesick and I wanted to come straight back to South Africa, once we'd reached Europe. In reply, they were persuasively adamant that I should not do so but that I ought to make the most of this unexpected chance to see and experience a world outside South Africa. Had I not acted on their sound advice, I certainly would not have had such a story to tell.

MV Soya Andrea. Swedish tanker, built 1952. My first voyage into the unknown.

While we were anchored outside the Portuguese East African port of Beira, awaiting a berth to take on some extra fuel oil, Bengt, now a firm friend and mentor, and I were detailed to paint the bow section of the hull. This meant standing on a ten-foot-long, nine-inch-wide wooden plank suspended at each end from the deck railings by a rope. As the bow of the ship curved inwards, another rope, strung behind the two vertical ones, pulled us in close to the side. I was at one end of the plank, Able Seaman Bengt at the other. We started off painting not far from the vast anchor.

As I concentrated on the task in hand and unnoticed by me, the tide was on the turn, the vessel moving imperceptibly with it, too. It was only a yell from Bengt – "look out, Peter" – that made me turn to my left to see the massive links of the anchor chain about to crush my end of the plank and probably me too. A plunge into shark-infested waters would have been the only other option.

Without thinking of his own safety, Bengt literally ran along the plank, grabbed me by the arm and rushed us back and half way up the rope ladder at his end. Less than a minute later, the chain crushed our makeshift platform to pulp!

While in Beira I found a tattered old copy of the prudish naturist magazine *Health & Efficiency.* It was the only English language publication I could find ashore, and it helped to draw my attention to the differences between men and women. But in Beira there was no opportunity to put into practice any of the thoughts that were suggested to my young mind.

At 11,425 tons, by 21st century standards the *Soya Andrea* was a very small tanker indeed. When we arrived in the Persian Gulf it was not only stinkingly hot, way over 100 degrees Fahrenheit day and night, but the Gulf was in a state of ferment, with a rising tide of nationalism driving out foreign workers. We anchored a mile off the tiny port of Mina al Ahmadi to await permission to tie up and load a cargo of crude oil. It took three weeks before that was granted and, in the meantime, we continued with our main ongoing chore, the painting of the deck. It was back-breaking work, not helped by the fact that, as fast as we put it on, the paint bubbled in the heat. It was certainly a huge relief to leave the Gulf and head into the Red Sea and Suez Canal, bound for our cargo's destination, an oil refinery in Rotterdam.

Shipboard life can be excruciatingly boring. That old ditty, 'we joined the navy to see the world and what did we see? We saw the sea!', hits the bull's-eye.

In 1952, Egypt and the Suez Canal were volatile areas. Bengt had become something of a surrogate parent to me, so much so that in the Suez Canal he was again to save my life. King Farouq had recently been deposed and the United Kingdom was perceived to have played a major, behind-the-scenes part in the destabilisation of the area. True or false, this had aroused huge local antagonism towards anything or anyone British.

At Ismailiya, the point in the canal where convoys of ships from opposite directions pass each other, we'd taken on board a collection of bumboat men. These were traders who sold knick-knack souvenirs of variable quality. Through passing acquaintance with every national flag which had a merchant marine, most could hold a conversation in anything up to 15 different languages. Also on board came a number of labourers who were responsible for tending the ropes which secured us to the shore whenever we were stationary in the canal. One of these, a swarthy, surly-looking character heard me speaking English to Bengt. When I was alone, he approached and asked me where I came from. I made a key mistake of saying, 'England'. His attitude immediately changed and, looking around to ensure that no one could overhear him, he hissed, "You English are trying to take my country. Because of that, I am going to kill you."

This was not why I'd run away to sea! As the *Soya Andrea* was a new ship, each person on board had the luxury of their own cabin but, in case of an emergency, none had locking doors. Also, to allow any seas that were shipped in bad weather to run away through strategically placed drains, there were two foot-high sills on the edges of the corridor which one had to step over in order to enter a cabin. That night, fearful of what might lie ahead, I bunked down on the floor. Sometime during the night, the door above me gently swung open and there, silhouetted in the corridor light, knife in hand, was the Egyptian! I yelled out. Not expecting a voice from deck level, the surprise unnerved him and he turned and ran off. It continued to be a sleepless night.

Next morning I relayed this to Bengt, who was varnishing some woodwork. "Which one is it?" he asked. I pointed out the man, then coiling a rope near the stern. My shipmate said nothing but just walked up behind the unsuspecting Egyptian, grabbed him by the neck and under the crotch and heaved him over the side and down some 40 feet into the Suez Canal!

"That should stop him, Peter," said Bengt, with a small smile as he sauntered back to his briefly interrupted task. I had no idea whether the Egyptian could swim or not. Frankly, I didn't look – nor care.

Ten days later in Rotterdam and during my usual 4 to 8 a.m. watch, I saw my first snow. Large, Christmas-card-sized flakes they were too, which stopped me in wonderment from my task of opening the huge hatch lids on deck to release the highly inflammatory gas left over by our now discharged cargo of crude oil. This was backbreaking work but even more taxing as it had to be done in near sub-zero temperatures.

But a surprising end was in sight. On its maiden voyage to Japan six months earlier, the *Soya Andrea* had taken a hit from an overzealous tug and sustained a small hole in the bow. It needed to be repaired. Luck was again on my side. The dry dock selected was Bailey's Shipyard in Barry, South Wales!

So, it had been Johannesburg to Wales. For me it had been almost door-to-door service.

When Roddy and I had set off from Johannesburg station on our journey into the unknown, I had two objectives. I'd made it into the school first cricket eleven, aged 16, but, because of my early flirtation with the clarinet, I thought this career might be worth examining, too. With music filling the house in Johannesburg, highly accomplished musical parents and a brother who was later to become a classical guitarist of repute, this was hardly surprising. Indeed, on the prompting of my parents, when I eventually made it to London, I did call into the Royal Academy and Guildhall Schools of Music to see about enrolling. But my playing standards were nowhere near high enough. and any aspirations in this field were soon extinguished.

Roddy also had a British passport so, after paying off the ship with me, my chunky, tousle-haired class-mate turned his face east. But before setting off for Moscow and his hoped-for audience with his hero Joseph Stalin, he went to see some relatives who lived in Newcastle-upon-Tyne. He got no further than that. A year or so later I learnt that during his visit north the Lord had got to him first. Roddy became a Christian and eventually a lay preacher, too. Later still, I learnt that he'd travelled back to South Africa and gone into the shoe-manufacturing business in Port Elizabeth. Industry's gain was Stalin's loss. So unlike me, and a complex character to boot, was my friend Roddy Clarke.

Although Bristol born, because of my father's upbringing in Cardiff I'd always regarded Wales as my ancestral home. The cricketing tuition I'd received from Allan Watkins and Dai and Emrys Davies had cemented this feeling. I thought I'd look them up, forgetting for the moment that, as the English county cricket season had ended three months earlier, they had all disappeared overseas again.

I had only a winter in the United Kingdom to look forward to.

CHAPTER 3

AROUND THE WORLD IN
A LOT MORE THAN 80 DAYS

Christmas 1952 was spent getting to know my paternal grandparents in Cardiff. This often meant joining a group of ancient Yorkshire-born ex-pats playing whist in a room above the old Capitol cinema in Queen Street. In between, I attempted to get a better understanding of the extraordinary mood swings of Eva, my maternal grandmother in Bristol. Her sister Milly had a daughter called Joyce, and their home in Kingsdown, Bristol, became something of a refuge for me. Milly prided herself on having the most highly polished brass door step in the street. Often when I called, she'd be on her knees with a tin of Brasso in one hand, shining away!

The damp and biting cold of the early part of a British winter compounded my growing feeling that the trip to Lourenço Marques had not been the brightest move I'd made so far in my short life. But what to do next?

If I wanted to escape freezing to death, there seemed to be little option but to go back to sea – or South Africa. In the month of January I scoured the Cardiff and Bristol papers looking for a job, any job. I did have a couple of interviews, but these came to nothing. Then luck played its part, with my father's eldest brother Richard providing the required helping hand. A seaman all his life, he served first in the merchant navy, then – during the War – in the Royal Navy. Back in the 1930s he'd spent four years, in two spells, in the Antarctic as first mate on the *John Briscoe* and *Discovery II* survey ships. During this time he had had a mountain named after him and been marooned on the mainland and reported lost with four colleagues during a blizzard which lasted three weeks. As the officer in command he had to organise a rudimentary shelter on a pebble beach under their upturned longboat with icy seas frequently dousing

Commander Richard Walker RN. An uncle who kept me afloat in every sense.

them. The food supplies soon ran out and, before their eventual rescue, they were forced to live off raw penguins they'd captured and skinned.

In his second two-year spell he found time to win the Polar medal – the equivalent of a peace-time Victoria Cross – for man-hauling a sledge with three others, in the style of Captain Robert Falcon Scott, to rescue American aviator Lincoln Ellsworth who had crash-landed while attempting to become the first man to fly over the Antarctic land mass. Quite a man was Richard.

While I was still hunting around for a job, Richard suggested that I should consider joining his old ship *Discovery II*. That sounded interesting but, when I heard that it would be for a two-year stretch surveying the Antarctic coastline in sub-zero temperatures, my interest quickly froze. I desperately felt in need of some heat. The idea of staying put, awaiting the distant return of an English summer and the cricket season, was an awful thought to a youngster used to a shorts and t-shirt lifestyle and often going barefoot too. But through his contacts Richard, then the Haven Master at Avonmouth and in charge of the Bristol Channel pilots, did turn up a trump card which provided me with a route out.

An ex-Royal Naval pal of his ran a shipping agency in Rotterdam. A call to him, and on offer came a placement as third cook on an aged Finnish oil tanker the *MV Aruba* which had just completed a three-month engine refit. Would I be interested? And how! – particularly as one of my souvenirs from my *Soya Andrea* days had been the chef's white, stovepipe hat.

MV Aruba. Ancient Finnish tanker which took me around the world. It provided an unlikely platform for developing my catching skills.

No longer having Roddy as a travelling companion, I was the only Englishman on board amongst 38 Finns and two other foreigners: a pocket-battleship of a Dutchman called Benny Laros, who inadvertently was to help to develop my catching skills, and a stateless able seaman from Czechoslovakia called Mike. Like the *Marie Celeste*, Mike seemed doomed to roam for ever the seas.

Two days out of Rotterdam our engines packed in, the first of many such occasions, and I had been unmasked as a 'cook' who could barely boil water! Demoted to galley boy, I spent the next five months peeling potatoes and stirring a Finish delicacy, a foul-smelling combination of pig's trotters and boiled cabbage. As our engine troubles continued on an almost daily basis, the trip through the Suez Canal – no sign of my intended assassin this time – to Ras Tannurah in the Persian Gulf to pick up a cargo of crude oil, took a month instead of the scheduled ten days.

Not even the flashing 'Welcome' sign of a café at the end of the Ras Tannurah jetty, advertising camel burgers, held the same appeal as an offer to jump ship and join an American tanker which had tied up alongside us. They were plying their trade between the Gulf and the Korean War. It sounded attractive, particularly as the wages were double the *Aruba*'s and there was a 100% loading on top of this because they were operating in a war zone where tankers carrying fuel were prime targets. However, the thought of spending up to a year on this run would have thwarted my ambition to get back to the UK in time for the start of the 1953 cricket season, so I held back. Surely, considering our engine problems, we were bound to return to the same Rotterdam dry dock, which would coincide nicely with the arrival of spring.

What happened next made me bitterly regret my decision not to join the Yanks. Tankers operate like trinket salesmen, prepared to go anywhere in search of a sale. The *Aruba* was a lumbering old barge of a ship, 30 years old at the time and with a top speed in a following gale of seven knots – that's well under ten land miles an hour. Steaming out of the Gulf, we awaited our next instructions via the ship's radio. Two days passed. Nothing. Then, to the officers' and crew's amazement came the instruction, 'Head for Los Angeles and await further directions.'

This would be a trip from the Gulf, across the Indian Ocean, through the Straits of Malacca, past Borneo and then across the whole vastness of the Pacific Ocean by-passing Hawaii. In all, a distance of around 11,000 miles and taking the best part of three months to achieve! As well as stretching our food supplies to the limit, hopes of a season playing cricket vanished.

My diary gives a graphic account of what happened next:

When these orders were received and handed out to the crew there was as near to a mutiny as one gets in the merchant navy these days. By an unhappy coincidence it was also the one night of the month when the crew were allocated a liquor ration. By ten in the evening an oppressive, aggressively sullen atmosphere prevailed in the crew's mess room.

When they've had too much booze, Scandinavian seamen are a notoriously ugly bunch. Their first reaction to a minor disagreement is almost invariably a major punch-up. When this happens, it's no place for a 17-year-old Englishman.

But at this point the relationship between me and the bosun, Dutchman Bernados 'Benny' Laros, was cemented. Pushing me inside his cabin, he stood guard at the door. We didn't have long to wait. A huge able seaman picked up a glass ashtray, smashed it on a table and attacked the bosun with it, because for some unjustifiable reason he had been blamed for the orders. There was blood everywhere as the rest of the crew joined in. The battles raged up and down the corridors, and twice Benny had to repulse boarders, felling one with a right, the other with a left hook which I later found out belonged to the one-time cruiserweight champion of New Jersey, USA. The officers meanwhile stayed put amidships until this particular storm had abated. The second mate, traditionally the medical officer, then began some rudimentary stitching and other repairs. The engines too eventually calmed down and, resigned to their fate, gave no further trouble until we reached the west coast of America. I returned to my sole solace, a clarinet which I'd bought in Bristol en route to Rotterdam. It was later to torture many a Glamorgan dressing room.

Benny Laros, almost as broad as he was high and an extrovert personality to boot, had an extraordinary background. He'd left school at 12, kicked around Holland leading a gypsy life, joined the merchant navy, jumped ship at the age of 19 in New York and, carrying a devastating punch in either hand, became a professional boxer. Without a work permit he won 12 of his 13 professional fights before being betrayed to the Immigration Department by a woman he'd let down. Three months in the notoriously tough Ellis Island deportee centre followed before he was shipped back to Holland where he returned to his previous life in the merchant marine.

This had happened five years previously. Without finance and without a formal education, Benny had acquired conversational skills in no fewer than 12 languages, including Arabic. Whenever he went through the Suez canal his speciality was to take what he regarded as 'some easy money' from the highly skilled Egyptian card-players who always came on board. As a master of most card games, Benny excelled at Casino, the most popular game in the canal. It required great powers of recall over the cards played and those still outstanding.

Benny was also mischievous. During our long, crawling progress across the Pacific and with the mate on watch half-asleep in the chart room, Bennie at the wheel steered the ship in a long, slow 360 degrees turn and back on course. This played havoc with the mate's calculation of dead reckoning – the actual distance travelled against the reading of the sextant which gave an altogether different figure.

Benny Laros was to teach me many things which were of immense use when a career in professional cricket came my way, above all self-reliance.

Three months is a long time to remain in a state of boredom. Sure, the clarinet helped. But, after the accordion-playing Chief Steward and I had regularly butchered an arrangement of a Weber clarinet concerto transcribed for piano and clarinet, we had to desist in order to avoid ourselves and our instruments being chucked over the side by crew members who did not share our taste in music. Evening hours in particular dragged by, even though I watched fascinated by the phosphorus in the sea glowing and sparkling and flying fish which passed us by at deck height as they glided often 40 yards through the air.

Little lightened the gloom. I experimented with covering a small box with the burnt ends of matches forming a delicate pattern. Although it did pass the time, it too was mind-blowingly boring. I was desperate to do something less cerebral and certainly more physical. Benny now provided both opportunities.

One day as we sat on the afterdeck chatting inconsequentially and looking at the vast, empty, blue Pacific he suggested, "Let's pitch each other a few catches." "Sure, but where and how?" I replied adding, "and anyway we haven't got a ball." "Follow me," said Benny. We went up a steel ladder leading to the boat deck. There stood two very large lockers containing, as I knew from my galley-boy duties, our substantial stock of potatoes. "You go port side and I'll take the starboard. And we'll keep throwing a potato to each other until one of us drops it, or more likely it goes over the wall. First one to drop five loses," smiled Benny. He turned and strolled over to the starboard rail saying over his shoulder, "Oh, by the way, I used to play a little semi-pro baseball when I was in the States."

We started. At first it was all very gentle and gentlemanly but it quickly became more intense, with national pride coming into play. Throws got flatter and faster. Then a little wider to each wing. Catching a potato became the single most important preoccupation in our lives. Irrespective of its size, weight or shape, if one had to take a tumble to reach and take a low catch, in the process taking a heavy fall on the metal deck, so be it. In the interests of self-preservation, I soon developed a technique of half-turning my body in the air so that I landed on the flat of my shoulder, not the point.

As we slowly progressed across the Pacific, the level of potatoes in the lockers gradually fell. Five days out of our destination at El Segundo, south of Los Angeles and to the fury of the chief cook, we ran out of them! My diary recorded an estimate of over 2,000 potatoes had gone to a watery grave. Hopefully the fish liked them raw.

Eventually we moored a mile or so out from the Californian shore and, from the seabed, hauled up the pipe which would transfer our cargo to an on-shore refinery. Bennie's former boxing skills were once again required. He was on deck-watch duty when his crew mates returned from a mammoth binge ashore. One of them sat on the edge of a hatch cover which was opened wide to allow the highly volatile gases to escape. He pulled out a cigarette and fumbled for a match. The former cruiserweight champion of New Jersey saved us all from being blown to smithereens. He came out of his corner at a run and KO-ed the unsuspecting sailor with a swinging right-hander which knocked him clean off the hatch! A useful man to have on board – in every sense – was Benny Laros.

Where next? Into the Panama Canal we went, headed to the rundown Venezuelan oil port of Punta Cardon for another load of crude oil. In the hot and humid lakes in the middle of the Panama, we anchored to await a convoy coming from the other direction. Moored about 300 yards away from us was the *Flying Enterprise II*. After sinking in a mid-Atlantic gale a few years earlier, its predecessor of the same name had attracted a huge amount of international media coverage. In classic naval tradition, after waiting for his crew to be saved, Captain Kurt Carlsson opted to go down with his ship. Although eventually persuaded not to sacrifice himself, as a result of his brave stand he became an instant, worldwide celebrity.

To escape the suffocating heat, so hot one could almost hear it humming, a group of us dived off the *Aruba* and swam over. As we arrived alongside, Captain Carlsson was on the bridge and shouted down, asking if we wanted to come aboard. But before we could accept, a couple of loud blasts from the *Aruba*'s foghorn summoned us back. It took us quite a bit longer to return, for peculiarly the waters of the lake ran in alternate hot and cold horizontal bands. With a 30-degree difference in temperature these quickly induced spasms of cramp. It was only afterwards that we gleaned from the mixed bag of Chinese, Indian and Caribbean negroes who were on board to shepherd us through the canal locks, that none of them swam in the lake – because of the large number of alligators present!

We nearly never made it to Punta Cardon. At 04.00 and only three miles from the port, we ran aground on a sandbank. Fortunately the tide worked in our favour and, thanks to a lot of gentle 'aheads' and 'full asterns' which kept the engine room best guessing as to what was happening, we eventually floated free six hours later.

Punta Cardon was a small, dirty, squalid town, lacking virtually every amenity. There was hardly a building of note, and the streets were poorly tarred and full of potholes. Being so close to the equator, day and night it was infernally hot and humid. The town gave me my first insight into life in a brothel, an experience which was to be repeated further down the line in Tampico, Mexico. In both I managed to retain my virginity, but more out of a fear of catching some incurable venereal disease than any moral scruple. Like any heterosexual teenager I was interested, if puzzled, by women and the way they thought and behaved. In a brothel, I was soon to find out, it was pretty one-dimensional.

The South American version had a standard layout. In the centre would be a small dancing area, with a deafening jukebox pumping out pop hits from yesterday. It had tables around it and cubicles off. The food served was quite appalling. As my ship mates tucked in to the various 'menus' on offer, I sat, if not glued to my seat, then certainly paralysed by fear. A lady of no great beauty and certainly no inhibitions swayed up and asked me to dance. When I shyly refused, she pulled at the hairs on my arm and enquired, "limpio?" (clean?). I later found out that had the hairs come out, then this was a sure sign I had the pox. She may have had it, too, so caution won the day. I decided to 'save myself' for something more wholesome and reliable. Well, that was my excuse anyway.

MV Aruba was five hours late leaving port as we waited for our own press gang to round up those still pursuing the readily available flesh of this truly miserable town. It seemed the gang had no luck. So a second party was sent out to find the first, and finally the captain and first mate went off in pursuit of the two missing groups. They found them all together, having a hell of a time in one of the countless brothels in the town which, during our three days in port, had become second homes to most of the *Aruba*'s crew.

Then it was off to New York for a 24-hour, off-loading turnaround with no shore leave permitted. Back south down the eastern seaboard of the USA we traipsed, headed we knew not where – until the usual radio instructions confirmed it was to be Tampico.

'Tampico, Tampico, on the shores of Mexico' is known and remembered mainly by the popular post-war song. It was only a notch or two more up-market than Punta Cardon. No matter where you told a taxi driver to go, he always took you to a brothel; after all, that's what every sailor craves, isn't it? An appalling stench hung over the town, a mixture of crude oil, rotting flesh and 'ganja' (marijuana), which everyone seemed to be smoking. The flies were man-eaters in size and, as we tied up, a massive fire was burning less than 100 yards from a large gasoline storage tank.

Almost to a man our crew dived into taxis and headed off to their traditional haunts. Two days later they straggled back from the 'Casa Pepe' with tales and wounds as proof of a bloodletting broken-bottle fight they had had with another crew, who had beaten them to it. Tampico was another South American hell-hole. Again I was relieved to escape from with life, health and hairs intact!

We sailed off into the Caribbean Sea, once again en route to New York. Suddenly, and for the first time in over three months, our engines again misbehaved. While we drifted and the engineers below struggled to get us under way again, the crew set up a fishing enterprise. As Finns waste nothing remotely edible, we had a lot of 'well past sell-by date' meat in the cold storage. With a large butcher's hook spliced to an inch-thick hawser attached to a steam winch in the stern, we fished for shark who always follow ocean-going ships to feed off refuse thrown overboard.

The excitement was intense when shark after shark took the bait, the steam winch was opened up – and up, up, out of the water, with I swear looks of amazement as they passed us by, flew the Kings of the Deep. None was less than five feet long. Under a baking hot Caribbean sun the eight we caught inside 30 minutes took several hours to die. Before then, if you approached too close and poked a stick into their mouths to check they had indeed expired, their jaws would slam shut. When eventually it was safe, our catch was skilfully skinned, taking care to avoid contact with their sandpaper-textured skins, for any grazing had to be quickly disinfected or it would turn septic. When definitely dead, the shark's backbones were removed, left to dry and then threaded onto a thin rod of steel. Strung back together in their correct order, they looked like a delicate piece of lacework and, as exotic walking sticks, they fetched a decent price on shore.

In their spare time seamen either read or play cards. Their world currencies are American dollars, cartons of 200 cigarettes or bars of soap. The shark walking sticks added something new to the *Aruba* crew's portfolio while, during our voyages between ports, tens of cartons of cigarettes would be wagered over a single hand of cards. We must have had on board enough cartons of Camel, Lucky Strike, Philip Morris, Marlborough and Texan cigarettes to guarantee lung cancer to half the smokers of New York.

Heading north again and almost within loud hailing distance of the bronzed and beautiful bodies on Florida's splendid beaches, I had my first glimpse of how the other half live. Around us too, like bees, buzzed a swarm of million-dollar motor cruisers. On their aft sundecks, each appeared to have an identity-kit collection of shapely blondes, martinis in hand. It was an eye-opener in every sense for a still chaste 17-year-old. I fervently hoped that one day I would enjoy that kind of lifestyle. It would certainly make for a pleasant change.

Soon after we'd passed through the Panama Canal, I'd realised that somehow I had to get off the *Aruba*. There was no guarantee as to where she would go once the Punta Cardon and Tampico cargoes had been delivered. Indeed, after I had paid off, it transpired that she went back through the Panama to trade up and down the west coast of North America. I could have been there to this day.

But how to escape? Unless a seaman was forced to pay off sick, no port in America would accept him without a visa. Benny's advice was, "Pete, there are only two ways off a boat in the States, on a stretcher or in a box." Unwittingly he'd suggested my exit route. I had no medical knowledge and couldn't talk to anyone who had, but I started to eat around a dozen eggs a day, hoping for what I had no idea. It sure made me constipated but, whether this helped or not, three days out of New York I felt unwell and my eyes had gone the colour of an egg yolk.

My 1961 diary recalled what happened:

The second mate, with that rare talent for diagnosis which is issued when they pass their master mariner's ticket, ventured, "You're sick. You must see the port doctor when he comes aboard." This was duly done; blood was drawn and sent for analysis. The results confirmed that I had a mild form of hepatitis and a 'chill on the liver' which needed 10 days of rest and a healthy diet to clear it up. The captain wanted a second opinion, quite rightly believing that I had a different agenda from his. Luckily the second lot of tests confirmed jaundice. I don't think the medical profession has ever had a more happy and contented new patient!

I was with familiar company for several of the *Aruba*'s crew, now itching below the belt from their efforts in Casa Pepe and other places, joined me on the Bay of New York ferry to the seaman's hospital on Staten Island.

During the 15-minute ferry ride from Lower Manhattan to the Island, I noted that there were a number of down-and-out looking passengers fast asleep in various corners. In case of need, I memorised this as a piece of useful information for I'd found out that the around-the-clock Staten Island ferry was the cheapest accommodation to be had in or around New York City. The fare of five cents entitled you to stay on as long as you liked, for one you didn't have to get off at either end!

Staten Island Marine Hospital was largely staffed by trainee or newly qualified doctors. It wasn't long before I realised that we seamen from many parts of the globe were guinea pigs, useful bodies upon which to experiment or try out new drugs and treatments. I was put in a ward of 16, my home for the next six weeks. It housed some extraordinary characters. Opposite me was Pop, an elderly Dane with a cherubic face and a halo of snow-white hair. He'd been the chef on the millionaire Vanderbilt family's yacht until a stomach ulcer had interrupted his culinary career – not much of a recommendation for his cooking skills! He had the softest of voices and, unless he whispered in your ear, you had no idea of what he was saying. But seamen have a great respect for age, and no-one took the mickey out of Pop as he patrolled the ward dressed in a red dressing gown looking like a clean-shaven Father Christmas.

Next to Pop lay another Dane. He had some form of diabetes and, throughout the whole time I was in the hospital, I can't remember him ever uttering a word, not even to Pop. In the day he would make cup after cup of thick, black coffee. After lights out at ten, the rest of us would lie in our beds waiting for him to mix his final beaker for the night. It was only after he'd stirred it with a deafening clack, clack, clack of his spoon that we could breathe a collective sigh of relief and settle down to sleep.

Pencil-thin Gabriel had his bed near the door. He was the only American I ever met who could name the then 48 States and their capitals too. He had colitis and talked faster than any of the Chipmunks. The more excited Gabriel got, and he was of a nervous disposition, the faster he spoke until he became all but incoherent to everyone, except presumably himself. At 22 he'd been married and divorced and had the mortification each evening of having his ex-wife bring her new man in to see him. So excited and depressed in quick succession were his mood swings before, during and after these visits that I wasn't surprised his colitis seemed incurable.

Perrera, a Portuguese deckhand, refused to leave the ward without someone to accompany him, while next to him Jennings was paralysed from the waist down. Despite this he insisted on crawling everywhere. He said that it had happened when he'd fallen into the icy Hudson river from a tug he'd been working on. A young doctor confided in me that this was nonsense; Jennings's liver had given in after years of alcohol abuse. He was the only one in the ward Pop wouldn't whisper a good morning to, because he considered him too lowbrow.

Bud was a short, swarthy Yank. Between five and six each afternoon, not a minute earlier nor a minute later, he would gather around him three fellow pinochle card players. Bud talked almost non-stop for the whole hour with a large cigar travelling from one side of his mouth to the other. Never once did he raise a hand to it, nor for that matter light it – for the Staten Island hospital had a strict 'no smoking' rule. Throughout the hour I used to watch fascinated at the progress of Bud's cigar. It was a bit of a giveaway; the better Bud's hand, the faster the cigar travelled. No wonder his opponents never objected.

Rodrigues, with the droopy eyes, had the then popular song 'Vaya con Dios' (Go with God) perpetually on his lips. He had so many ulcers inside and on his body that I felt sure that his wish would soon be granted.

Then there was Jerry. A Kentuckian optician by training, he had developed a drink problem. In trying to break the habit, Jerry had gone to sea as a second cook. But methylated spirits caught up with him on the high seas and he was in Staten Island hospital drying out, trying to reclaim his liver. It was his second visit! Jerry professed a great love of England and things English and, although I'd been schooled in South Africa and talked like a colonial, he thought I had "a beautiful English accent, just like my mother's."

A true southern gent was Jerry and, when he was discharged a few days before me, he made me promise to look him up at his small apartment in downtown Manhattan.

Still with yellow tinged eyes but otherwise feeling in pretty good shape, I was eager to claim my free repatriation to Europe paid for, as American law required, by the *MV Aruba*'s American agents. I travelled back on the ferry to Manhattan and walked up through the avenues of sky-high buildings, surrounded by fast-moving and even faster-talking New Yorkers. It was, and to me is still, the world's most dynamic, exciting city.

I called in to register my hospital discharge at the U.S. Immigration Department, and then it was on to the *Aruba*'s agents. Within half an hour they had found me a passenger berth on the *Georgic*, a Cunard liner due to leave New York on 15th August 1953 bound for Southampton via Le Havre. The cricket season may have been nearly over, but I was on the way back.

I now had nearly ten days to kill before I sailed. In the New York of the 1950s a Finnish seaman's daily wage could just about buy a cup of coffee and a haircut, so I made a beeline to what I'd been told was the cheapest bed in town – other than a night on the Staten Island ferry. It was the Seaman's Hostel on West 20th Street. Aged movie buffs will recall Marlon Brando's powerful performance in *On the Waterfront*, a story of one man's battle to survive in the Mafia-controlled jungle warfare that was an integral part of the union-dominated dock labour force. The hostel was smack in the middle of this.

In those days New York was a city which steered immigrants with similar backgrounds into one-nation ghettoes. Harlem had a majority black population, Brooklyn a preponderance of Jews, Italians congregated in the Bronx – and Chinatown, in downtown NY, near the impoverished Bowery had, well, Chinamen by the thousands.

The Hudson River docklands area, on the west side of Manhattan, was dominated by Puerto Ricans. I checked in to the hostel, producing by way of proof, my Seaman's Union card. "Right, buddy," said the gum-chewing, heavily tattooed male receptionist. "You have two choices, it's a dollar 75 cents for a bed in the dormitory. You'll be sharing with 20 other guys. Or, you can take your chances in the room right opposite for 50 cents a night. You look about the right height."

I was puzzled by what he meant by that last remark, but as I had but 15 dollars to my name, the choice was pretty obvious. I opened the door to the 50 cents a night accommodation. It was a room some 30 feet by 15. From one diagonal corner to the other and some five feet from the ground, with a central supporting pole, ran a rope. It was mid-morning but I could see at a glance what my half a dollar had bought. Three men were draped over it, the rope running under their arms in support. They sort of hung there, knees bent, probably dozing, for, as I was to find out, proper sleep in this position

31

was well nigh impossible. Lying down on the floor was forbidden. If you were awake, you sort of strolled around until you tired; then it was back for another session doing the rope trick.

A call on Jerry became of pressing urgency. I went out into West 20th and back up towards the centre of Manhattan. I hurried past groups of lounging, gum-chewing, marijuana-smoking Puerto Rican youths who gave me a visual once over but let me pass. Even though it was mid-day, a couple of hookers plied their trade along the pavements, their pimps hovering within calling distance. A few overnight drunks slept it off under metal staircases which gave access to the upper floors of decaying apartment buildings lining both sides of the street. The whole area reeked of decay and deprivation. It was awful and certainly not the New York of my imaginations.

Jerry's tiny flatlet was the Ritz by comparison. "I'm afraid I can't give you room on the settee," sympathised Jerry, "as I've got a pal from Kentucky staying for three nights. But after then you're more than welcome to doss down here until your ship sails."

Those nights across a rope, and the abject poverty I shared with my fellow hangers-on, shaped my future attitudes. I vowed never, ever again would I be that short of money. Somehow those nights, and the days in between, passed. I lived on cups of 'kawfee' plus a doughnut a day. If it rained, I sat in a café or a 24-hour fleapit cinema. Manhattan is a huge island but I went everywhere on foot to shows, museums and events where the entrance was free. Walking back to the hostel after dark I'd been warned by Jerry to avoid the sidewalks, stay in the middle of the road and never, but never, to stop. One night I found out why.

Sullen, menacing groups of unemployed Puerto Ricans stood on most street corners. They would shout abuse in Spanish to any 'gringo' who passed. Heeding my friend's advice, I looked straight ahead and lengthened my stride. Suddenly there was a swishing sound, followed by a thump. Directly to my left a knife had embedded itself in an apartment door. Disobeying orders and looking to my right and longing to break into a run, I saw that on the other side of the street stood a Puerto Rican boy, no more than 15 years old. He smiled at me even though I had interrupted his practice session, honing his knife-throwing skills! That night the rope never had a more grateful body suspended from it.

The move to Jerry's apartment transformed my remaining days in New York. He introduced me to a tall, gangling, ginger-haired lad in his mid-twenties called Ernie – but known to all as 'Coco'. A truly extraordinary character, he was one of several hustlers I met during my stay in the 'Big Apple'. Coco had never worked in his life and, at a guess had a vocabulary of around 300 words. Despite not having any obvious source of income, he rarely appeared in the same outfit twice. He was forever 'going home to change, Jerry.' Home, according to him, was across the East River in Brooklyn. But according to my host, 'home' was somewhere Coco hadn't been to for years, and then only to steal something.

During the day he was out and about on the prowl in search of sellable goods, particularly clothing and luggage and, if he was lucky, cash. He once left us wearing a t-shirt, jeans and sneakers to return three hours later in an expensive, bespoke tailored suit, open-toed sandals – but no socks. Whatever shoplifting techniques he used, he must have been a master of them. Jerry told me that in icy New York winters Coco would trawl around the expensive Central Park apartment area, leave his outer clothing hidden in a paper bag in the foyer, ring a doorbell and, if a woman answered, plead for a bit of bread to eat. Gullible New York socialites would often not only provide him with that but, seeing him shivering in the cold, occasionally hand over one of their husband's barely used camelhair overcoats and other bits of expensive clothing and tell Coco to "wrap up warm."

Jerry, Coco and Peter on top of the Empire State building, New York 1953.

In his own field of operation, Coco had style. Being somewhat short of clothing myself and because we were about the same height and build, I asked Coco if he had anything 'at home' that might fit me? "Buddy, that's a cinch," he said. "I've got the very thing hanging up in my wardrobe, and our feet look about the same size so I'll bring some shoes, too. Just hang out here till I get back."

He returned two hours later, a sharkskin suit over his arm. It fitted perfectly. He asked for three dollars, then worth around £1, but apologised for not bringing any shoes. Coco was later to bring from 'home' enough clothes for me to have to ask if he could find me a cheap suitcase to replace my small grip and, if possible, those shoes too. "Come with me and we'll chose something," he said. Curious to see him at work, but planning to keep a decent distance in case the NY Police Department hove to, off we went to the Bowery on the southern tip of New York City. It was getting dark, but already that area's collection of out-for-the-count-on-cheap-redeye-booze hoboes had taken up their stations in sheltered doorways. We strolled casually amongst them until, remembering my need for some shoes, Coco spotted a tall figure slumped against a lamp post. No doubt, here was a size-11-shoe man. With two flicks of the wrist they were off his feet and into Coco's carrier bag. They too turned out to be a better than average fit.

We walked past a shop selling cheap luggage. I pointed out the kind of thing I wanted for the voyage, and we moved on. Next day he pitched up at Jerry's, carrying a suitcase which looked very familiar. Sure, it was made of cardboard, but not only did it do the job but it is with me to this day as a reminder of Coco, New York City and hard times.

I never met anyone with less idea or less concern about the value or importance of money. But Coco really had no need to worry for his income and lifestyle lay all around, available on demand. One day Jerry and Coco took me to meet one of New York's most successful 'fences', a Fagin-like, hooded-eyed figure who was introduced to me as 'Jack'. When we arrived at his off-Broadway apartment, Jack was sitting cross-legged on a king-sided double bed surrounded by quality merchandise provided by the likes of Coco. Jerry had told me that, when Jack had once paid my 'pal' 10 dollars for a 1,000-dollar suit, even my beanpole friend realised he'd been short-changed. A few days later he'd brought around a number of umbrellas. Again ten dollars exchanged hands. It was only when Jack came to open them up to check their condition that he discovered each one had holes punctured in it! All square – but Coco had to lie low for a few weeks until harmony was restored, thanks to a free pair of hand-stitched 800-dollar crocodile-skin shoes which fitted Jack as if they'd been made to measure.

Before leaving New York I was determined to see an American League baseball game. At that time the Brooklyn Dodgers' home stadium was at Ebbets Field and, when Coco suggested we go to a game there against the Philadelphia Phillies, I jumped at the chance. "Don't let Coco know how much money you've got on you," warned Jerry. "If you do, he'll make you pay for everything." Forewarned, I took his advice and sure enough, after we'd each paid for our own ticket in the bleachers section, the cheapest available, from then on Coco gorged himself on endless Coca-Colas and cartons of popcorn. Each time he stocked up, he first asked me to pay as he had no money. The faster I said "neither have I", the faster dollar bills kept appearing from his various pockets.

When my time in New York was up and the boat taking me back to Britain was calling, I found it quite an emotional wrench to leave gentleman

Jerry and street-wise Coco, two men who, in their vastly different ways, had shown me a New York not many visitors would have seen or known about.

As I walked up the *Georgic* gangplank to the luxury of being a passenger, a fit of homesickness hit me. I'd been away from South Africa for over a year and it was time, or so I thought, to go home.

But on board, and for the first time in my life, I fell in love. Mary was a dark-haired 24-year-old from Santa Monica, California, a devout Christian travelling with a large party of similarly inclined American college girls en route to a cultural tour of Europe. Looking back, she must have found the inexperienced fumblings of a 17-year-old amusing and harmlessly innocent. Then, the day before we docked in Le Havre, a subdued Mary told me that the night before she'd been raped by one of the passengers.

Deeply shocked and with me struggling to mouth the right words of dismay and sympathy at this unexpected disclosure, we started a correspondence which was to last nearly a year. Mary wrote beautiful letters without any bitterness against the rapist and full of hope for our possible future together. Encouraged, I made plans to travel to California.

Re-reading her letters fifty years on, I realise that I'd obviously provided her with some desperately needed support. However, this took quite a knock when, eight months after our trip on the *Georgic* and she now back in States, Mary confessed to being pregnant after a one-night stand with an Italian exchange student at Berkeley University!

Although my illusions were shattered by this news and my pride certainly dented too, we did keep writing to each other right through the traumas she was going through as to whether or not she should keep the baby or have it adopted.

He was born on December 28th 1954. I have no idea of his name, but Mary did not hand him over. She bravely chose instead to face the then massive social stigma of having a child out of wedlock, particularly living as she did within a deeply religious family.

But, as Simone de Beauvoir wrote, 'Love at a distance is a fantasy'. The letters between us first became less frequent and then stopped. It was a sombre ending to my first romance.

CHAPTER 4

TO HELL AND BACK

But what or where to next? After my first experience of a shipboard romance and broken heart, I had a need to 'get away from it all'. While I still harboured my schoolboy ambition to become a county cricketer, I had a pressing need to make some money first.

Through his local connections, my uncle Richard quickly found me another job, this time as a cabin boy on a 5,000-ton tramp steamer called the *Birmingham City*. It was due to sail from Avonmouth on its regular scheduled round trip to the east coast of North America. It was to be the hardest, busiest and unhappiest six weeks of my life.

SS *Birmingham City* sailing out of Avonmouth. Hell on the High Seas.

In those days, there were four ports any non-local merchant seaman would not voluntarily sail out of: Glasgow, Liverpool, Tilbury … and Avonmouth. All had a reputation for toughness and roughness. Crews originating from there seemed to need confirmation of this on a daily basis. By now I had fortunately acquired enough savvy not to flag up that I'd got my job, albeit the most menial one on board, thanks to the influence of my uncle, the Haven Master of Avonmouth! Had I done so, life would undoubtedly have been even worse than it turned out to be. My salary was ten pounds per month for a Seaman's Union agreed 84-hour working week. From this was deducted one pound ten shillings for union dues. During the voyage to the eastern seaboard of America and back, I did an additional 110 hours of overtime at one shilling and threepence an hour, 6p in today's currency!

With its frequent mid-winter gales, crossing the North Atlantic Ocean in a small ship is a frightening experience. There were vertical climbs and steep descents up and down mountainous swells with crested waves often breaking over the bow, shipping huge amounts of seawater down the funnel amidships; it felt like the end of the world had arrived. It was like being on a Blackpool funfair roller-coaster – minus the fun. Added to this, the ship rolled appreciably from side to side, occasionally reaching a list of 42 degrees. At over 45 you stand a good chance of turning turtle.

My main tasks were to clean the officers' cabins amidships, make their beds and, over an open deck, bring their food in heated containers from the galley at the stern. This could only be done by linking an arm over a rope strung from the galley to the dining room, for the deck in-between was often awash and therefore highly dangerous to traverse. I also had to scrub the floors of the cabins and the mess room and polish all the many bits of brass work. These were lengthy, exhausting daily chores. Another tiresome task was to make, on demand, endless cups of tea for the Chief Steward, a miserable, vindictive sod who was always complaining and forever insisting that otherwise perfectly satisfactory jobs had to be done again. By a warped coincidence, years later I discovered that he was the father-in-law of the Chairman of Glamorgan's Cricket Committee. I was to have an uneasy relationship with him, too!

Right at the stern, I shared a stark, furniture-less cabin with Francis, a fresh-faced, 16-year-old Londoner who was making his first voyage to sea. He had signed on as the galley boy where he was at the mercy of the chief cook's violent mood swings With two trips to my name I was senior to him, so I nabbed the bottom bunk with its wafer-thin mattress, and he had the top. When hurtling down a huge swell the *Birmingham City* would go into a nosedive, and the ship's propeller, separated from us by just one bulkhead, would break surface. Such was the vibration this caused that we had to hang on to our bunk supports to avoid being tossed out onto the carpet-less deck floor.

Despite all this, Francis was a cheery soul, and in our brief time together he used to entertain me by playing any tune I requested by bouncing the handle of his toothbrush against his front teeth in the manner of a Jewish harp, changing the note through the positioning of his lips. To this day I can never hear Frankie Lane's version of *High Noon* without remembering my former cabin mate.

Every day of the week we both had an 05.00 wakeup call. This was administered by a cruel, soulless able seaman called 'Lofty' Adams, hopefully now long gone. No cup of tea and a 'wakey wakey, me hearties' from Lofty. He took a sadistic delight in loudly rattling a cane against the metal frame of our bunks and then thwacking us across whatever part of our bodies surfaced to make sure we were alive, if not well.

One of Francis's regular tasks was to take the 'rosy', the slops bucket, to the leeward side of the ship and empty its contents overboard. Five days out of Avonmouth and at the height of what seemed to be the storm to end all storms, he went outside to do this chore, swung the heavy bucket up and over the rail – and, coinciding with the stern flipping out of the water, his momentum took him overboard, disappearing with the rosy into the cauldron of the sea. There was no turning back. He would only have survived a few minutes in the icy waters.

Battling into the teeth of the storm, we once made only 13 nautical miles in a day. Berthing in Halifax, Nova Scotia, it felt like we'd arrived in Shangri

La – even though the miserable town, stuck on the bleak Newfoundland coast, was more Wild West than paradise. In port the hot water system on board the *Birmingham City* broke down. With the outside temperature hovering around minus 20 degrees centigrade, a bucket of snow had to be thawed over the galley stove before I could tackle the daily task of washing up piles of coagulated, egg-stained plates in water just above freezing point. If you have a masochistic streak, try it sometime.

The detergent we used on the ship was called Teepol. It came in five-litre cans. The combination of this stuff, and the temperature of the water, caused the skin on my hands to crack as if it were dry parchment. Thereafter, putting them into water of any temperature was agony. Fifty years on, I can close my eyes and still feel the pain.

New York was more like it, familiar territory. We had tied up around 03.00 on the New Jersey side of the Hudson River. When I came on deck at 05.30, the city skyline was enveloped in dense fog. A couple of hours later, after brewing several cups of tea for the Chief Steward, and the brass work gleaming, I ventured outside again to find a seagull sitting on the stern's flagpole. The fog at ground level was still hanging around. I looked upwards some 80 degrees. There was the top of a building. I looked back at the seagull, my eyes now level with the deck. Surely this was a mirage? But no, when the fog finally lifted, there, directly opposite our berth, was the Empire State, then the world's tallest building. What a sight!

During my short spell of shore leave, as a lover of modern jazz, I naturally made my way to the Birdland nightclub in Manhattan. Be-bop was the new sound on the block, and I saw and listened to legends in the making: Art Blakey, Philly Jo Jones and John Coltrane as well as the George Shearing Quartet who were performing in more genteel cocktail bar surroundings. I couldn't afford cocktail prices so stood at the back, enthralled by the group's virtuosity.

Returning to the ship late one night, and ahead of a well-oiled, swaying shipmate, two shots rang out behind me at the entrance to the shed alongside which we were berthed. I had just shown my seaman's card to the security guard and been allowed to pass, but my colleague had failed to do so and had broken into a trot towards our gangplank. The shots brought him to an immediate halt, a swift about-turn and an even speedier journey back to make his peace with the gun-toting guard.

Our next ports of call to off-load and take on cargo were Philadelphia, Baltimore and Norfolk in Virginia, home to the US Navy. Then it was a non-stop return leg to Britain. This time we had the following Gulf Stream to enjoy and thankfully a relatively docile sea so the passage back was uneventful.

It was late August when we docked in Avonmouth and from there it was but a short hop to Cardiff by train. This time I was determined to see if my vision of a life in cricket could become a reality.

In those days the Glamorgan County Cricket Club offices were at 6 High Street, two floors above estate agents Stephenson & Alexander. I climbed the stairs full of expectation and hope but, by the time I reached the second floor, this had largely evaporated. "Peter," I said out loud – for talking to myself had become second nature on the *Soya Andrea* and *Aruba* – "behind that door could be the life you wished for back in South Africa." I made two abortive journeys up and down those stairs before my nerve finally held. I knocked and walked into the cricket club's offices.

The offices were a rundown set of linoleum-floored rooms, with piles of files on antiquated desks and chairs. On the walls were fading photographs, including one of the Glamorgan side who had won the County Championship in 1948. Since then no further successes had come the club's way – and it showed. However, directly in front of me, my eye was drawn to that photograph of Dudley Nourse being caught by Allan Watkins, the catch which had originally inspired me. Seeing it gave me the confidence to ask if I could make an appointment to see my hero.

Mrs Renée Saunders, who was to become almost a foster-mother to me, was one of the club's two long-serving secretaries. She said that, if I followed her into the next office, she could do better than that. There, in deep discussion, were Allan, Wilfred Wooller and Johnnie (never Johnny) Clay, a member of the '48 side and now a trustee of the club. It turned out that in the 1920s he had known my father during his Cardiff C.C. playing days. These three senior figures in Glamorgan cricket politely chatted to me, asking about my life in the merchant navy and my cricketing ambitions before suggesting I take a stroll around the city and come back after lunch.

My diary recollection of that day is worth repeating:

While I strolled around Cardiff's main streets, doing as I was told, Allan must have given the other two some background details on my cricketing abilities from the time he'd coached me at school in South Africa.

As I came back through the door, Mr. Wooller came straight to the point: "I want you to have a trial in our indoor school at Cardiff Arms Park." "When?" I managed to croak back. "No time like the present," said the Glamorgan captain and secretary. Before sending me on my way, he gave me instructions on how to get to the ground, a mere 300 yards away. There I would be met by George Lavis, the club coach.

'School' was a something of an exaggeration for it was just two rubber mats divided by a net on the top floor of the later-to-be demolished North Stand of the famous rugby ground. Except for George Lavis, himself a former Glamorgan player and now its coach, for the first half hour there was no one else present in what turned out to be a session quickly organised solely to run an eye over me.

To loosen up George had asked me to bowl at him. It had been a year since I'd last turned my arm over and I was all over the place, hardly bowling a decent ball. I was beginning to feel very embarrassed when heavy footsteps up the stairs announced the arrival of Messrs. Wooller and Clay, the latter, as always, dressed in a brown pin-striped suit and deerstalker hat.

Suddenly, my luck as well as my direction changed. I bowled between 15 to 20 balls to George, all on a length on or outside the off stump with some slight turn on the smooth, hard surface, a sure sign I was spinning not rolling the ball out of my fingers.

"Right," said Wilf, "you'd better have a knock." Wearing ill-fitting pads and gloves and using a bat I'd had to borrow from the Glamorgan Colts kit bag, I had 10 to 15 minutes against the bowling of Wooller, Clay and Lavis. Mr. Wooller then called a halt and went into a conclave with Messrs Clay and Lavis in the primitive dressing room adjoining.

I waited anxiously but thinking, what the hell, in the circumstances I'd done better than I could have hoped for. It only took a few minutes before Wilf returned and said, "We're in agreement, we've liked what we've seen so we'll offer you a summer contract for next season and the one after. In that time it'll be up to you to show us you can make it as a county cricketer. You'll be paid £4 a week. By the way, you may have to do National Service in this country."

And that was it. I had suddenly metamorphosed from a footloose, seafaring 17-year-old kid into a potential county cricketer! The Glamorgan trio must have seen something they recognised as talent.

However, although my schoolboy dream had suddenly come true, it was to take me two and half years before I finally made the grade.

As to the National Service issue, Wilf and the Club President, Sir Herbert Merrett JP, both had influence in many circles and they managed to convince the Home Office that because of what I'd done in South Africa – a drummer boy in my school's cadet band – I should be placed in the exempt category. In those days in Wales, few argued with Messrs Wooller and Merrett.

But my seafaring days were not completely over. Winter was coming on fast and the urge to go back home to Johannesburg, to play some club cricket before returning to Cardiff in time for April's pre-season nets, was strong. While the thermometer was falling, dreams of fame and fortune on the cricket fields of England would have to wait.

There is rarely such a thing in the merchant navy as a one-way ticket, that is unless you have an old sea dog for an uncle. Haven Master Richard had seen in one of his nautical magazines that the South African Railways and Harbours were waiting to take delivery of a new Glasgow-built, coal-fired sand dredger, which was going to be based in Durban harbour. A couple of phone calls later and I was on my way to a shipyard on the Clyde to become part of a crew signed on to deliver the new vessel. I was to be a sort of general factotum on the catering side and was given a copy of the 'Terms of Employment' to read and accept. Leaping out of me in bold type was: 'this contract to be employed on the voyage from Glasgow to Durban shall last for a period not exceeding two years.' Two years, wow! It took the Union-Castle mail-boat thirteen and a half days to reach Cape Town. What sort of tub was I joining? As it transpired, our voyage 'only' took two months.

Memories of a week in dockside Glasgow waiting for the final fit to be completed are of miserable, chilling rain emptying continuously from dull grey skies which at least helped to dilute the overpowering smell of whisky and urine. To save money the so-called 'new' dredger, named *The Bontebok* after an antelope common throughout Southern Africa, turned out to have been built to 60-year-old plans! It was shaped like a bathtub and very difficult to tell at first which was the bow or the stern. Most of the interior was a huge empty area called a hopper. This would store the dredged-up sand which would keep the entrance to Durban's splendid harbour navigable to ocean-going liners. *The Bontebok* had no running water, just a few smallish tanks on deck, and was powered by old-fashioned, coal-burning boilers.

As it was not designed for anything other than work within the confines of a harbour, its storage bunkers for coal were too small to cater for a 7,000-mile ocean journey. In consequence, every square inch of space on deck had to be filled with sacks of coal.

To save further on costs, only two of the six boilers were fired up and our top speed was therefore a maximum of five knots – around six miles per hour.

If the voyage on *Birmingham City* had been a nightmare experience, my new short-term home proved to be anything but. There were 14 crew only, six of them Glaswegian stokers, and all bar me with the guarantee of flights back to Britain from South Africa when, and if, we survived to deliver *The Bontebok* to its new owners.

We eventually lumbered off down the Clyde river and into the Irish Sea, the huge weight of coal on deck causing the water to be barely below the legal Plimsoll line. We soon found that, even in the gentlest of seas, we were more submarine than ship. We looked and felt a leading contender for the ugliest vessel afloat award.

No sooner had we emerged from the Scottish mainland than a force eight gale drove us to shelter in Belfast harbour. Marooned there for two days until the storm abated, we then inched our way south, through a thankfully benign Bay of Biscay, past the Canary Islands and, with coal running out, put into Dakar, French West Africa, for replenishments.

As long lines of Africans came on board carrying sacks of coal on their heads, it reminded me of pictures of the porters David Livingstone used in his journeys through Africa. At the same time a huge dockside crane also deposited loads of loose coal into the *Bontebok*'s bunkers. Each time this happened the old tub listed violently to one side.

There was precious little by way of rank distinction on board; everybody mucked in for whatever task needed extra pairs of hands. After a meeting

The Bontebok. The South African Railways and Harbour's new dredger arriving in Durban from Glasgow. At sea they don't come any slower!

in Dakar with the six Glaswegian stokers who were feeling the pace, the skipper decided to take on two local ones.

Off we went again. Like the earliest Portuguese explorers in the 15th century, we were trying to keep the coastline of Africa in view in case we foundered. Once, after we'd been blown out of sight of land by a light squall, the skipper asked the inexperienced third mate, who was responsible for navigation, what was our position? With a wry smile the mate offered, "Well skipper, my dead reckoning says we're 30 miles up the Amazon River!"

In the tropics we used to cool off by swimming in the vast hopper. To give the bobbing cork that was *The Bontebok* some stabilising ballast, this had been filled with seawater. Out in the Atlantic fifty or so miles from land, paddling around, circling the metal stanchions which divided the hopper compartments, was a surreal experience. However, after most of us developed sore throats and occasional mild fevers, the discovery that the primitive toilets on board emptied directly into the hopper, brought a halt to these dips!

Time dragged. The two Africans, taken on as support for our Scottish stokers, found it all too much, particularly when the heat of the boilers was added to that of the tropics. This meant that the rest of our crew, from the captain down to the cook, had to take turns raking out and throwing on new coal.

It was a job that required more skill than one would imagine. On opening the furnace doors the heat was like a punch on the jaw, while hauling out the still red hot coals before adding fresh fuel meant risking being burned alive if you pulled too hard. The rest of us quickly came to regard the six original stokers as a very special breed of men.

The skipper was a lover of a particularly repulsive-looking fish called snoek. He thought it a great delicacy and liked it dried out in the sun and eaten raw. As our arrival deadline was not important, he decided one day to reel in the small propeller that was attached to a length of rope which ran through a pulley at the end of a pole stuck out some 20 feet from the side of the vessel. At the other end of the trailing rope a rev counter was attached to provide a record of the distance we'd travelled.

On a normal voyage this is an important navigational tool. Not so on *The Bontebok* where time and distance travelled hardly mattered. So the skipper then tied a couple of hooks to the end of the rope, baited them with food he believed would entice a snoek and gently lowered them back over the side, playing it out until the rope went taut. To give him warning that a fish had taken the bait, he substituted the distance counter with a bucket full of, yes you guessed it, coal. His idea was that, when a snoek was hooked, the person on the bridge would be alerted by the bucket rapidly lifting off the deck and discharging its load, making a hell of a racket in the process.

The idea seemed to have some merit and, on board any vessel, the skipper always has his way. A day or more went by; nothing stirred. The hooks were re-baited and let back out again. Still all quiet. Interest and expectation from us all, including the skipper, waned. Suddenly, just before sunset and with a tremendous clatter, the bucket flew upwards, coal flying everywhere. Now it was all hands on deck. There was undoubtedly something big on the end of the line for trying to pull the rope in was a task fit for Hercules. It took eight of us twenty minutes working in short shifts, before the rope line was vertical under the pole. A few more heaves with us thinking we must have at least a Great White shark on the end and then ever so slowly appeared from the ocean – an empty coal sack, now full of sea water! The captain went absolutely ballistic, threatening to keelhaul the practical jokester responsible when found.

Thankfully his sense of humour did eventually return, but he gave up trying to land his favourite snack until we reached our next port of call, Walvis Bay, where he knew the local fish market stocked it aplenty.

In Walvis Bay, then in South West Africa, now Namibia, we took on another deckful of coal and a couple of extra unsuspecting local firemen after the two from Dakar did a runner. We sailed slowly but certainly not majestically on to repeat the same bunkering formula in Cape Town before rounding the Cape on the final leg of our journey.

My abiding memory of Christmas Day 1953 is of getting up in the morning and seeing the Natal town of Port Shepstone off the port bow. Such was the head-on strength of the South Equatorial current that, when the sun went down, Port Shepstone was only just abaft our stern!

On Boxing Day we limped into Durban, task completed. No fanfare or ticker-tape to welcome us, just a huge relief that we'd made it. On the quayside stood my waiting father.

Our reunion was a strange mix of emotions. I pressed into his hand the £20 he'd advanced me 15 months ago at Johannesburg station where he'd waved me an unsuspecting goodbye. It seemed a lifetime ago.

As I did so I said, "Thanks, Dad, now we're square. I've done it all myself."

The 17-year-old lad who returned his warm embrace on Durban's dockside was no longer a boy.

Father and elder son reunited on the quayside of Durban docks, December 1953.

CHAPTER 5
INTO THE UNKNOWN

With a lot of play and very little work in three months of socialising, the days flew by in South Africa. Soon it was March 1954 and time to travel back to the UK, to pick up the first of the two summer-only contracts with Glamorgan.

An Italian tramp steamer, the *SS Pegaso*, was due to sail from Durban to Bari near the south-eastern tip of Italy. OK, unlike the *Soya Andrea*, it wasn't Barry in South Wales, but it was more than half way there. Thanks to my father having a pal who had a twice-monthly contract to ship South African coal to Italy, I was able – along with three other young South Africans – to book a berth in one of the *Pegaso*'s three twin-bunked passenger cabins. The 20-day voyage, with full board and lodging, cost us each one pound a day! There were, however, conditions attached.

We were expected to help out, if required, doing simple jobs either on deck or in the galley. Typically Italian, once we'd sailed, they either forgot this obligation on our part or didn't think we looked as if we'd be up to any task they had in mind. However, one of the sailors, a Maltese named Mike, did tutor me in one of the few domestic skills I now possess, the ability to iron a long-sleeved, collared shirt and to fold it correctly.

Disembarking in Bari, we four spent a day in Rome before taking a 24-hour train ride to Paris. Then it was rail again on to Calais and a ferry ride across a stormy English Channel where, to counter any seasickness, our still-functioning sea legs allowed us to weave and sway on the open rear deck to keep our balance. Landing at Dover, we purchased rail tickets to London where we split up. Then solo I trained it to Cardiff to start what turned out to be a 18-year relationship with Glamorgan County Cricket Club.

Any sports-mad youngster would have envied this dream scenario: being paid to play a game you loved, out in the fresh air. This was certainly true – except the salary of four pounds a week, from which I had to find board and lodging, didn't leave much over to enjoy the good life!

Ahead of my arrival in Cardiff, my paternal grandmother had managed to find me digs at 31 Penhill Road, directly opposite the vast and magnificent Llandaff Fields. In the latter part of the 19th century these had been given to the citizens of Cardiff for recreational use by the Marquess of Bute. My wages just about covered the three guineas a week charged by landlady Miss Coles, but I found to my joy that this also included a substantial evening meal. For a few extra shillings she also took care of my laundry. Fiftyish Miss Coles, a small, mouse-like scurrier of a woman, must have had an unfortunate early-life romantic experience, for the only strict rule of the house was 'no women allowed across the threshold'. At that stage of my life this was not a difficult condition to meet, if not so easy later on.

I found myself sharing a bedroom with Vernon Booth, a slightly off-the-wall ex-World War II fighter pilot. He was to become my most loyal friend and fan. 'Eccentric' summarised my new pal exactly. Dogmatic in the extreme, he used to drive to distraction his twice-weekly bridge-playing friends, all of whom were internationally rated players. When they came round to our house to play, I used sometimes to stand behind him and watch as he steadfastly refused to be rushed when considering his next bid or card to play.

Vernon worked in the accounts department of a Treforest company called Aerozip. In all weathers he travelled there, resplendent in full leather pilot's gear and goggles on his 500cc Triumph motorcycle, piloting it like a Spitfire. Riding pillion with him required a strong stomach and an unswerving faith in the protection of the Almighty.

Each summer evening Vernon and I would cross the road into Llandaff Fields and take turns hitting catches to each other. He was the proud owner of a pre-war Don Bradman autographed bat, the handle of which he'd shortened by sawing it down to within six inches of the splice! In consequence, the bat had no balance nor sweet spot 'middle'. It was like wielding a pickaxe handle, but Vernon staunchly claimed it gave him greater control and refused all my offers to replace it with one of my own.

Reporting for my first day at Glamorgan's Cardiff Arms Park nets in early April was both exciting and daunting. I found myself in the company of many household names in Welsh cricket, including my mentor Allan Watkins. But in the first few days all we newcomers were required to do was retrieve balls hit out of the nets by the county's frontline batsmen. The excitement of doing this soon waned for me and the other juniors on the staff. These included West Walian Alan Jones, later to become the county's heaviest scorer, Billy Davies of Barry, Tudor Hargest from Neath, Wyn Walters who hailed from Pontardulais near Swansea and the gloriously named George Bernard Shaw whose home village was Treharris.

Cardiff Arms Park cricket ground, 1954. Scene of a lot of toil, tears and frustration.

45

Our GBS was no relation to the famous playwright. Despite his youth George had a full set of false teeth, top and bottom, which used to clatter together whenever he laughed. An off-break bowler, he'd modelled his action on his boyhood hero, Glamorgan's JC Clay, but their backgrounds could hardly have been more different.

Johnnie Clay was a member of the Glamorgan hunting, shooting and fishing set. At the age of fifty, he'd been a key member of the 1948 championship-winning side. In his playing days and forever after, his tall, gaunt figure was a familiar sight on Cardiff streets as he walked along, squeezing a squash ball and spinning it from hand to hand to keep his fingers strong and supple during the off-season.

Although of similar build, cricket's GBS may just have been a baker's son from a village near Merthyr, but he earned the admiration and envy of his fellow junior pros by courting and eventually marrying Maureen, the elder of two beautiful blonde sisters who worked in a Cardiff arcade wool shop. As is said in cricketing parlance, it wasn't long before I 'played and missed' at Betty, the more voluptuous of the sisters. The most amiable of souls, George featured occasionally in the county side in the middle 1950s. Later he emigrated to Australia where he was killed in a car crash near Melbourne.

While still retaining our ball-retrieving roles, we newcomers were soon being employed as net-bowling cannon fodder for the senior batsmen. Billy Davies looked to have a very promising career ahead of him as an opening bat and back-up seam bowler, but he was to be ruined by his compulsory two years of National Service where some bad habits in his batting technique became indelibly ingrained. On his return Billy, unlike Tudor and Wyn, did play some games in the Glamorgan first eleven, but his youthful promise had evaporated.

The more senior pros had wives or mothers to make them lunchtime sandwiches which they ate in the same dressing room as that used by the Welsh rugby team in the Five Nations international winter programme. We juniors, however, used to go out through the Gwyn Nicholls gates at Cardiff Arms Park (now moved up Westgate Street to opposite the Angel Hotel) to Moseley's café in Quay Street.

As we walked in, the large, motherly figure of Mrs. Moseley would shout out to the kitchen, "four plates of egg, beans and chips, tea and bread and butter." It cost us one and threepence (6p) each. Occasionally I'd join a small group of Cardiff club cricketers. They lunched on jellied veal, though for years I thought it was jellied eel. Among the friendships cemented there was one with a young architect John Webb, who went on to design the revamped Arms Park rugby ground before its last transmogrification into the magnificent Millennium Stadium.

We juniors bowled at the first-team county players for two hours in the morning and a further two after lunch. We were rarely given a chance to bat except right at the end when, tired out to the soles of our boots, we had to bowl at one another. It wasn't long before I had my first run-in with the club coach, George Lavis. Remember, in terms of worldly experience I was 18 going on 35. As a former county batsman obsessed by the niceties of technique, George was a stickler for style over result. After bowling in the net for an hour or more, I liked to sidle off, usually taking with me at least two of my mates, to practise on the wooden slip-catching cradle, then the only piece of close-fielding training equipment on the market. George, rightly seeing me as the ringleader, would soon yell, "Come on back and bowl and stop messing around", thus dragging us back to the nets.

I'm sure I must have seemed a real pain to George Lavis, and unfortunately he made my progress through the Colts and second eleven more difficult than it needed to be, by batting me low down in the order and giving me few chances to bowl. Despite this, watching up close first-class professional cricketers honing their skills provided me with a fascinating learning curve.

There was, of course, Allan Watkins and my other former coach, Emrys Davies. 'The Rock' he was called, because of his solid defence and quiet manner. 'Em' was a left-hand opening batsman and slow left-hand bowler good enough to do the double of 1,000 runs and 100 wickets in 1935 and 1937. For many years he also held the Glamorgan club aggregate run record (26,102), which was eventually broken by my former junior colleague, Alan Jones.

Before I'd set off from South Africa for my first season on the Glamorgan books, it had been typical of Emrys that he should reply to a letter of mine sent to Rondebosch Boys High School in Cape Town where he was coaching at the time. I had sought his advice as to what I should bring with me by way of kit. He wrote back, saying he had contacts in the UK where I'd be able to get it cheaper than in SA. One passage read …

I'm leaving here on the *Pretoria Castle* on the 26th February for what will be my 31st season with Glamorgan. I have loved every minute of it and would most certainly, if I lived my life over again, do the same thing. I'm sure you will enjoy it too. We are a grand lot of lads and I know you will like them as well. Being left-handed I may be able to tell you a few things when you start. Do please convey my best wishes to your Dad who I remember playing with in the Cardiff Cricket Club side back in the '20s. Look forward to seeing you soon in Cardiff.

During the 1954 season Emrys turned fifty, and early that summer his slowing reflexes were to hasten his retirement from the game.

The other established players included Gilbert Parkhouse, an elegant, right-handed opening batsman who could make fast bowling look medium pace. On the often unpredictable, uncovered pitches of his time he also had the soft-hands technique needed to counter spin bowling. Gilbert was the bon viveur of the team. Saturday evenings in the old Bush Hotel in his home town of Swansea always saw Gilbert and his wife Dorothy enjoying a steak, accompanied by a bottle of Beaujolais. When I eventually made it into the first team as an uncapped player, I would sometimes go there too, but I could never afford the wine! After all, Gilbert was on £800 a year. 'Parkie' was a high-class player who, in a more fashionable county, would undoubtedly have made more than his seven scattered appearances for England.

Gilbert's opening partner was Bernard Hedges, small of stature but big of heart, a man so obsessed by playing within the spirit of the game that he once gave himself out lbw when only one person, and he square of the wicket, had appealed! Without bothering to look at the umpire, Bernard walked off for he believed the ball would have gone on to hit his stumps! A fine full-back for Pontypridd RFC with, so I was told, 'the safest pair of hands in Wales', he was – in cricketing terms – a surprisingly poor catcher and fielder.

Willie Jones was a diminutive, chain-smoking attacking left-hand batsman of a highly nervous disposition. As a young man he'd also been an outstanding rugby fly-half and a marvellous kicker of the ball. After a few pints at the end of play, even nervous Willie occasionally became brave enough to challenge his captain Wilfred Wooller to a kicking contest. Wilf had played for Wales in a full rugby international when he was still a sixth-former at Rydal School – he'd stayed on so long at school that he was 20 at the time – and later appeared as an amateur centre-forward for Cardiff City AFC, too.

Both were around-the-corner kickers, not toe-enders as was the norm then, and we'd all troop next door onto the old Cardiff Arms Park rugby pitch to watch as Willie and Wilf placed the ball on the corner flag and curled their kicks between the posts. Bearing in mind that they were doing so with an irregular-shaped, heavy leather ball and several pints inside them, they did so with extraordinary accuracy.

When I eventually got into the county side, I was on the field one day when at deep square leg Willie dropped a catch off Wilf's bowling. Willie was inconsolable but, so help me, a couple of overs later another catch came to him off Wilf's bowling – and down went that chance, too. Now he could barely stop shaking; what would Wilf be thinking and surely it couldn't happen again? But it did. This time the batsman absolutely middled a powerful sweep and, like a 303 bullet, the ball flew at head height straight at Willie. Seeing another probable dropped catch hurtling his way, Willie stood stock still, opened his arms wide and shouted, "Hit me." Luckily the ball merely brushed the top of his cap en route to the boundary, and even Wilf joined in the general roar of laughter which followed.

Because of his between-overs, ungainly waddle of a walk, wicket-keeper Haydn Davies was known to all as 'The Panda.' He was something of a life philosopher as well being one of the most astute readers of the game. When it came to gathering the ball, he had an unusual technique of lining up the ball with his right hand and, as it entered, dropping his left over it like a rat-trap. Even in the days of Kent and England's Godfrey Evans, there was no better keeper to off-spin bowlers than Haydn.

We had two high quality off-spinners then, Jim McConnon and the legendary Don Shepherd. It was Haydn who, together with Wilf, assured Don's future in the game by persuading him to turn to medium-pace off-breaks when his career as a fast-medium swing bowler was in terminal decline. Funnily enough

Haydn always stood back to Don, reckoning that at his speed he wasn't likely to get many stumpings but certainly there were any number of catches to be had wide down the leg side. As was so often the case, he was right.

On and off the field I learnt a lot from Haydn Davies. One day, when we were discussing close fielding skills, he asked me, "What do you catch with, Peter?" My reply, "Obvious isn't it, my hands." He smiled condescendingly. "No you pillock, it's your eyes! They tell you where your hands should go. That's why I keep after you to stand still at short square leg to give your eyes a chance." It was the kind of advice which was to bring me nearly 700 catches in first-class cricket. Wherever you are Haydn – and I hope it's up above – thanks a lot.

Impressions made on a young mind are often indelible. Besides the now venerable Emrys Davies, two men finishing their careers as mine was starting were Norman 'Pete' Hever and Len 'Fruity' Muncer, both imports from Middlesex. A real Cockney, Hever swung the ball into right-handed batsmen more than any man on earth while Muncer, a fine off-spinning all-rounder, retired at the end of the 1954 season and went back to London to run his sports shop near Lord's. His signature stroke, the 'Muncer chop' as it was known around the county circuit, was a late cut delivered with a tremendous axe-like downward blow that put terror into the hearts of wicket-keepers standing up – and first slips too.

Glamorgan 1957
Back (left to right): Edgar Truran (scorer), Bernard Hedges, David Evans, Jim Pressdee, Peter Walker, Frank Clarke, Brian Evans, Don Ward, John Evans (physio).
Front: Don Shepherd, Gilbert Parkhouse, Wilf Wooller (capt), Allan Watkins, Jim McConnon.

Glamorgan, looking into the not too distant future, were keen to find a replacement behind the stumps for Haydn Davies, then in his late forties. Wilf always asked Haydn his opinion of those who came for a trial. The Panda's usual pre-season practice amounted to emerging two days before the start of a season, putting on his wicket-keeping gloves and getting one of us youngsters to throw him a dozen or so balls before announcing, "OK, that's it, I'm ready!"

To be fair to Haydn's memory, he did spend each winter at the Cardiff Squash Club as their professional coach. As a result, and despite his build, he was supremely fit and easily maintained the essential hand/eye sharpness needed by wicket-keepers. In 1958, his final season, the first day of our match at Cardiff against the New Zealanders was rained off. Haydn, by now aged 46, took on three of the tourists at squash, all of them provincial standard players back home. I can see him now in his thick maroon tracksuit, leaving each of these super-fit Kiwis exhausted as he beat them 3-0. He had hardly a bead of sweat on his brow!

During this search for his replacement and protecting his corner, Haydn would dismiss almost every trialist, finding failings which sometimes only he could see. There were two exceptions. One was a Cardiff-born, RAF trainee pilot, Alex Cohen. Tragically, soon after his appearance at the Glamorgan nets, Alex died when the fighter plane he was piloting developed a fault and crash-landed in a field near a housing estate. The inquest came to the conclusion that, rather than bale out, Alex had stayed with the aircraft to steer it away from the built-up area until it was too late to save himself.

The other who might have taken over from Haydn was Trevor Royal. He hailed from Essex and was tall, strong and could bat. He was not short of self-confidence, either.

County cricket then was still pretty feudal in its structure, amateurs and professionals more often than not changing in separate dressing rooms and, in some cases, staying in different hotels, too. Captains were always addressed as 'Skipper' or 'Mister'.

In the nets, Trevor gave an immaculate display behind the stumps, so much so that even Haydn was unable to find a major fault. However, at the end Trev blew his chances by marching up to the bowling end and saying, "Well, Wilf, I was pretty pleased with that. I'm sure you'll agree. When do I start?" That afternoon Chingford man was on the 17.25 train back to Paddington.

Physically, Wilfred Wooller was a giant of a man and, for over fifty years, of equal stature and influence in all matters to do with Glamorgan. To many he was a bigoted, one-eyed despot, but on a cricket field Wilf was a born leader who expected his team to follow unconditionally his personal example.

Before the war Wilf had been a hell-raising Cambridge student, whose antics are still enshrined in Christ's College folklore. Two undergraduate stories filtered down to me. In one, after a rugby match in Leicester, Wilf was refused entry by the night porter at the Grand Hotel as he attempted to escort a young lady into a lift. He returned later, went up four flights of stairs, picked up an enormously heavy pottery vase, leant over the balcony and dropped it down some fifty feet where, with a huge crash, it smashed into a thousand pieces at the feet of the dozing porter! For twenty years thereafter the Cambridge rugby team was not allowed back to that hotel. The second story involved another fit of pique, this time after Wilf was gated for having missed a deadline for the submission of a piece of academic work, never Wilf's first priority in life. By way of revenge he cemented up the toilets in the tutor's quarters.

During the war in the Far East, he was taken prisoner in Java. Incarceration in the notorious Changi POW camp in Singapore probably helped to calm the more impulsive side of Wilf's nature. But after three years in Changi and other camps, his weight too had undergone a substantial change, dropping from a powerful sixteen and a half stone to just eight. But even so, after his release and demob, this had no effect on his driving ambition nor his will to win.

Years later Wilf told me that he regarded himself as 'in loco parentis' to me – I suspect that it was about the only Latin phrase he knew – and, after two undistinguished seasons, I've no doubt he was solely responsible for steering through a third year's contract for me against the majority wishes of an unimpressed GCCC committee. Thankfully I was able to repay his show of confidence with interest in that year, but it wasn't until the late 1970s when I'd been five years out of the game that I could bring myself to call him Wilf.

Thinking back, those first two summers must have been a great disappointment to both Wilf and Johnnie Clay. I, too, was often close to despair. I found runs hard to come by on under-prepared, irregular-bounce, Welsh club pitches. Having grown up on true South African batting surfaces my defensive technique was nowhere tight enough, nor was I helped by some ropy umpiring decisions. But thankfully I did keep taking wickets.

To get playing experience at weekends, like the other junior pros I was allocated to a Welsh club side. In my first year I was billeted with the Cardiff Club. Playing amongst a grand set of lads and given opportunities with both bat and ball by captain Haydn Wilkins, it was one of the happiest spells in my formative years. My particular pal, the architect John Webb, spent much of his time unsuccessfully trying to mend the huge, ever-expanding holes in his knee-length, long-sleeved sweater, so wide it would have blanketed Quasimodo. John was an extremely unorthodox batsman who, to the dismay of all who bowled at him, swept virtually every ball. He had a wonderful eye which, down the years in another field, enabled him to acquire a magnificent collection of antique porcelain and Victorian paintings.

In the following year Llanelli, then the furthest point west with an affiliation to Glamorgan, became my weekend cricketing home. There I played under the captaincy of Peter Davies, Emrys's son. Although a right-hander, in terms of personality and time spent at the crease he was very much a chip off the old block. Llanelli was a two-hour, fume-ridden, bumpy N&C coach ride from Cardiff, which sometimes required an enforced stop outside Ammanford so I could puke up into some roadside bushes.

It was during this period that I first went head-to-head with the fiscal strictures imposed by Glamorgan's then assistant secretary, Phil Thomas. He was an ex-policeman and a stickler for detail. In the American humorist Damon Runyon's wonderfully descriptive phrase, Phil could well have been described as being 'as loose as concrete with his money.'

For my return coach fare to Llanelli I put in a claim for two shillings and nine pence. I was summoned to the 6 High Street offices for interrogation. Timetable in front of him, Phil pointed out that, if I'd left on a bus before eleven in the morning and returned before seven pm, the return fare to Stradey Park, Llanelli, was two shillings and six pence, not two and nine as I had claimed, a saving of three pence! While a two-hour bus ride before eleven from Cardiff was certainly a possibility, I pointed out that, as league matches often finished around eight in the evening, it would be hard for me to come back before seven. Phil was unbending. So, out of my £4 per week salary, I had to take the three pence hit.

To save money, and if he was playing in a club game near mine on Saturdays, I used to cadge a lift with Londoner Stan Montgomery. Stan had an in-and-out sort of summer career with Glamorgan but in football, as a 'stopper centre-half' he was one of the best in the game. Nothing, man or ball, got past him in the Cardiff City defence – or at least not more than once! In those days 'The Bluebirds' were in the First, now the Premier, Division and even feared and combative centre-forwards like Nat Lofthouse of Bolton Wanderers and England and Trevor Ford of Sunderland and Wales would give Stan, tall and rangy with sharp, bony points all over his body, a wide berth. Stan was always good for tickets to the City's home games and, although now long gone to clog no doubt a few passers-by in heaven, he too is part of Glamorgan CCC's folklore.

Batting with Stan in a county match in the north of England, Wilf once called him for a suicidal run. The centre-half raised a hand and yelled back a footballing refusal which left Wilf, stranded half way down the pitch, run out. Wilf was furious, so much so that at the end of the game he sent Stan back to Cardiff with instructions to practise his running between the wickets. So, under the eye of coach George Lavis, on three consecutive days, for an hour in the morning and another in the afternoon Stan, fully padded up plus bat and gloves, sprinted between stumps pitched 22 yards apart on the Cardiff Arms Park outfield. At the end of one session Monty, a real Cockney, said to us juniors watching this performance, "Cor, fuck me, mate; give me football any day. I'm absolutely knackered."

On the way to our Saturday jaunts to our respective clubs in West Wales, Stan, who owned a small, battered, two-door Ford Anglia, would be full of optimism. However, that particular season virtually every week he seemed to be given out lbw. The ride back to Cardiff was bruising in every sense because accompanying every nuance in his latest story of crooked and blind umpires would come a sharp elbow dig into my ribs to emphasise the point he was making. At the end of each trip my sympathies were most definitely with Nat

Lofthouse, Trevor Ford and others who had to spend ninety minutes with Stan as their shadow.

When I became a regular in the county eleven, I used to travel to away games in a variety of senior players' vehicles. Actually I drove; they almost invariably slept. One senior player had a deserved reputation as a highly accomplished womaniser and so was in special need of his rest. Once, after a Cardiff match which went all the way to six o'clock stumps on the last day, the other players had quick showers before setting off on the seven-hour, pre-motorway journey to our game next day in Sheffield. I waited patiently for my designated partner to emerge before he said, "Hang on just a minute. I need to pop over to the Westgate Street flats to see a friend." Off he went to return over an hour later.

It was now nearly half past seven. Pretty irritated by this, for I didn't want to arrive late and tired out, I jumped behind the wheel and off we set. My passenger next opened his eyes fifty minutes later as, still inside the Welsh borders, we drew level with Raglan. "Pull into the main pub in the village," he instructed. We did so. A barmaid of generous proportions greeted him like a long lost lover – he undoubtedly was that – and it was 10.30 'stop tap' closing time before we set off, heading north again. So help me, just after midnight as we were passing through the Worcestershire town of Malvern, he stirred once more and navigated me to a four-storey building just off the main road. He threw up some gravel to rattle a second-floor window, which eventually opened, and a blonde head appeared. "Let me in," he said in a stage whisper worthy of Romeo. "I only want to talk to you." It was a lengthy conversation, for by the time he reappeared the sky was lightening and we were less than half way to Sheffield! We made it just before the toss, but only just. He was as fresh as the proverbial daisy, his driver absolutely knackered.

In my third year on the staff I came to terms at last with the necessary technical adjustments to my batting and bowling that were needed to succeed on uncovered pitches. I mastered the art of watching the ball right onto the bat and playing it with soft hands. I also realised the necessity of bowling a far fuller length than I had in South Africa. Because of this I started to turn in some half-decent scores and bowling analyses in the Colts, the Glamorgan second team, and club cricket. At Jimmy McConnon's suggestion, I experimented with medium-pace seamers, a switch which initially helped me to get into the county side.

One day Wilf called me into the office. "We" (meaning himself of course), "are pleased with the way things are going, and the committee have decided to increase your salary". My chest swelled; fortune, if not yet fame, had arrived. "Yes," he went on, "instead of four pounds a week we're going to raise it to four pounds, ten shillings." I walked out feeling like a millionaire.

All in all, I had found the going tough in my first two years on the junior staff and in my appearances for Cardiff and Llanelli. My next two clubs were Neath and Maesteg Town, but I made only infrequent appearances for them, as by that time I was starting to gain a toehold in the county side. But they remain important, career-shaping years.

No-one felt prouder to wear the daffodil of Glamorgan and Wales.

In July 1956, two 50s in a second eleven match at Worcester earned me my chance in the first team on 2nd, 4th and 5th June against Leicestershire at Llanelli, a game we eventually won by 40 runs. For financial, rather than old times' sake, I travelled down the afternoon before on an N&C coach with Frank Clarke, a large, raw-boned young fast bowler from the St. Fagan's club who was also making his debut in county cricket. Frank now lives near Brighton and, surprisingly for a man of his bulk, has become one of the world's leading antique furniture restorers, a trade which needs great delicacy and certainty of touch.

For me, it was not the most auspicious of debuts. Batting at number eight I was bowled Jackson, 0 in the first innings and bowled Palmer, 2 in the second.

In those days it was customary to give a debutant or a player in his benefit season 'one off the mark'. When I came out in the second innings I had to pass Leicester all-rounder Maurice Tompkin, standing at mid-off. "Hit it to me, son, and run," he said with a smile. First ball I faced and, presumably to make up for the failure to comply with tradition in the first innings, that kindest of souls Charles Palmer served up a gentle full-toss. I pushed it firmly in Maurice's direction; too firmly, I thought, to run. But fair play to him, he made a theatrical hash of trying to stop the ball. It went through his legs and to my enormous relief I had made the first of my 16,510 runs for Glamorgan!

One more run later and I was on my way back to the pavilion, bowled by the self-same Palmer.

In that match against Leicestershire I didn't get a bowl, but in their second innings I caught Leicestershire opening batsman Maurice Hallam off Don Shepherd, the first of 656 catches for the county and the first of the 178 I was to take from the bowling of the finest spin bowler Glamorgan has ever produced.

Just before this happened, I had found myself at second slip alongside my erstwhile coach and hero, Allan Watkins. I asked him where I should stand. He was in the middle of telling me when Frank Clarke ran in to bowl, and he paused. Gerry Lester, the other opening bat, flashed at the ball and it flew fast and low, bisecting Allan and myself. In a split second Allan dived to his right, catching it almost after it had passed us both. He got up and tossed the ball back to Frank, who was jubilant at his first wicket in county cricket. He then turned to me to continue his positioning instructions.

I was still rooted to the spot. It was my first experience of just how much quicker the action was at county level, compared to club cricket.

That season I was selected for a further six games, getting into double figures (11 in each innings) in the next game against Nottinghamshire, another 11 against Hampshire and a personal best of 15 against Middlesex at Lord's where I also got my first first-class wicket: Peter Delisle, caught by Haydn Davies behind the stumps.

So in September I headed off to Southampton and the mail-boat back to South Africa, pleased that I'd made it into the first team and inwardly confident that I could do better next year.

My growing self-belief was further boosted by at last consummating a shipboard romance, this time with Betty, an older and certainly vastly more experienced campaigner than me. It helped to round off an eventful, happy summer.

For the next seven British winters I commuted each six months between Britain and South Africa. Returning to a sporting life with the Balfour Park Cricket Club team in Johannesburg both matured and toughened me up as a player. The club scene there, while wholly amateur, was well above UK Minor County standard. Recent past and current Springboks like Johnny Waite, Neil Adcock, Peter Heine, Hugh Tayfield and many others all took a regular part in the weekend league programmes.

I was very often the only Gentile in the predominately Jewish Balfour Park club side and never tired of their quick-fire, self-deprecating sense of humour. In many ways it was like being a bit player in a cricketing version of *Guys and Dolls*. During this period, besides some freelance writing of very forgettable three-paragraph rugby reports for the *Sunday Express* newspaper, I made a modest living by following in the footsteps of Allan Watkins and Emrys and Dai Davies, by doing some afternoon coaching for the Transvaal Cricket Union at selected secondary schools. It was short in hours, long in boredom. Thankfully the sessions were frequently curtailed by Johannesburg's regular summer afternoon thunderstorms. It was almost possible to set a watch by them; at four minutes past four the heavens would darken and ten minutes later came a torrential downpour.

If the rain didn't come as saviour, my method of coaching could sometimes be a painful experience. During a particularly tedious session with a succession of indifferent and/or marginally interested batsmen, in an effort to capture their attention I grabbed a stump, pushed the batsman to one side and said, "Look at the ball and do it this way."

There were some big and fairly brisk 17-year-old fast bowlers, waiting to launch themselves at the other end. At first they trundled down some medium-paced deliveries, but they were galvanised when I yelled down the pitch, "Come on, bowl properly." Until then, with this one stump, I'd middled all the balls bowled to the growing admiration of both bowlers and the watching batsman. This was to change when, responding to my shout, one of the bowlers at 80 mph nipped a delivery back off the seam and struck me full square on my unprotected left shin.

The pain was excruciating – but I dared not show it. I fended off a couple more before getting the schoolboy batsman to take guard again. Trying hard not to limp as I left the net, I somehow managed to carry on. Later, when rain brought a relieving halt and the students had all gone, I had a chance to look under my trouser leg. There was a lump the size of a small unicorn's horn on my shin. Nearly fifty years on, it's still there, albeit somewhat reduced in size.

Because of its ethnic base, Balfour Park's first eleven always seemed to get involved in the fiercest of contests. We were certainly a mixed bag in every sense. For instance, our wicket-keeper I knew as Harvey Nash. His actual name was Harold Nochamowitz. He had a full brother called Bennie Norman, a mother named Mrs. Lipschitz and a blood father whom I always knew as Mr. Cohen. The last two had been married forty years!

Then there was Kenny Siebert, a fine opening bowler on the fringe of provincial honours. A tail-end batsman, he'd also been a former South African amateur heavyweight boxing champion. I once found him standing under a running shower, holding his bat up to the spray. "What are you doing, Kenny?" I asked. "Well, I reckon, if I soften up the edges, the umpires won't hear any snicks," seemed his not unreasonable reply.

Joe Blewitt, of the high-pitched squeaky voice, hardly ever appealed because in his excitement in hitting the pads he reckoned that his shout would have been above the maximum range of the human ear.

We never saw Dirk van Blerk, a true 'Dutchman' he, ever eat. A fine bowler who even at Johannesburg's 6,000-feet rarefied altitude could swing the ball both ways, he was a committed brandy-drinker. As to why no food, his simple retort was, "I don't believe in eating on an empty stomach."

Boris Schroder, known to everyone as 'Bubbles' after a recent female murder victim of the same surname, was our scorer and main critic. His loud observations on our performances often led to umpires calling out from the middle for him to pipe down or leave the scorers' box.

But our principal supporter, often a useful threat if the opposition fans got too abusive, was the huge, menacing figure of Abe Wiseman (real name, Abe Snoyman). Abe billed himself as 'the Jewish heavyweight wrestling champion of the world'. No one dared challenge Abe on his claim, but he really was the most amiable of souls with an endless line in stories about his lengthy wrestling career both in South Africa and abroad. Despite the fact that he'd only won one contest in over 300 so-called fights, in those days all-action Abe was big box office. "I always play the villain," he told me. "If I ever thought I could beat whatever hyped-up polecat they imported to fight me, I'd quickly remember that my deal with the promoter was that, if I won, I didn't get paid."

His only victory came after a mental block on Abe's part when a pre-arranged move for his opponent to toss Abe out of the ring came badly unstuck. Struggling under our cricket supporter's 19-stone weight, Abe had to assist his opponent's move with a spring-heeled leap timed exactly at the right moment. Judea's finest duly fell into the lap of a woman in the front row who happened to be his opponent's mother. (Earlier Abe had met her in the dressing room when he and his opponent rehearsed their moves in what the fight's pre-publicity had billed as a 'grudge' contest.) She promptly stubbed her cigarette out on Abe's substantial buttocks. Enraged by this, our man slid back under the ropes and KO'd her son with a haymaking right hook. Realising what he'd done and with it the disappearance of his appearance money, Abe frantically tried to revive his comatose 'foe' with a series of phoney strangle-holds, but to no avail. His opponent remained out cold so, to his great chagrin, Abe was declared the winner!

I once went to watch Abe wrestle a tallish Texan called Sky Hi Lee. Billed as being six foot seven inches in height, he may actually have just topped six foot but, as he wrestled in high-heeled cowboy boots, the illusion was sustained. Abe had tipped me off that in the third round he was to be hoisted up onto Sky Hi's shoulders, who would then go into a propeller-type spin before throwing 275-pound Abe out of the ring. All went according to plan, except that connoisseurs of the grunt and groan game would have noticed that Abe seemed to be actually climbing on to his opponent's shoulders to allow this to happen. Into the spin went Sky but, staggering to support Abe's weight, he collapsed with Abe on top of him and was knocked unconscious. With the Texan down and out, the timekeeper, recognising a crisis for all, rang the bell a full minute before the scheduled end of the round. Sky was dragged back to his corner while, in the other, a concerned Abe wondered how he might get back on script. With a flash of inspiration he dashed across to his opponent's corner, gave him what appeared to be a mighty punch as he sat on his stool – but was really only an open-palmed slap – and, much to Abe's relief, he was promptly disqualified!

They were wonderful, carefree, humorous days spiced up by my having a series of excellent seasons with the club. In one of them a Johannesburg nightclub owner promised me a free evening for every 50 made or five wickets taken.

At the time I had a tall, elegant girl friend who rejoiced in the exotic name of Thirl – and an equally exotic job as a diamond sorter. I didn't get much in return in those anxious pre-contraceptive pill days but we did dance the summer nights away, often until dawn was breaking.

This off-field 'run of form' came in a spell when I attracted the kind of girl with her hands certainly on wealth, if not actually owning it. The following year, after Thirl had traded me in for a less exhausting partner, a Balfour Park team-mate of mine named Lou Harris asked if I'd take his visiting sister-in-law out on a blind date. He painted a glowing and persuasive picture of her beautiful face and figure. I took the bait.

She had another unusual name, 'Zan'. We had a brief, torrid affair until, after travelling to pick her up from her flat one Saturday night, I was halted at the door by six mean-looking policemen. They gave me a long grilling before I managed to convince them I was merely a caller on social business. Despite this they suggested I turn around and scarper. Stony-faced, fully-armed Afrikaner policemen tended to have their suggestions listened to, so I went.

Next morning's *Sunday Times* newspaper had a banner front-page picture and story of the Jo'burg police having arrested the prime suspect they'd been trying to corner for a number of years who headed up a multi-million pound, illicit diamond-buying syndicate. Yes, it was Zan. She eventually did a long stretch in prison.

But not all of life was so exciting, satisfying or unexpected. As a professional cricketer, albeit initially as very much a beginner in the trade, I was often approached by club cricketers for advice. Two occasions in particular remain in my memory. One involved a Balfour Park club mate, then still at school, who went on to become a lifelong friend. During a practice session he asked me what I thought of his grip on the bat. He was a predominantly on-side player, and I told him that unless he got his bottom right hand a lot further around the handle, he'd never make a batsman except as a shoveller on the leg side. He wisely ignored this well-intentioned advice and went on to become one of South Africa's leading Test batsmen, its captain and the world's most influential cricket administrator. His name? Ali Bacher.

The other sought my guidance at a net practice at Witwatersrand University. The blonde-haired student all-rounder belted the ball in and out of the net, missing some, edging others and being bowled at least half a dozen times. He then had a spell with the ball, swinging it away from the bat at fast-medium pace but all over the place in terms of length and direction. Afterwards he came up to me, oozing the kind of self-confidence that was to become his trademark. "What do you think, coach? he said. "How long do you reckon it'll be before I make it at the top level?"

I can remember my reply to this day: "Do you play any other sports?" I asked. "Well yes, actually last season I played outside-half for the Junior Springbok rugby team," came his swift reply. Drawing breath I came back with, "Well, if I were you, I'd stick to rugby."

Two years later this bouncy, bouncy young man was the best white all-rounder in world cricket. His name? Eddie Barlow. It wasn't so much a case of "Don't put your daughter on the stage, Mrs Worthington," rather "Don't let your son anywhere near that coach!"

There were any number of memorable matches in my years with Balfour Park during which time I also played for the province of Transvaal. But it's not the results, it's the stories surrounding the games and players involved which stick in my memory.

In a match to decide the league championship we played our arch-rivals Jeppe Old Boys, a team with four Springboks in their side and three provincial players to boot. It was at Jeppe's home ground. We arrived to find, at the bottom end of their sloping pitch and on a length, the grass had been left long and green as an encouragement – as if he needed it – to their ace fast bowler, the feared and ferocious Neil Adcock. The upper end's length had been shorn almost bare of grass and roughed up too to provide assistance to Athol Rowan, their skilful off-spin bowler who had only recently retired from the international scene.

We lost the toss and were put in to bat. When we received the news, our dressing room went uncharacteristically quiet. Captain Kenny Matthews, seeking to promote some confidence, looked at me and said, "Peter, you're a pro in England. Instead of batting at number four, today I'd like you to open." I had no choice; the others did. "And to open with you..." He glanced around a dressing room where suddenly everyone had found something important they needed in their cricket bags, pretending not to be listening. To break the impasse, Kenny found a typical Jewish solution: "We'll play cards for it. First one to draw a black deuce goes in with Peter."

The cards were dealt. The two of spades fell in front of our smallest player, five-foot-two-inch Joey Hersowitz, normally our number nine batsman and occasional spinner. As Joey made a dash for the door, he was rugby-tackled by his team-mates and held down while his pads and gloves were forcibly attached.

Looking like Peter Cook and Dudley Moore, we went out to the middle. I hadn't long been a pro but, when asked about how he tackled the fastest bowlers in the world, I'd learnt enough to subscribe to Len Hutton's maxim: "the best way to gets runs against a great fast bowler," he would pause for effect, "is from the backing-up end!"

So I said to Joey, now visibly shaking at the prospect of what lay ahead, "you take the first over because Neil won't be fully warmed up and it'll give you a chance to get a feel of the pace of the pitch and get your eye in." "Thhhhhhanks," stuttered Joey and did as he was told. Adcock had a 25-yard run-up. He raced in, if not at full throttle, then certainly well above half-pace. It pitched on a length and Joey, frozen like a rabbit in the headlights of a car, barely moved before it hit him under the heart. Down he fell. We gathered around, all except Adcock who was keen to get on with a ritual disembowelling. Joey got to his feet. "Are you OK?" I asked. A weak nod of agreement and so in came the Jeppe and Springbok's main strike bowler to deliver the second ball. It was slightly shorter but a lot quicker than the first. It hit Joey in the pit of his stomach, decking him again. This time he took a longer count before recovering. When he eventually got to his feet, all I could think of saying by way of encouragement was, "Well done, Joey, you're getting right behind the ball, just what we want. Keep battling on."

In came Adcock again, this time at full throttle. He tried to bowl Joey a genuine bouncer, but it pitched in the roughed-up end and skidded. It hit Joey straight amidships, and with a loud yell of anguish – in his anxiety he'd forgotten to insert his box – my opening partner fell in a heap, writhing in pain. Before any one could move to his assistance, our chairman Tuxie Teger grabbed a white towel on the pavilion balcony and threw it out onto the field, yelling out like a caring boxing manager, "My boy's had enough!" We stretchered Joey off. Oh, by the way, Jeppe won the match.

Before I set off back to Britain, I was able to satisfy one of my two remaining life's ambitions. I bought my first Parker 51 fountain pen. The other, to get myself a made-to-measure Savile Row suit, I'm still saving up for.

CHAPTER 6

WASHING MY HANDS OF THE SEA

As it turned out, I had not completely severed connections with my life in the merchant navy.

In the first two years of my contract with Glamorgan, the club agreed to pay for my passage out to South Africa, £45 for a place in a four-berth cabin, on the Union-Castle mail-boat which sailed from Southampton to Cape Town every Friday. It was then my responsibility to make it back to Cardiff in time for April's pre-season nets. So, ahead of the 1955 season, I travelled from Johannesburg to Cape Town in a two-door Morris Minor car with three friends, each of whom was also over six feet tall. Making this journey possible was Morris Charnas, a Balfour Park colleague of mine. Morris was a very talented slow left-arm spinner, who had represented Transvaal on several occasions and lacked only the self-belief that would have enabled him to make the next leap upwards to international level. A generous, amiable man, who once described himself as being "the only poor Jew I know", he had recently landed himself a new job selling insurance. With it came the Morris Minor and, when I suggested that he might like a break and drive me the 1,000 miles to Cape Town where I planned to get a job on a Union-Castle ship headed back to Britain, to my astonishment he readily agreed.

Dirk van Blerk got wind of the idea and asked if he too could come along as he was off to Europe on holiday. No problem. Then Morris – or Maish as he was known within the Jewish community – flagged up a problem: "I must take someone to share the driving on the way back." This was a fair point, but who would be dull enough to volunteer for the 2,000-mile round trip? Simultaneously we all thought of a pal of ours who played for the Old Maritstonians club. He was known, not without some justification, as 'Punchy' Boschoff.

Picture the scene when we arrived at Punchy's house to start the journey. Dirk and I had jam-packed the tiny, underpowered car with our luggage and the borrowed roof rack was fully loaded, too. Punchy came to the car, carrying a suitcase big enough to house Imelda Marcos's shoe collection! As one we demanded, "what the hell have you got in there for four days away, Punchy?" He opened it. All it contained was a t-shirt, a pair of underpants, two packets of Texan cigarettes and a 'tickey', a South African threepenny piece. And that was it! After some heated discussion we reached a compromise and set off with all of Punchy's kit now in a pillowcase. He propped this up against the front passenger-side window and, before we'd even left the Johannesburg city boundaries, he'd fallen fast asleep, waking only fitfully during the 24-hour journey to Cape Town and then only to light up a cigarette.

After his return to Jo'burg, Maish wrote to say that Punchy had slept all the way back and still had two Texan cigarettes and the tickey in his pillowcase!

In Cape Town, Dirk and I were forced to go our separate ways, he as a paying passenger on the Union-Castle mail-boat *Athlone Castle*, while I had no problem in signing on as a steward, or winger as they are known in the merchant navy. For me it certainly proved to be an interesting 14-day trip.

I was shown into my accommodation in the foc'sle, and warning bells rang in my brain when the cabin door opened and I found that the normally bare, single overhead light bulb had a lampshade and there was a rug on the floor. The cabin had six bunks, four on one side in stacked pairs, the other two on the opposite bulkhead. The cabin was empty when I entered. I checked which bunk appeared free; it was top left. I swung my suitcase up on to it and waited to meet my cabin mates. Not long afterwards they came in all together and introduced themselves.

"Hi," said the tall, thin, peroxide blonde with an unmistakable lisp and hip-swinging walk. "I'm Lillian," thoughtfully eyeing me up and down. "Welcome aboard," said the diminutive but muscular figure alongside him. "Call me Trixie." The sad-looking 50-year-old who badly needed a shave said, "My name's Jeannette but everyone calls me Jean." And the last member of the group, an archetypal Royal Navy stoker look-alike grunted, "And I'm Connie." All were dining-room stewards in the first-class saloon.

Those were the days when homosexuality was a criminal offence. Catering departments on passenger liners provided one of the few environments where they could break cover unmolested – in a manner of speaking. Although I had by now become a fully paid up, practising member of Heterosexuals United, I'd gained previous knowledge, if not personal experience, of what life below decks was like on passenger ships so I shook hands firmly with my four new shipmates – hoping this would get through to them that the 'mates' part of our short-term relationship would not include me.

That night we sailed from Cape Town en route to Las Palmas and Southampton.

In our cabin Lillian, Jean, Trixie and Connie threw a candlelit leaving party for their respective on-board boyfriends. It was a true bacchanalian evening. In some trepidation and, still with my jeans zipped up and tightly buckled, I crept into my top bunk and tried to sleep while shadowy figures danced and swayed below me. I must have dropped off, but I awoke with a start to find the cabin in darkness and a clammy hand stroking my chin from behind. It was time to make my position clear. I sat up and swung a punch into the darkness. It hit something soft, there was a grunt and then silence. My message had thankfully got through and, from then on, there was a truce between us. After all, they knew I was only on board for a fortnight.

A year later, the next working trip I made on the *Pretoria Castle* was nowhere near as exciting. On the *Athlone* my duties had entailed looking after the ship's engineers with a schedule which began at 05.30 and ended with the scrubbing out of their dining room floor around 22.30. But on the *Pretoria Castle*, I joined as a scullion, a word I thought had died out in the 17th century. I was stationed in the 'plate house' where the waiters used to charge in from the dining rooms and dump their used plates, scraps and all, onto a long trestle table. The other scullions and I would then be responsible for scraping off the residue of food into refuse sacks and then washing the crockery and cutlery in large vats of very hot soapy water. There were no effeminate rubber gloves issued in those days. At the height of a meal, when around 300 first- or second-sitting passengers were being served, plates were dumped on us at a fast and furious rate. If he got behind, one of my fellow scullions had a formula. Grabbing a stack of some ten plates, he'd dip them en bloc into the water and then, in one movement, swing them up into the drying racks, the middle sections almost completely untouched by water. When under real pressure, another old hand used to open a porthole and throw a heap of unwashed dishes out for the sea to clean and store!

I reckon in the 14 days I must have washed around 10,000 plates without dropping one. I regarded this as a positive indication of my developing catching skills.

On each of my two Union-Castle trips I paid off in Southampton 15 pounds lighter in weight but £25 heavier in my pocket as wages. These trips were to be my final stints as a seaman, ending a series of voyages which had begun in 1952 as a 16-year-old runaway schoolboy.

In 1957 I had either to consolidate my position within the Glamorgan first team, or to think about diverting into some other profession. I'd always enjoyed writing diaries and the occasional newspaper article, no doubt a gene handed on to me by my father and his father before him. After two erratic years on the Glamorgan junior staff it was time to get serious and work at cricket, a game at which, despite my own misgivings, a few influential people obviously thought I had some talent.

Where this book all began – Cardiff Arms Park dressing room, 1957.
Wicket-keeper David Evans wondering what on earth I've found to write about.

Wilf Wooller's stock reply to public and press criticism of Glamorgan's failure to repeat its championship success of 1948 was to say, "We're in a transitional period." For most of my career, bar an extraordinary, purple patch between 1968 and 1970 when we finished third, first and second, the playing staff had little idea as to where we were in transit from – or to!

Wilf could take real umbrage at media criticism of his players. I witnessed one memorable example of this when, after yet another defeat, Peter Moss, a well-respected cricket writer on the *Daily Mail*, tapped on the dressing-room door and asked Wilf if he could get a quote from one of the Glamorgan batsmen who was experiencing a bad run of form. Wilf leapt across the dressing room and, to our astonishment, grabbed Peter by the throat and wrestled him to the floor, pushing him under the large table in the middle. The senior players managed to pull Wilf off, and a dishevelled Moss rapidly exited. Peter could so easily have laid a charge of GBH against Wilf, but he didn't. However, particularly to the junior members of the team, it was a graphic illustration of what would happen if we crossed the captain.

Wilf was a dynamic captain, the best I ever played with or against and certainly so early in my career on the rare moments when Glamorgan got into a winning position. On the much more frequent occasions when we were losing, often inside two days, Wilf would become a tenacious, dogged rearguard-action scrapper. As a World War II POW survivor, he was physically brave too. In 1954, Wilf had listened to 50-year-old veteran opening batsman Emrys Davies come back into the dressing room after facing Northamptonshire's Frank 'Typhoon' Tyson who had, almost literally, exploded on the scene. He had been bowled for 0, and he announced his retirement from the game with the chilling words, "Skipper, I'm finishing, I can't see the ball." Wilf, already 41 years old himself, had no hesitation in taking on Emrys's opening role for the rest of the season and the next two.

In the run-up to this incident, we'd all heard on the player grapevine of Tyson and his amazing pace. He and Northants wicket-keeper Keith Andrew had come out before the start of the match to warm up. On the outfield, in front of the Glamorgan dressing room window and from a mere three-yard jog, Frank fired one down at Keith some thirty yards back. It comfortably cleared his head one bounce! A hush had fallen over our dressing room, particularly amongst the first five batsmen. It had been a superb piece of softening-up psychology.

In a later game against Northamptonshire, I was batting with Wilf when Tyson took the second new ball. He went back to the start of his 25-yard run, bounded in and hit Wilf a fearful blow under the heart. The 17-stone, ex-Welsh rugby centre buckled at the knees and leant forward on his bat handle, taking deep breaths. Everyone, including Tyson, rushed down to Wilf's end. Looking up, the batsman's eye first lit on the concerned 'Typhoon' who asked anxiously, "Are you alright skipper?" Wooller, whose face had drained of all colour, glared back. "Why don't you fuck off, Frank; you're not quick enough to hurt me." I couldn't believe what I was hearing. If you retained an interest in staying alive, this was certainly no way to talk to a genuine fast bowler.

Suitably aroused, Tyson went back to the end of his run and, if anything, next ball bowled an even faster delivery which reared from just short of a length. Most mortals would have been treading on the square-leg umpire's shoes, but not Wilf. He was right behind the ball, bat and gloves up in front of his face, 'no surrender' exuding from every pore.

Then, in a game against Surrey and despite having a right index finger broken in the previous game, Wilf opened the batting at The Oval to find himself on the end of an intimidating, around-the-wicket bouncer barrage – numbers unlimited in those days – from the hostile and mean-spirited England fast bowler, Peter Loader. The pitch was a rock-hard, green-top 'flier' freshened still further by a shower of rain. "I've waited years for this," growled Loader who felt he'd been unfairly treated by the England selectors of whom Wilf was one. Our captain never flinched, even when struck on his injured hand, and, believe it or not, but typical of Wilf, he and Loader shared a convivial beer or two at close of play.

There were so many other incidents involving my first county captain which remain vivid memories. In a game against Nottinghamshire at Trent Bridge, after damaging another finger, he put me in his usual position three yards from the bat at forward short leg. Their opening bowler Arthur Jepson had a reputation of being a powerful tail-end hitter. Off-spinner Jimmy McConnon flighted one up to him, and it went past my right ear and, with two bounces, over the boundary rope. I moved back a couple of feet. The following ball got the same treatment and, believing my time had come, I retreated still further to give myself a better chance of taking evasive action. But next ball, Jimmy beat him in the flight; Jepson changed his mind and prodded forward. The ball hit the inside edge of his bat and looped from his front pad to where I'd begun the over. I dived forward and just failed to get my right hand under the ball.

Before I could get up, a booming voice behind me from mid-on shouted, "Stay where you are." I lay there, arm still outstretched. Wilf came up, compared the position to which I had retreated to where he'd originally placed me. He then proceeded to scratch a line which, I swear, was no more than two yards from Jepson. "Move from there, and you'll never play for Glamorgan again," said my skipper, turning on his heel.

What happened? Not unexpectedly Arthur had an almighty swish at the next ball, missed and was bowled. If he'd connected, I wouldn't have been around to write this book.

Wilf used to have endless verbal battles with opposing captains. Players on both sides became reconciled to the fact that they were taking part in a private game between the two skippers with the remaining twenty of us mere bystanders. His particular bête noire was Robin Marlar of Cambridge and Sussex. There was one particular game when Robin came out to bat. Wilf had taken the previous wicket and was waiting to bowl to him.

Before facing a ball, Robin called down the pitch in a loud voice to his partner, "You stay that end, I'll handle Wilf." This from a man with a career batting average in single figures! At the intended jibe, Wilf lost his cool. He ran in to bowl his medium-fast away-swingers with even greater purpose. Robin proceeded to play and miss at four balls an over but somehow survived. After this had gone on for some while, Wilf paused in his follow-through and said, "Robin, which way is the east?" Marlar waved in the direction of square-leg. To gales of laughter, including Robin, Wilf got down on his knees and bowed three times in that direction. I tell no lie, two balls later he had his old foe edging one – caught behind!

The bowler Wilfred Wooller. A giant of a man and a leader of men.
Batsman Jack Robertson of Middlesex, fielder Emrys Davies.

Although his prowess at the summer game was certainly inferior to that at rugby union, in 1954 Wilf did the cricketing double, 1,000 runs and 100 wickets. In the penultimate match of the season at Edgbaston, and despite suffering from a strained Achilles tendon so bad that he had to come down the hotel staircase backwards to minimise the pain, he still needed six wickets to reach his hundred and complete the double. As always Wilf took the new ball and, heavily strapped up and ignoring the pain, bowled 32 overs in Warwickshire's first innings, 28 in the second, and in the process managed to take the six wickets he needed.

When he reached the milestone, the Warwickshire chairman walked out to the middle, carrying a bottle of champagne and some glasses, and everyone drank to the health of one of the game's most gutsy characters.

Then, in the final game of the season against Derbyshire at Chesterfield and still strapped up, he bowled a further 35 overs straight off and took five for 45!

I never met anyone else who could give one the most fearful bollocking on the field – and shut the door on the incident at close of play. Wilf was not a man to harbour a cricketing grudge nor let fierce debate affect a relationship. But he was always prepared to test the mettle of the opposition and, in particular, his own players.

I had first-hand experience of this early on in my career. At Bristol in 1957 I started a spell of bowling; at this stage I had rather lost my spinner's natural action and had converted myself into a medium-pace swing bowler. I got a fairly early wicket and, five hours later, was still bowling, my eventual analysis being 50.3 consecutive overs, 10 maidens, 116 runs and 7 wickets. *Wisden* called it 'an exceptional feat'. Not once did Wilf ask me how I was feeling or whether I wanted a rest; I think he was waiting for me to fall over with fatigue. It was his way of putting me to a test that I'm sure that he himself would have taken on, even then aged 44.

He belonged to a different breed of men did Wilfred Wooller; a skipper who, if he felt a player was not giving of his best, could be quite ruthless and cutting in both criticism and action but kind, forgiving and supportive to those having a hard time on or off the field.

During the summer of 1958 the Glamorgan committee decided it was time to find a successor to Wilf, who by then was nearly 46 years old.

They unearthed the 34-year-old AC 'Tolly' Burnett, who felt he would enjoy a break from teaching science at Eton College! This was despite the fact that his only first-class cricket had been eight years earlier as a Cambridge undergraduate, where his record as a batsman had hardly been impressive.

He duly arrived in Cardiff to play in the last eight matches of the season, the first six under Wilf's leadership, the last two as captain in his own right. Batting at number six, Tolly's contributions were: 9, 0 (in a Glamorgan total of 26 against Lancashire!), 12, 8, 0, 17, 2, 9, 4, 0 and 10. His final match was at Ebbw Vale where in the first innings he was blown away for 0 by Frank Tyson; then in the second, as captain, he dropped himself further and further down the order, waiting until Tyson had been removed from the firing line!

He was an accomplished pianist but, when Wilf asked him to play *The Eton Boating Song* in our Weston-super-Mare hotel lounge, he claimed not to know it! In more than one sense, Mr AC 'Tolly' Burnett's cover was blown and he was never seen nor heard of again on our side of the Severn Bridge!

In the 1950s most youngsters coming into a county side did the out-fielding. Men who had come through the war had lost much of their fleetness of foot, so we kids did the hunting of leather and the long-distance throwing. At the start I was no different. It was Wilf who changed that.

In 1957 I got into the county side in the middle of June. In my second match we played Warwickshire at Cardiff Arms Park and, much to Wilf's annoyance, were bowled out for 176 on a good pitch. It was a blazing hot day and, by late afternoon, we were fielding with the game slipping away fast.

The Arms Park was a massive ground, no 75-yard boundaries in those days. I was running between overs from third man to third man, a journey of some 200 yards each way. My diagonal cross-field route took me past our profusely sweating, less-than-pleased-with-life captain who, after an unproductive opening spell, was about to put on off-spinner Jim McConnon.

As I crossed the pitch and eager to please, I asked, "Where would you like me to field, skip?" Wilf turned a baleful eye on me and said, in a phrase which was to change my cricketing life, "Oh, for Christ's sake, Peter, spit in the air and go where it lands." He immediately lost interest in my whereabouts and set about placing the remainder of McConnon's field.

One rarely argued with Wilfred Wooller, most certainly not on the field. So, as a junior player, I did as I was told, moved to the edge of the pitch, lifted my head and spat in the air. It fell at short square leg. I went there and, second ball from McConnon, Warwickshire batsman Norman Horner pushed forward and got an inside edge. I dived to my left and caught it at full stretch two inches above the ground.

I was to spend the majority of the next 16 years in that position!

If I can claim immodestly to have made any indelible imprint on the game of cricket, it must have been in close catching. In 469 first class matches, I ended up with 697 catches, well behind Frank Woolley's all-time total of 1,018 – but then his career spanned 33 years, not far off twice as long as mine. But for Wilf, I might never have got even that close.

In 1999, when long retired, at the National Exhibition Centre in Birmingham I was asked to deliver a workshop session on close catching to coaches from all over the cricketing world. They had been invited there by the England and Wales Cricket Board as part of their plan to nurture grass-root level cricket in every country where the game was played.

As with sex, each new generation of cricketers believes that the ones preceding it were either naive and/or incompetent. Batting and bowling techniques and equipment may well have evolved and undergone substantial changes, but catching a ball is the same today as it was in W.G. Grace's time.

Here is an abridged version of what I put in that paper handed around to those coaches. I think it still applies to this day ...

Chapter 7

CLOSE ENCOUNTERS

CLOSE TO THE WICKET FIELDING
– THE NEGLECTED ART

Close to the wicket, any high-class fielder should be able to catch equally well with both hands. As a natural left-hander I spent a good deal of my early professional career practising taking catches to my right as well, making stops and swiftly returning the ball to the stumps from close range from both wings. This training routine continued on a daily basis during the season and throughout my 16-year career in the first-class game.

By the time I had established a reputation in the game as a close catcher fit, so critics and my peers said, to be ranked with the best of all time, I actually slightly preferred the ball coming to my right-hand side!

Preferred, I might have. Anticipating it would do so, NEVER!

Why? Because it is impossible to pre-determine accurately the thickness of an edge, the ball's pace off the bat or its trajectory, particularly if it deflects off the batsman's pad too. All the finest catchers I ever played with or against, and indeed have subsequently observed, stood very still at the moment the ball was played. They then reacted instinctively to what happened after the batsman had made contact.

Of course co-ordination between eye and hand and lightning-fast reflexes are essential if you are to become a top-class close catcher. These can be speeded up with improved concentration levels and planned practice sessions. Remember, you have about 0.5 of a second, (if you've really close to the bat it can be only 0.3), in which your eyes have to relay the message to the brain as to where the ball is and tell your body and hands where to go!

One little exercise I developed certainly improves hand/eye co-ordination and reflex speed. Start with two 50-pence pieces. Lay one towards the end of your fingers, the other on the butt of the palm. Straighten your arm out to shoulder height, palm upwards. Gently, and I mean gently, and keeping your arm straight, flip the coins slightly into the air. Quickly turn your hand over so that the palm now faces downwards and then, one at a time, snatch each of the coins back into your hand. The whole operation should be completed before the coins have dropped to chest height.

This exercise must be done without bending the knees, following the coins downwards and of course, not dropping the first coin in pursuit of the second.

When you can catch four coins (the third resting at the base of your fingers, the fourth on your wrist), WITH EACH HAND, you will have matched the reflex action of all the finest close catchers in cricket's history!

STANCE: I suggest you spread your feet a fraction wider than your shoulders. Do not splay them outwards which weakens your base. If anything, I'd prefer to see a fielder stand slightly pigeon toed. Try this for yourself. With toes pointing out at, say, 10 to 2 on an imaginary clock face, you'll find it difficult to obtain sufficient leverage to push off sharply either left or right. Now "toe in" and, with your weight slightly forward on the balls of your feet, you'll be immediately aware of being able to generate much greater propulsion from this stronger platform.

HEAD AND BODY POSITION: Because of the way the powerful muscles in the back work, from a semi-crouched position it's far easier to extend yourself rapidly upwards or sideways than it is to try to bend down quickly. So, with your forearms just off your thighs, keep your hands relaxed and reasonably close together, fingers pointing slightly downwards, chin up, head still. Your weight should be spread 70-30 onto the balls of your feet.

EYES: Remember, you catch the ball with your eyes. So, in order to give them the best chance of sending a clear and concise message first to your brain and on to your hands, it's vital to keep your head STILL, particularly when the bowler is on the point of releasing the ball. Just watch a jockey's head on board 30mph of pounding horseflesh. Despite all the moving action beneath him, it remains virtually still.

Whether you watch the roll of the front pad, the bat's edge or, if you're fielding in a near straight line to the bowler, as at first slip, and prefer to look at the bowler and then track the ball down the pitch, do please only allow your head to move fractionally from side to side, not up and down. It's difficult not to overstate the importance of minimising the amount of head movement, particularly at the moment the ball hits the bat. This is the "moment of truth" which, within the blink of an eye, affects everything that follows.

ANTICIPATION: DON'T! No human being can possibly anticipate the thickness of an edge, the angle or height the ball will come off the bat, nor its speed. If in your mind you have subconsciously thought to yourself, "this ball is going to my right," you're in

Catching Geoff Clayton of Lancashire at Cardiff Arms Park.

70

big trouble if it doesn't, for even if your body has stayed still, your chances of catching the ball if it goes left will be substantially reduced because your brain has been pre-programmed to move your hands and body to the right.

Watch top-class goalkeepers if you need further convincing. They invariably anticipate which way a penalty kick is going to go; if they guess wrong, they're left high and dry.

PHYSICAL CONDITION: By all means work in the gym to improve your overall fitness levels, but make sure a high percentage of your time isn't wasted on pure aerobics and pumping iron. Instead concentrate on exercises which improve your flexibility. Indoors, use gymnastic mats to provide a cushion. Learn how to dive and break your fall, either with your free hand or by twisting in the air to land on the back of your shoulder. I learnt to do this the hard way – throwing and catching potatoes with a fellow crewman on a ship's metal deck – no mats there!

One of the most tiring training exercises ever devised is to take a position in between two gymnastic mats and get a colleague standing around five yards away to throw or better still hit a tennis ball with a racquet wide to your right or left while trying to disguise which way he's going to direct the ball. Get it back to him as quickly as you can and, equally swiftly, take up your stance again. Using a tennis ball at first is a good idea as it tends to bounce out of one's hand unless caught cleanly in the fingers. After training with a tennis ball, a cricket ball is so much easier to hang on to.

Three non-stop minutes of this exercise and you'll swear that you've just run a sub-45 second 400 metres!

Glamorgan v India at Swansea 1959
Catching Abbas Ali Baig. If the photographer had been a split second faster on the shutter, my left arm would have been fully extended.

71

PRACTICE: The old wooden slip 'cradle' is coming back into vogue although the modern fashion of one player throwing the ball waist high and fast to another with a bat, who then slices it into the waiting cordon of slip fielders, now predominates.

I much preferred using a rectangular four-to-five-foot square metal frame with a taut nylon webbing which springs the ball back to the thrower. The downside is that the return angles are usually predictable, but it does mean that you can practise alone at various distances, in the process improving your throwing with either hand, too, as you hurl the ball back at the net. Again, a tennis ball is ideal for you can stand close and vary the action by throwing the ball not just at the middle but the corners, too, which give a more unpredictable return.

COURAGE: Fielding anywhere close in front or square of the bat, particularly on the leg side, needs courage. It's like the ability to bowl fast, either you have it or you don't. No coach or manual can instil this in you. These days, while helmets, chest and shin pads make life safer if not more comfortable, they inevitably hamper agility. Some of the bravest players of quick bowling become timid souls when fielding near the bat. You have to stand there to find out if you've got the bottle – or stupidity, some would say.

CONCENTRATION: We all have different methods of concentrating. Mine was to take a mental break after every ball, chat to a nearby fielder, or the batsman if he's so inclined, look at any passing "talent" on the boundary edge, think of a limerick, count the blades of grass between your feet … until the bowler turns to run in, do anything that takes your mind away from the next ball. Then the 'light switch' in the brain goes on.

If you only touch the ball competitively a dozen times, you should find you come off the field at the end of a day mentally very tired. To a close fielder, the last ball of the day is as important as the first. A half chance taken at 6 pm could turn – or win – a match.

WHERE TO STAND? The finest catchers stand closest to the bat. There's a simple reason. The closer you are to the batsman the more edges – or shots off the middle – will come straight at you. Go back a yard and the catching area to be covered widens. It's pointless standing too close if a genuine edge is going to fly past outside your reaction time. How deep you stand will depend on the pace and bounce of the pitch. You also need to have faith in the accuracy of your bowlers, something not always possible to guarantee at professional, let alone club level.

CHECKS AND BALANCES: Part of my 'check list' routine, particularly in the first few overs, would be, after a ball had passed through to the wicketkeeper, I'd brush the backs of my hands lightly across the grass underneath me. If I couldn't touch the ground, then it meant that I'd stood up slightly around about the time the ball passed the batsman. My eye line therefore must have been on the move, too. Throughout the day, but in particular right at the start, I always wanted the keeper to throw the ball to me to relay on back to the bowler. Feeling the ball hit into your hands breeds familiarity, not contempt – as well as confidence.

If, irrespective of speed, the ball kind of melts into your hands, then your timing is spot on. You'll know if this form is true the very first time you touch it. If the ball doesn't feel a part of you as it enters your hands, then make very sure you quickly get hold of it again and then throw it from one hand to the other until it does.

EQUIPMENT: I'm old-fashioned. I don't like to see helmets worn by close catchers. It makes average fielders braver than they should be for their own safety. Also, a helmet is a very heavy object. Diving for catches requires suppleness and agility. Any superfluous weight or padding acts like additional deadweight on a horse in the Grand National steeplechase.

ATTITUDE: Try for everything! There just isn't the time available to weigh up whether or not a fast-flying edge is within range. Ingrain in your subconscious the belief that every single ball bowled is coming your way. You'll quickly turn this excellent habit into your norm and in the process catch some that nobody, including on reflection you yourself, believed you had a hope of getting anywhere near.

Slip fielders at club level often use the ancient method of sticking their arms out to measure a perceived correct gap between them. By all means do this, but I would suggest that, having done so, each fielder then takes a further step away from his colleague. This fixes in the mind that, wherever the ball travels, 'it's mine!' Everywhere should be your territory. Staggering the line of the slips, too, is a must. You don't want to be aware of someone at your shoulder and in your eye line. You are the only one who matters. Fielding can, and indeed always should, be ultra-competitive.

Remember, too, that close fielding is not just about hanging on to catches. It's about run saving as well, particularly in the gully and on the leg side, backward and short square-legs. Top-class fielders in these positions can save up to 20 runs in a day, in the process making a major contribution to restricting the opposing side's total. This is a key area, particularly in the early stages of limited-over cricket where fielding restrictions, wicket-taking and especially runs saved are important factors.

Like great batsmen and bowlers, outstanding fielders create their own aura of skill and invincibility which puts extra pressure on the batsman at the crease and on those watching a tight contest from the dressing room. Think of South African Jonty Rhodes, and you'll know what I mean. Close to the bat, a wonderful short-leg fielder or gully is just as much of a menace!

On a good day, when one or more brilliant catches or run-saving dives have brought you the adulation of your team-mates and possibly the media, too, all your practice, determination and courage will be receiving its just reward.

Chapter 8
THINGS FALL INTO PLACE

During the period I was transiting in and out of the first team, it took me a long time to score my first ever century. It came at the BP Llandarcy Refinery ground near Neath, for Glamorgan Colts against the South Wales League Select XI. At the end of the match Les Harris, who was their opening bowler and who back in the 1940s had had a few games for the Glamorgan county side, came up and congratulated me. He said that I'd have a long career in the game. It was a small but important gesture to a youngster who, despite an extrovert exterior, was inwardly something of the opposite, with all the inbuilt lack of confidence that goes with such a split personality.

When I finally established myself in the Glamorgan first team, things began to improve at a far quicker rate than, I suspect, even my mentor Wilf Wooller thought possible.

Being awarded a county cap was an important milestone for a player. Up to that point one was in a constant state of uncertainty, usually pogo-sticking in and out of the team. A cap was the club's recognition that you had arrived. One could then afford to have a poor run of form but still be retained in the first team. There used to be a fairly straightforward formula about being awarded a cap. First, establish a regular place in the county side; then produce a match-winning performance. Once that happened, it followed – albeit not automatically – that ten years later one would be granted a benefit season. This would be a committee decision, based on the concept of loyal service dating from the awarding of the cap. It was feudal in concept certainly, but much valued nevertheless.

In the days when no cricketer in the land earned £1,000 a year, the long-standing post-war benefit record of £14,000 by Lancashire's Cyril Washbrook represented riches to rival Croesus. A benefit was a one-off chance to amass some capital. It was tax free, too, and remains so to this day, thanks to a 1926 decision in the House of Lords. In Relf versus the Inland Revenue, their lordships found that, as it was not written into Relf's contract, it should be regarded as a gift for past services rendered, not a contractual entitlement from the club to the player.

My cap was awarded early in 1958 at Northampton. It was not a particularly memorable match for me, but it followed a run of useful scores, a handful of wickets and a number of high-quality catches which earned me the press nickname of "Flypaper Fingers" Walker. It was customary for a newly capped player to buy his team-mates a drink. So, on the way back from Northampton, we stopped at a pub in Stow-on-the-Wold. The round made a great dent in my week's wages.

Through the experience of sleeping over a rope in New York, I had developed a reputation of being, shall we say, 'frugal' with money. That round of drinks came as a severe financial blow. Before having my salary doubled after the award of my cap and the bonus levels considerably upped too, I had been on a basic salary of four pounds ten shillings a week with three pounds per match for a first-team appearance and a further three pounds if we won – which we only did five times that season.

My benefit was actually awarded eight years after receiving my county cap. It realised £4,500, which in those days wasn't far off a Glamorgan record. Nowadays, leading players frequently top a quarter of a million pounds. Even allowing for inflation, that's a quantum leap. My net figure actually was £3,250 because I lost £1,250 on a pop concert held at the old Capitol cinema in Queen Street, Cardiff despite putting on a bill including top-ten groups like Gerry and the Pacemakers and Billy J Kramer and the Dakotas. It had been fixed for me, at a discounted cost, by Vic Lewis, a London-based cricket nut. Vic was a former bandleader and a manager who handled The Beatles and was repaying favours for the times when I had been in London and played for his team in Sunday charity matches.

Why did such a big-name bill 'bomb?' Who knows, for despite a great deal of publicity, hardly anyone turned up!

I remember standing on the steps of the cinema afterwards and sadly realising that an event which everyone who knew about such things told me was an odds-on, huge money-spinning winner, had in fact cost me a third of my benefit!

Different expectations then, different returns now in the 21st century.

But the joy of playing a game I loved compensated me for the financial loss. Cricket brought far greater intangible rewards within the Glamorgan team and friendships amongst other counties' players which last to this day. You can't put a value on these. At receptions and parties, people frequently asked me what I did for a living. When I said "I'm a professional cricketer", noses would occasionally be wrinkled either in surprise or disdain. I had a query in return, "Do you look forward to Mondays?" Few would nod 'yes', at which I would quickly add, "Personally, I can hardly wait for the weekend to be over." Saying this helped to confirm my own sense of worth.

I spent one October, living the life of a beatnik on the then almost deserted Mediterranean island of Ibiza, starting and failing to complete a novel based on the romantic idea that the ancient Greek city of Atlantis had sunk beneath the waves. This I'd started the year before after spending a couple of pre-season weeks in Las Palmas, another Spanish island off the North African coast. There I'd got friendly with a Swedish girl who had been abandoned by her boy friend who ditched her to set off solo across the Atlantic in his 42-foot yacht. Unsurprisingly her eyes reflected a look of deep sadness. She'd remarked one day how interesting it was that a lot of the indigenous people of Las Palmas had blonde hair and blue eyes, whereas the nearby coast of Africa was either African or Arabic. This sowed the idea of my book about Atlantis.

Together with my Glamorgan club mate Billy Davies who had spent the winter with me coaching in Johannesburg, we then spent three days on a small cargo ship from Las Palmas to Cadiz. On board were a group of 20 desert-hardened Spanish Sahara legionnaires, who all looked like character actors out of the film *Beau Geste*. The evenings were whiled away sitting in a circle on deck with one legionnaire playing guitar as accompaniment to the others singing flamenco songs. It was magical.

In the British winter of 57/58 I had played a couple of early season games for Balfour Park in Johannesburg before getting itchy feet. I had met up again with my old Cardiff flat-mate Vernon Booth who had emigrated to South Africa the previous year, and in October I borrowed his ancient Citroen car to set off for Cape Town. I decided on a 'small' detour going via Durban, making it a round trip – Jo'burg back to Jo'burg – of not far off 2,300 miles!

Soon after I'd arrived in Cape Town and at my father's suggestion, I looked up an ex-newspaper pal of his. His daughter Patricia opened the door – in more senses than one. At the time of our meeting she was 18 and on the point of going to Cape Town University. Three decades later Pat Kavanagh had become, and remains, one of England's most respected literary agents.

In a matter of hours, not days, Pat and I became inseparable. But then, when I'd only been in South Africa's 'mother city' three days, a message came through that I'd been selected to play for Transvaal against the touring Australians. I delayed my 1,000-mile direct return trip to Johannesburg to the very last minute and, with the proverbial heavy heart, set off 48 hours before the start of the match with a deadline to make the Transvaal practice nets at the Wanderers Stadium the day before the game was due to begin. After nearly 24 hours behind the wheel, broken only by two short sleeps in the middle of the semi-desert Karoo and in a plantation near Bloemfontein, I arrived a mere half an hour before the session was due to start. This was not ideal preparation, particularly as I was first man into the nets to face our opening attack of Neil Adcock and Peter Heine!

During the match itself, won comfortably by Australia by nine wickets against the best provincial team in the land, I hadn't particularly disgraced myself, catching Peter Burge at short leg from the bowling of off-spinner Hugh Tayfield. But, shortly afterwards, disaster struck when, in the same position and off the same bowler, I made an absolute sleep-walking hash of an easy chance. The batsman was the young Bobby Simpson, later to become his country's captain, coach and selector.

Inexperienced Bobby had started the tour badly and was only just into double figures when Hugh beat him in the air and the batsman got the thinnest of inside edges; I thought, it's mine! The ball, however, had slightly brushed Simpson's front pad and that fractionally slowed it on its way towards my hands. They shut a moment too soon, and the chance was dropped. Bobby went on to make 103, which launched him on a long and distinguished career in the game. On the rare occasions we now meet, it's the first memory we exchange.

To compound my discomfort, at a cocktail party for both sides on the last night, Ian Meckiff, the Australians' fast left-arm 'chucker' opening bowler, rubbed in the fact that he'd got me lbw in Transvaal's first innings by also seducing away Antoinette 'Tony' Botha, my Audrey Hepburn look-alike girl friend at the time.

Dropping Australian Bobby Simpson from a dolly of a catch off the bowling of Hugh Tayfield at the Wanderers, Johannesburg. Transvaal v Australia 1958. A miss which launched Simpson on a distinguished international career.

Not a good match to remember, for sure! Cricket, too, could be a fickle mistress.

There was a sort of PS to my brief encounter with Pat Kavanagh. Prior to the start of the 1958 season and en route back to the UK on the *Winchester Castle*, I sat on deck drinking a Castle lager out of a bottle. I missed her. At the time we were some 40 miles off shore from Spanish Morocco, rounding the bulge of Africa. So I got some writing paper from the ship's lounge, scribbled a short love letter using a biro pen and on the outside of the envelope put her address in Cape Town with mine on the back. In my rudimentary Spanish I also wrote on the outside, 'Would the finder of this please take it to the British Consul." I then made a tube of it and squeezed it into the now empty beer bottle. I retrieved the lift-off metal cap, smacked it back into place, kissed the bottle and threw it over the side of the ship, thinking it would drift onto the African mainland.

As they say in cricket, not for the first time in my life, I'd 'picked the wrong line'.

Soon after my departure from Cape Town for the less romantic cauldron of county cricket, Pat had attracted a new admirer, a bearded architectural student at Cape Town University. As time passed, I forgot about the bottle – but not about Pat. Then, some fifteen months later, I received a copy of a letter sent to her by the British Consul in Ciudad Trujillo, the capital of the Dominican Republic in the Caribbean.

July 24th 1959

Dear Miss Kavanagh

I have pleasure in enclosing a letter addressed to you by Mr. Peter Walker (of 188 Llandaff Road, Cardiff, Wales) which was picked up in a bottle found in Scotch Bay (Bahia Escocesa) on the north-east coast of this island, (latitude 19 degrees, 25 mins north; longitude 69 degrees 53 mins west) and delivered to me on July 16th 1959 by the Dominican naval authorities.

The bottle was dropped in the sea by Mr. Walker on April 8th 1958 off Oran, Algeria. He gave his position as 35 degrees 10 mins north and 0 degrees 20 mins west from the SS Winchester Castle. It must have drifted through the Straits of Gibraltar and was then carried across the Atlantic by the Canaries current and North equatorial current following roughly Christopher Columbus' first voyage.

I have sent copies of this letter to Mr. Walker and the Admiralty, London.

Yours truly.

W.W. McVittie   (H.M. Ambassador)

When I told Richard, my seafaring uncle in Bristol, about this, he said that although my navigation was poor – I'd given completely the wrong longitude and my knowledge of currents was faulty too – my casual toss over the side was one of the longest bottle drifts ever recorded. It seems that even hermetically sealed containers gently put over the side from specialist survey ships are rarely found; they either spring a leak or sink after having their tops pecked open by seagulls. I can only assume that the birds either didn't like the taste of the dregs of Castle lager, they couldn't read or, most likely, the power of love kept it afloat.

Back-tracking a little, shortly before returning to the UK ahead of the 1958 season, I'd unexpectedly been approached by an Indian businessman in Johannesburg to round up a team of overseas professionals to play against his own invitation, non-European team. Remember, this was in the days of apartheid when in public inter-racial gatherings needed a government permit. I duly contacted the English professionals who were coaching in and around Jo'burg. We played the match (with a permit) on a matting pitch and sand outfield at Natalspruit, a non-white designated sports field on the outskirts of Johannesburg – and were soundly beaten. To their eternal credit, two white Springboks, batsman Ken Funston and all-rounder Tiger Lance, had rung me and asked to be included in the side – but they made no difference to the result.

We smuggled a few cartons of beer into the ground which, at the end of play and much to our opponents' amazement, we insisted on sharing with them in their dressing room. We had to do this away from the prying eyes of the white security cops who were scattered around the ground and whose job was to try to make sure there was no inter-racial fraternising.

In the opposition team were two talented Cape Coloured players, later to feature in English cricket: Cecil Abrahams, who went to the Lancashire leagues and whose son John played for and captained Lancashire, and Basil D'Oliveira. who starred for Middleton, Worcestershire and eventually

England. After the South African Nationalist government's refusal to accept him as an MCC touring team member, claiming that his selection had been politically motivated, Basil's omission became a major weapon in the battle to defeat the devil of apartheid.

The summer of 1958, which began with my winning my cap, also provided me with my maiden first-class century, against Surrey at Swansea. Three weeks earlier at Coventry I had run myself out for 99, but in July– against a Surrey attack that included Peter Loader, Tony Lock and Jim Laker – I made 104 not out. As I cautiously inched my way to that hundred, Loader – with the second new ball in his hand – came down the wicket to me. I was on 85, and he said with barely concealed malice, "You'll have to fetch the next 15 fuckers." He was right, too, for he bowled boomerang out-swingers outside my off stump for four overs, and I had to scramble the required runs at the other end.

Going back to that match at Coventry, Warwickshire had drafted in a West Indian-born, fast-bowling Birmingham bus driver called Shirley Griffiths. He was mighty quick for a few overs and came racing to the crease from a 30-yard run-up. It had been a blisteringly hot day and, with Glamorgan in the process of building a massive total, late in the afternoon he was chucked the second new ball. He set off on his lengthy run for his 32nd over of the innings but, half way to the wicket, slowly ground to a halt. Bending over and putting his hands on his knees he announced in a loud voice, "Man, ma legs is too tired for ma body," and tossed the ball back to his captain, Mike Smith!

Receiving gold cuff links and a bottle of champagne for most catches in the month of May, 1959. *Left to right:* Phil Thomas (Glamorgan Assistant Secretary), Jimmy Hill, Allan Watkins, Peter Walker, John Evans (Glamorgan physio).

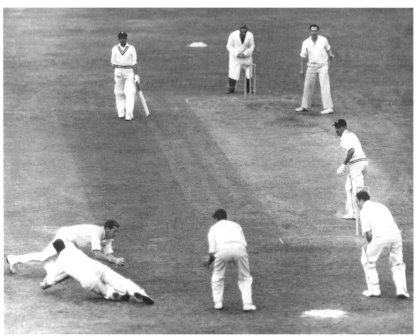
Nari Contractor, caught Walker, bowled Shepherd. My 50th catch of the season which broke Maurice Turnbull's Glamorgan record set before the War.

I scored 1,052 runs in 1958, and I took 36 wickets and 34 catches. But the summer of 1959 was even better for me with 1,564 runs, 80 wickets and 69 catches. For the first of three consecutive years I carried off the national Brylcreem Award for the most catches by a fielder in a county season.

With my fiftieth catch that year I broke the Glamorgan record of 49, set in 1937 by Maurice Turnbull. It was at St. Helen's, Swansea on 1st August, when I caught India's opening batsman Nari Contractor in the gully from the bowling of Don Shepherd. My father sent me a short telegram from South Africa with a biblical quotation, "The Lord is thy shepherd, thou shalt not want."

But, as always in sport, there's a darker side to any full moon. Every player has a nemesis; even Geoffrey Boycott, for instance, could hardly lay a bat on the gentle medium-pace of India's left-arm seamer Solkar. In my case, Ian Buxton of Derbyshire and particularly Ian Thomson of Sussex only had to shrug their right shoulders, and I was on the way back to the pavilion. For instance, coming in at number four on a perfect batting strip at Hove, I duly bagged a 'pair of spectacles': caught Parks bowled Thomson 0 in the first, bowled Thomson 0 in the second.

However, despite this Achilles heel, towards the end of my most successful campaign to date, I was selected as England's twelfth man for the final Test against India at The Oval. The future looked pretty rosy.

Chapter 9

THINK BEFORE YOU JUMP

Towards the tail-end of the 1950s I saw parts of Africa I'd never before visited.

My father had a recurring daydream about buying some land and building his own house. He drove me to the mountainous kingdom of Swaziland and identified four acres not far from the capital of Mbabane, which he could have bought for around £200 but didn't. I think he preferred not to wake up from this particular fantasy. Another trip took us into the heartland of Zululand near Eshowe, not this time in pursuit of Shangri La but to see a wizened, old Zulu called Umtooli who sculpted the most beautiful life-like clay wild animals. From his days with the Institute of Race Relations, my father had grown to have a huge interest and respect for this once most warlike of African tribes, something which I inherited and built on in my post-cricket days.

Back in Johannesburg, a great pal of mine, Mike Challis, born in Botswana and at heart still a 'man of the bush', had part-funded his architectural course at Natal University by working for Ken Momsen, a professional crocodile hunter on the Zambezi river upstream from the Victoria Falls. When Mike suggested I might like to join him on one of these excursions, I jumped at the chance. In my green Wolseley car we headed north out of Johannesburg, crossed the border with Southern Rhodesia at Beit Bridge and altered course north-north-west on what were now strip roads, two narrow lines of tarmac roughly the width of a car's wheels. Driving on these needed concentration and nerve, particularly when approached by a rare oncoming vehicle in which case each kept the driver's side wheels on the macadam while the passengers took their chances on the dirt fringes. The more adventurous would sometimes delay their swerve until the very last second, pretty frightening when the combined closing speed could be around 100mph! Mike was driving while I dozed alongside in the passenger seat.

We'd been on the road for nearly ten hours headed for our final destination, Kasane on the Caprivi Strip. The Strip is a narrow finger of land dividing Rhodesia, now Zimbabwe, and Botswana. It is roughly 60 miles down river from where Ken had his hunting concession. It teemed then – and still does – with big game.

A gentle swishing noise caused me to stir. It was the sound that way, way down south led the Zulus to name one of their main kraals, Eshowe, a word which imitates the sound of wind blowing across open grass prairies. Opening my eyes, brushing against the window, was dense, five-foot high, elephant grass! Where the hell were we? I shot a glance at Mike behind the wheel – he was fast asleep. At 40 mph we had drifted some 30 yards off the road and into the bush. Thankfully we were in boulder-free, treeless country and were being gradually slowed by the grass.

What a shock! I grabbed the wheel, Mike jolted awake and I swear neither of us blinked again until we reached Kasane.

We were now in a major recruiting area for cheap labour to service the

Johannesburg gold mines. We got on a powerful barge run by WNLA, short for Witwatersrand Native Labour Association, and set off up the Zambezi headed for Katima Mulilo (*put out the fire*) where we were to meet Ken. To cool off, we jumped over the side and held on to the stern of the barge, passing safely by herds of somnolent hippos. The helmsman had reckoned that no crocodile could keep up with us – at least that's what he said.

In times of flood, it's impossible to see across to the other side of the Zambezi and, even in times of drought, it remains a massive river. We were now truly deep in 'darkest Africa'. At Katima Mulilo, as we off-loaded our kit and a few miners returning home, I thought that my hearing had been affected by our trawl at the end of the barge. Surely it couldn't be the sound of a game of tennis? But it was. Behind KM's small collection of huts and shacks, a sand court had been hacked out of the bush. There, playing what turned out to be their daily set of tennis, were the elderly white District Commissioner and his wife. The ancient couple had a group of six barefoot piccanins acting as ball boys and, to keep the scorching sun at bay, the DC wore a 19th century Raj-type pith helmet. I thought, 'Welcome to the other side of civilization.'

Over the 2,000-plus miles of the Zambezi, only eight men had licences to hunt crocodiles commercially. Ken took us out at night in what was really no more than a big canoe powered by a small outboard motor. He sat in the prow with a rifle across his knees. He had a miner's lamp attached to his head and would sweep the river looking for the tell-tale gleam of a crocodile's eyes, which reflected back when the beam picked them up. Through experience Ken was able to tell the size of a croc by their width and height out of the water. Believe me, to a Jo'burg townie, it was pretty scary as, with engine switched off, we stealthily drifted up close enough for Ken to get in an accurate shot. Then it was a swift restart of the engine and a rapid acceleration in to prevent the carcass from sinking before he could gaff it.

Getting a deadweight crocodile on board meant tilting the canoe to one side and rolling the reptile in. I'd heard tales of merely stunned crocs waking on the return journey to KM. For anyone sitting in the stern facing its jaws, this must have caused one hell of a lot of consternation. Thankfully that didn't happen to us. What did, however, was something which still sends a shiver down my spine.

One day Mike and I stood fishing on the banks of the Zambezi looking to hook 'Tiger' which, as its name suggests, was a great fighting fish. Every now and then one of our lines would get snagged in some underwater obstruction so Mike and I would take turns to jump in and swim the few yards out from the bank to shake it free. A few days after we had left for home we heard that, right where we'd been fishing, the local natives had caught and killed an 18-foot crocodile which in the past few months had taken a number of cattle and a few of the villagers, too. Try to imagine the girth of a beast that size. It would be a struggle to get your arms to meet around it!

Mike said that we'd been mighty, mighty lucky. Crocs, which are mainly fish-eaters, tend to forage along banks, moving very slowly up or down a river. How close must that 18-footer have been when we were taking those dips!

Chapter 10

THE VIEW FROM THE TOP – AND BOTTOM

The summer of 1960 was a remarkably topsy-turvy one for me.

My stint as twelfth man in the 1959 final Test against India at the Oval had included a daily chore of bringing England wicket-keeper Roy Swetman his lunch and tea in the dressing room, as well as fetching and carrying to satisfy every whim of the rest of the team. I felt mentally catapulted back to my merchant navy days as a steward and general dogsbody, but the experience had given me a taste for, and a desire to be part of, the 'big time'.

Due to winters playing on fast and true pitches in the Transvaal, I usually made a slow start to a UK season, needing time to readjust to the slow, low turning strips of Wales and beyond. In the second match of 1960, against Leicestershire at Swansea, I had a good game in the field, taking five wickets for 25 in their first innings and holding five catches in the second. But my batting didn't get going at all. In fact, when I went out at Lord's in the second innings against Middlesex, I had scored 31 runs in six innings and was on a hat-trick of first ball ducks. It was desperate stuff, but I chose the bold approach, cracking my first ball through cover for four with the *Western Mail* recognising my 'spirit of adventure'!

My form the previous summer, and the fact that Wilf Wooller was one of the England selectors, may have led to my being picked to play for the MCC versus the touring South Africans at Lord's on 21st May. My summer had been erratic, but I knew that a good performance in this match might just lead to my winning a place in the England team.

In 1957 and '58 I'd achieved a modicum of success with bowling medium-pace 'seam up', which had come about because Glamorgan were short of men who could either swing or move a new ball off the seam. Indeed, those 51 consecutive overs without a break at Bristol were in that style. However by 1959 I'd reverted to my original finger-spinning mode, and this had attracted the attention of the England selectors. They were looking to find a replacement for Tony Lock, who was in the process of remodelling his action after further instances of being called for throwing.

In fact, the issue of throwing dominated the summer. During the South Africans' match against the MCC at Lord's, their fast bowler Geoff Griffin was called three times for throwing by umpires Frank Lee and John Langridge. It was the first time a touring bowler had been called in England. Meanwhile I took three for 36 runs in 27 overs, including the top order wickets of Johnny Waite and their most dangerous attacking batsman Roy McLean. Batting at number eight, I came in when we were 126 for 6 and made 57, which proved to be the top score in our first innings. All round, this didn't do my England prospects any harm.

During this match, both teams were invited to an evening reception at Clarence House, the home of the Queen Mother. We duly pitched up and were ushered into three large reception rooms with sliding dividing walls. Everything was, as they would have said at Balfour Park, very 'kosher' in that, if you saw something that looked like a Ming vase, it was a Ming vase, not a copy. While drinks were being served, I drifted around looking at the room's many paintings before halting in front of one. It was a view, looking up a short, stone-ridden slope to the crest of a hill. I can't explain why, but it grabbed my attention. Moving closer, I saw the signature at the bottom was Monet! I felt a tap on my elbow. It was an equerry. "Are you interested in painting?" he asked. I nodded. "Then perhaps you'd like to follow me." We walked back across the entrance hallway and into a smaller room. On the wall were 26 different watercolour views of Windsor Castle by John Piper. A baby grand stood in a corner. "This is the piano which Princess Margaret played most evenings to her dying father, King George the Sixth," said my helpful guide before escorting me back into the middle reception room.

It was full of people, and a small woman, broad in the beam and with her back turned, stood squarely in my way. I paused for a minute or so and then, as she seemed to be unaware of my presence, tapped her lightly on the hip. I said, "Do please excuse me, may I pass?" She turned and gave me the kind of glacial look that in times of yore would either have turned me to salt or sent me to the Tower for keeps. It was Princess Margaret!

I was cautiously optimistic at the end of the match against the tourists, *The Times* calling me 'a cricketer of high promise', and, to my great joy, I was to hear that I was in the twelve for the first Test at Edgbaston. This was announced the day before the South Africans came to Cardiff to play Glamorgan in their last game before the Test. Previewing this game, JBG Thomas, rugby and cricket correspondent of the *Western Mail*, wrote: 'I feel that providing Walker shows good form against the South Africans, particularly as a batsman, he will get into the side.'

My local, The Criterion pub in St. John's Square, Cardiff.
Publican Dennis Reardon presenting me with a tankard celebrating my being picked for England.

Unfortunately I made the proverbial pig's ear of things, scoring 19 and 0 with the bat and being pasted around the Arms Park by Jackie McGlew and Trevor Goddard as they put on 256 for the first wicket.

However, on Wednesday 8th June 1960 I reported for duty at Edgbaston for the customary net practice ahead of Thursday's start. From a virtual no-hoper in 1956, here I was but four years later in with a shout of playing for my country, alongside the likes of Ted Dexter, Colin Cowdrey, Fred Trueman, Brian Statham, Ken Barrington, Mike Smith and Ray Illingworth.

In those days, the England team stayed at the Raven Hotel in Droitwich. On the eve of the match, the players and selectors – no coach in those days – traditionally dined together. At the end, after a few words from chairman Gubby Allen, the selectors withdrew. Bob Barber, then captaining Lancashire, and I were the new kids, very much strangers in the camp. Our captain Colin Cowdrey outlined the importance of getting off to a winning start so as not to let the South Africans dominate. Their morale was pretty low after the Griffin no-balling affair and, in Colin's view, a shortage of runs from their middle-order batsmen made the touring team vulnerable.

To my astonishment, and before taking the opinions of the highly experienced international stars, ten of whom had toured the West Indies the previous winter, Colin turned to me. "Peter, you've played a lot of club and provincial cricket in South Africa against most of their lads, what do you think are their strengths and weaknesses and how should we attack them?" Me, tell the likes of Trueman, Statham and Illingworth how to bowl and Barrington, Dexter and our captain how to bat against the likes of Neil Adcock, Trevor Goddard and Hugh Tayfield? Surely not! I can't recall exactly what I said, but I had an attentive audience.

During the winter I'd played for a Transvaal 'A' side against Natal 'A' at Pietermaritzburg, and I'd faced Geoff Griffin, who had been called before for throwing in his own country. I ventured the thought that, with Syd Buller and Frank Lee due to stand as umpires in the second Test and as it was common knowledge on the county circuit that they had both expressed concerns about Griffin's action, it could be an eventful series. But not even I could have anticipated quite how eventful.

The following morning we drove into Edgbaston, had a loosener in the nets and a few catches on the main arena. The rest of the morning remains something of a blur. After we'd returned to the dressing room, Cowdrey went out to toss. Indoors, Bob Barber and I sat together. We exchanged several glances and tried to appear unconcerned. Who was playing? No indication had been given in the run up to the 11.30 start. Colin came back in. "I've won the toss, and we're batting." Still no clue as to who the final eleven were, even though our skipper had exchanged his team list with the Springbok captain Jackie McGlew.

Bob and I looked around the dressing room, sharing an identical thought: "One of us must be unlucky." Then through the dressing door came Gubby Allen, in his hands a large open-topped, brown cardboard box. He walked anti-clockwise around the dressing room, handing out some ties. He paused first at Jim Parks, then Geoff Pullar and Raman Subba Row, wishing each of them a brief "Good luck". Then he came level with Bob and me.

He stopped in the gap between us. "What are your cap sizes?" he asked.

It was the first indication we had that we were both in the team. Ken Barrington, of all people, had been left out! Waves of joy and relief washed over us, but what an extraordinarily flippant way to tell us that we had become the 399th and 400th men to play Test cricket for England!

I think Gubby, very much a Lord's establishment figure, added something like "Congratulations to you both. Go out there and do your best." But I was hardly able to take it in. I do recall looking down at the cap in my left hand, with the three lions on the front, and the England tie in the other, and hardly daring to look up in case he'd made a mistake. Then, led by Colin Cowdrey, came the congratulations to us both from the rest of the team.

As I got to know him better, I was to discover that Colin had a quiet, off-beat sense of humour. I wonder now if he had purposely avoided telling the two debutants ahead of the toss, just to keep us on edge.

As to the match itself, England won comfortably by 100 runs with just over three hours of the fifth day to spare. When my turn came to bat in the first innings – at number nine in a strong batting line up – we were 255 for seven. I took guard against Neil Adcock, an old adversary from our club days in South Africa and a team-mate in the Transvaal squad. Off the field we were good friends, but not now. That day, the pencil-slim, indefatigable, six-foot-three-inch Adcock was en route to taking five wickets for 62 in 41.5 overs of sustained hostility. Mine was his fifth.

As he raced in towards me, I had no doubt in my mind that my first ball was bound to be a 'welcoming' bouncer, delivered from around 18 yards away at over 90 mph! (Under the old no-ball law quick bowlers, with pronounced back foot drags, were quite a bit closer to the batsman than they are now.) Instead, it was a full length delivery, pitching just outside the off stump.

The ball hit my bat while I was still picking up! But thankfully it ricocheted harmlessly along the ground to gully. I was still there, and I was now an England cricketer.

Looking back to that moment, I'm reminded of a story about Eric Russell, a great Middlesex buddy of mine and a fine player who, in less competitive times, would have been a regular England opening batsman. He made his Test debut at Lahore in October 1961. The first ball, bowled by Hampshire's 'Butch' White, passed harmlessly through to wicket-keeper John Murray, who relayed it to his Middlesex team-mate in the gully. Eric caught it, looked down at it, looked up and said, "Well, lads, they can't take it away from me now; it's Eric Russell, Middlesex and England."

So it was for me when at Edgbaston the ball went off my bat into the gully. Now it was Peter Walker, Glamorgan and England. I eventually inside-edged one past backward short-leg to get off the mark and somehow I reached nine before I was caught by Goddard in the slips.

Our final total was 292. In South Africa's reply of 186 all out, Bob Barber and I had but six overs each, costing 26 and 13 runs respectively. However, in my six I did have John 'Pom-Pom' Fellows-Smith caught behind by Jim Parks, only for him to stand and await umpire John Langridge's decision: 'not out.' At close of play that evening John, one of cricket's old-fashioned gentlemen, sought me out and said, "I'm sorry, Peter; in county cricket I'm so used to batsmen walking if they edge the ball that, when Pom-Pom stood there, I thought he couldn't have hit it. But on reflection I was wrong."

With England suffering something of a batting collapse in the second innings, I came in at 112 for six, soon to be 118 for seven. Helped by a rapid 25 from Fred and an equally boisterous, if less skilful, 22 from our number eleven, Brian Statham, I stayed at the wicket while 90 runs were added, my own 37 turning out to be the innings' top score. We eventually totalled 203, giving us an overall lead of 309. Trueman, Statham and off-spinner Illingworth then got three wickets apiece as South Africa fell 100 runs short in their second innings. My contribution was two catches at backward short-leg, one each off Trueman and Statham.

With only a further four overs required from me, John Langridge's decision cost me what would have been my only Test wicket.

But I went back to Wales on something of a high. 'Walker has all the gifts to make a Test all-rounder,' John Arlott wrote, while the following year's *Wisden* recorded that 'Walker distinguished himself in his first Test with powerful off-drives and leg sweeps.'

After so much pre-match conjecture, neither of the Edgbaston umpires, John Langridge and Eddie Phillipson, had apparently seen anything wrong in Griffin's action, a great relief to the touring side who'd gone into the game apprehensive over the legality of one of their front-line bowlers. I returned to the Glamorgan side for the games with Middlesex and Somerset, making scores of 8, 5, 8 and 37 and taking only two wickets. But I'd done enough at Edgbaston to hold my place in the England set-up so it was up to London for the second Test at one of my favourite and luckiest grounds, Lord's.

England won the toss and batted, with that fine player Ken Barrington replacing Geoff Pullar who had had his wrist broken by a particularly ferocious Adcock bouncer at Edgbaston. To take advantage of both his home ground and the notorious Lord's ridge just short of a length at the Nursery end, Middlesex quick bowler Alan Moss came in for my fellow Edgbaston debutant, Bob Barber.

England won the match by a comprehensive innings and 73 runs, with more than a day to spare. Brian Statham and Alan Moss – aided by Fred Trueman – totally overwhelmed the South African batting in both innings.

But the result was overshadowed by two dramatic events, both involving the South African fast bowler Geoff Griffin. Eleven times he was no-balled for throwing by umpire Frank Lee, the first time a bowler had ever been called for throwing in a Test match in England, and in the middle of all this he also completed a hat-trick!

England team, 2nd Test at Lords, 1960
Back (left to right): Jim Parks, Ray Illingworth, Peter Walker, Alan Moss, Mike Smith, Ken Barrington.
Front: Ted Dexter, Raman Subba Row, Colin Cowdrey (capt), Brian Statham, Fred Trueman.

As a result of my efforts in the first Test, I had been promoted above Ray Illingworth to number seven in the batting order. Arriving at the wicket at 227 for five, there was still work to be done. I joined Mike Smith and together we put on 120 in two hours and twenty minutes, our partnership swinging the game in England's favour.

During our stand, in and around us raged the battle between Griffin and the umpires. Geoff actually delivered 30 overs in that one England innings and, having faced him head on, there was absolutely no doubt in either Mike's or my mind that he threw virtually every ball. However, I do not believe this was intentional on Geoff's part; it was exactly the way he'd always 'bowled' and, except for one or two isolated incidents, his action had been passed as legitimate by South Africa's leading umpires.

In one delivery he was called simultaneously for throwing by Frank Lee at square leg and for overstepping the mark by Syd Buller at the bowler's end.

With the score on 347 for five, Mike Smith was on strike for the last ball of a Griffin over, with 99 to his name. Unfortunately he flashed outside the off stump and was caught by Johnny Waite, the wicket-keeper.

The over was complete, and out to join me came Ray Illingworth. I now faced the accurate medium-paced, left-armer Trevor Goddard, who was bowling from the Nursery end. His stock ball was the in-swinger to right-handed batsmen, and his first two balls both drifted down the leg side, allowing me to waft them over long leg for six each, taking me to 51. It was my one and only half-century for England. I enjoyed a lengthy round of applause and off the last ball of the over I pushed a single out on the off side to pinch the bowling. I now had to face a fired-up Geoff Griffin.

Encouraged by the wicket of Mike Smith, he raced in towards me. I expected something short of a length. Instead, it was well up on my leg stump. I was late on the shot, and the ball cannoned off my pads and onto my stumps, bowled by Griffin for 52.

Made it at last! En route to a half century in the 2nd Test at Lord's v South Africa in 1960. Johnny Waite the wicket-keeper.

Out for 52, bowled by Geoff Griffin in the middle of what was about to become an historic hat-trick in a Lord's Test

As I walked towards the pavilion steps, I was passed by next man in, Fred Trueman. "Well played lad," he said as we crossed. "I'll give this fooker some stick!"

The dressing rooms at Lord's are on the first floor. I had barely time to make it up the curved staircase to receive the team's congratulations when Fred had a great swing at his first ball and his middle stump went somersaulting out of the ground. With all the drama of Mike Smith's dismissal for 99 and my two sixes, it was a moment before everybody realised that Griffin, who had suffered so much press and public hostility, had become the first bowler to take a Test hat-trick at the home of cricket. Forty-six years on, he is still the only one to have done so.

Then on a helpful pitch, in a truly magnificent exhibition of fast bowling, Brian Statham took eleven wickets for 97 in the match, which ended during the fourth afternoon. With the Queen and Prince Philip due that afternoon there was then a hastily arranged exhibition match during which I took over as wicket-keeper from Jim Parks. It brought further humiliation to the unfortunate Griffin. *Wisden* records, 'Griffin's only over consisted of eleven balls. S. Buller no-balled him for throwing four times out of five. On the advice of his captain, McGlew, who had spoken to Buller, Griffin changed to underarm bowling, but was promptly no-balled again by Lee for forgetting to notify the batsman of his change of action.'

40 years on, a reunion of the four men involved in the Test hat-trick at Lord's.
Left to right: Geoff Griffin, Mike Smith, Fred Trueman and Peter Walker meet at Old Trafford.

Back at Glamorgan, storm clouds were gathering around me. There were mutterings amongst my team-mates and louder rumblings in the local press and among supporters over my abysmal performances for the county. I had just made a fifty in a Test at Lord's, yet by this stage of the summer I had played ten matches for Glamorgan and had scored only 201 runs at an average of 11.16 and taken 21 wickets at 33.23 each.

Why couldn't I reproduce my England form for Glamorgan? Had I lost interest in playing for my club and, by definition, for Wales? Had success at international level gone to my head, etc, etc? I couldn't explain it then – or now. The harder I tried, the worse my county form became. About the only facet of my skills that remained unimpaired was close catching where, for the second year in a row, I was in the lead in the country's fielding statistics.

Returning from the euphoria at Lord's to Stourbridge for the county game against Worcestershire, I made a miserable five in the first innings. Because of injury Wilf Wooller missed that game, and our opening batsman Gilbert Parkhouse captained us. When he in turn injured his hand, he pushed me up the order to open our second innings with Bernard Hedges. There was nothing pre-meditated about what happened next, but something inside me snapped.

Worcestershire had a formidable pace attack: Jack Flavell, Fred Rumsey and John Aldridge, the first two going on to play for England. I stood firm-footed at the crease and just slashed, heaved and slogged at every ball bowled at me.

Somehow I connected more times than I missed and, to the accompaniment of oaths such as "and you call yourself a fucking England player" from Don Kenyon the Worcester captain, the ball flew everywhere, once even out of the ground! John Billot in the *Western Mail* called it 'one of the most startling displays ever of unorthodox batting by a Glamorgan player.' I hit a six over Flavell's head and eleven fours, and I was eventually caught by Kenyon off Rumsey for 68, scored inside an hour, out of a total of 81. So disgusted with my performance was my fastidious opening partner Bernard Hedges that he refused to talk to me out in the middle or for some weeks thereafter.

Many years later, at a dinner for former England players at the Café Royal in London, I sat next to Jack Flavell, one of the meanest, most hostile quick bowlers I ever played against. He somehow managed a tight smile and shook his head sadly as we relived that extraordinary innings. He left me in no doubt that even thirty years on it still rankled within his breast.

I was retained for the third Test at Trent Bridge. It was another overwhelming win for England by eight wickets, with a day to spare. But here again there was an incident which, when compared with behaviour patterns in the modern game, illustrates how much cricket changed within one generation.

After winning the toss England mustered a laborious 287 with me contributing to the tedium by scoring 30 in 95 minutes. When South Africa batted, it was 'Fiery Fred' Trueman's turn to dominate with nine wickets in all including five for 27 in the first innings as the visitors were shot out for just 88. I took two catches at short square leg, the one off Fred with which I dismissed Sid O'Linn being described by *Wisden* as 'brilliant'.

However, the incident for which the match is most remembered was the controversial run out of South African captain, Jackie McGlew, as he was leading his country's determined fight-back in their second innings. *Wisden* recorded it thus:

> The left-handed O'Linn played a ball from Moss to extra cover and went for a reasonably quick single. Moss dashed across the pitch to chase it and McGlew ran into his back. He stumbled and darted for the crease, but Statham had picked up and with unerring aim hit the stumps. Cowdrey and the other England players near the broken wicket promptly appealed and Elliott, the square-leg umpire, signalled out. Elliott's decision was correct because Moss had not deliberately baulked McGlew. McGlew never hesitates when given out, but as he hastened towards the pavilion the crowd voiced their disapproval of the circumstances of his dismissal. Three times Cowdrey called him to come back, and when he did the England captain asked the umpires if it was possible to change their verdict, but they were adamant.

Can one imagine that kind of sporting gesture happening today?

I was only required to bowl three overs, but I left Trent Bridge feeling that, although I'd had practically no opportunities with the ball in the three matches played, I'd done enough to be retained for the fourth Test at Old Trafford. It was not to be.

Life at Glamorgan was going from bad to worse. Between my innings at Stourbridge and the third Test I had been dismissed for 1 and 9 against Essex at Westcliff. After the Test I joined up with my team-mates at Bath where on the first day I took one for 99 as Graham Atkinson and Peter Wight put on 300, a new third-wicket record for Somerset.

The next day, a Thursday, was a nightmare. As I had done at Stourbridge, I tried once more to hit my way out of trouble getting off the mark with a six that only narrowly cleared a mid-wicket fielder, but I was out for 23. Although there was a level of sympathy for me among some of my team-mates, others were not so supportive and the atmosphere in the dressing-room that day was not welcoming.

To my face, former England players Gilbert Parkhouse and, most hurtful of all, my former schoolboy mentor Allan Watkins were pretty forthright, not so much about my form, which in all players is transitory at some stage in a season, but my attitude. They felt that my less-than-professional approach to the demands of county cricket and responsibilities to my team-mates was having a bad effect on dressing-room morale. They were absolutely right. In this period of private despair I was morose and uncommunicative, a real pain to be near, let alone in the close and intimate confines of a dressing room.

In many ways I did have a cavalier, rather than a roundhead, approach to cricket, and often this did not sit comfortably with my county colleagues. With my background I was really more of an amateur in spirit, and sometimes I found the life of the professional cricketer constricting. Indeed, it's no coincidence that two of my most lasting cricketing friendships, during and after my playing career, were with Glamorgan captains, Ossie Wheatley and Tony Lewis, Cambridge men both. In business, music and current affairs they had wider interests than just matters concerning bat and ball; with them, the often claustrophobic, narrow conversational boundaries of a cricket dressing room were left behind at close of play.

The pressure had been steadily building up on me. It was getting oppressive, difficult for me to handle. Walking through the streets of Cardiff and Swansea became something of an ordeal. Whereas once there would be smiling nods of recognition, during this topsy-turvy 1960 season I felt something of an outcast, imagining that everyone who passed was looking at me with a critical eye. I didn't help myself by leaving the ground as soon as play was over for the day and rarely joining my Glamorgan team-mates at away games when they set off for some lighter entertainment than I was providing. No-one fitted the description of 'paranoid Pete' better than I did.

There was only one thing that brought me some solace: the clarinet. It had played a similar role during the many long and boring days at seas. Although too short of practice to produce a pure tone, I would often spend the evenings tootling away in the grounds of our hotel. I must have cut a very strange figure to the other guests, let alone my puzzled team-mates who never quite came to understand this calming balm during my periods of deep depression.

The often claustrophobic atmosphere of a county dressing room did not help. Team spirit is a very fragile beast, easily bruised and changeable after losing a match or two. Although cricket is a team game, batting, bowling and indeed fielding are very solitary activities with each carrying its own responsibilities.

The impact of failing to deliver what your colleagues believed you could, and should, weighed heavily upon me. While there is always a measure of sympathy awaiting those whose luck is out, my mood swings during this bleak period must have given the outward impression that I didn't care one way or the other about the team's needs.

At Bath we were all out for 247 and had to follow on just before the close of play. Wilf sent me out to open the batting with only a couple of overs to be bowled, and I was out immediately. The *Western Mail* said that I 'essayed a strange stroke and was caught.'

I was at rock bottom, and the hostile dressing-room atmosphere was greater than ever. Some idea of what was going on in my head at this time can be gathered from an article I wrote a fortnight later for the now defunct *Empire News*, a Sunday paper that was a real ragbag, full of sleaze, titillation and innuendo. Their Welsh edition editor Gareth Bowen, a future colleague of mine at BBC Wales, was a man with good antennae when it came to a story, and he got me to 'confess' as to what was going on:

NEUROTIC! (That's what they call me)
by Peter Walker

Head case! Nutter! Neurotic! Times without number I've heard phrases like that flung at me – particularly in the past couple of weeks. I fancy you critics are mostly right, you have good reason to wonder what goes on inside me. And looking back I can see that many of my statements and gestures in dressing-rooms and hotels in which we stay must have brought strange glances from my Glamorgan colleagues.

....

I often feel that the game I love is fast turning me into a neurotic; or so it would appear. You see, cricket will always be to me a game. I can never approach it as a cold-blooded job for £.s.d. and this lack of dedication sometimes brings me into conflict with my fellow professional players. My mind (and surely all things are basically played in the mind), with its early indoctrination of the arts, will not accept the often stultifying effect of cricket. For the job, as opposed to the game, makes demands on us which leave little time for any action or thought outside cricket.

The normal office worker leaves his job on the desk at 5 p.m. For us often the most detached and pleasurable part of the day is when we are on the field. The moment we leave the "shelter" of the playing area we are besieged by well-meaning observers intent on giving us their interpretation of the day's play as they saw it.

Here again the sense of the basic futility of professional cricket comes home to me. We are supposed to be paid entertainers. Yet so often what we do on the field seems lost on the people who pay to see us play. To a person of my highly-strung nature it sometimes seems the equivalent of trying to get something important across to a group of people who speak only a little English. The need to get across to them is great, but there seems to be no common medium to convey it. That is why the occasional sense of frustration overflows in me. Every time I go out on the cricket field I want to project to the watching public and Press whatever cricketing talent I may have. Very often when deeds and actions are misinterpreted I get an acute feeling of depression.

This outlook may seem hypersensitive to many. But to me the sane, sensible professional approach at the end of a bad day of not worrying is foreign to my nature. I will always worry if my team or I do badly, and constant failure by either will always make me irritable and short-tempered – even with people outside the game.

That evening in Bath I had had enough. To say I was pretty disillusioned with life and cricket in particular would be a massive understatement. We were booked in at the Royal Hotel in Bath. Most of the lads went their separate ways in pursuit of food or crumpet, or both. I found my steps leading me to Bath Abbey. It was around nine o'clock in the evening and, to my surprise, when I pressed against a side door, it opened to my touch. While never a regular attender, churches have always fascinated me. I could appreciate and understand the comforting blanket of peace which envelops believers who seek sanctuary therein. I sat down and took stock. I don't know to this day if I was silently 'spoken to', but my thoughts went along these lines: "Peter, you've achieved everything you wanted to do when you ran away to sea. You've become a professional cricketer and reached the highest level you can hope for. OK, the clarinet has somewhat fallen away, but what's left?"

Although there was no audible answer, something inside me said "nothing".

In a more relaxed frame of mind, I stretched out on a pew and almost immediately fell sleep, waking only when the early morning cleaners came in. They must have thought that I was some sort of heavenly apparition, but I now most certainly had both feet on the ground. Like Saul on the road to Damascus it was very clear to me that major changes in my life were required and in the foreseeable future these did not include either cricket or music.

I suppose I have always been a rather quixotic character. I had run away to sea when I was sixteen, and now, in a way, I was ready to run away again, to look for some fresh adventures. At the ground I sought out Wilf Wooller and told him that, with immediate effect, I wished to resign. But, as we had a rearguard action on our hands to try to save the match, he had more pressing problems on his mind. He merely asked me to think it over and, if I still felt the same, to put my request in writing so he could present it to the committee. We were on tour, so any decision had to wait until the team got back to Wales.

We saved the game, thanks to a characteristically dogged 93 by Alwyn Harris, and went on up to Liverpool to play Lancashire, who were then in the running for the championship. Wilf didn't come with us. He had the team for the fourth Test to select and, with Allan Watkins the senior professional not keen to take on the captaincy, Don Shepherd skippered us.

We had not won for over a month, and morale in the team was at rock-bottom. But during our three days in Liverpool, we played with real spirit.

It was a pig of pitch, and I was out to Brian Statham in both innings, for 6 and 18, but I took four wickets and two catches on the last afternoon and we won an exciting victory. In the *Empire News* I wrote:

> At Liverpool I cannot remember ever being in a Glamorgan side that played so much as a team. Every player did his stuff. The effect of this great team-work was our wonderful win. To Don Shepherd, our skipper for that particular match, must go a great deal of credit for our mid-season revival. Being a bowler himself he knew how the rest of the bowlers felt and gave us encouragement whenever we flagged. Don Shepherd is a great *player*, and one of the finest *gentlemen* it has ever been my privilege to know both on and off the field!

Unfortunately news came through during the game that I had been dropped by England. The Test series had been won 3-0, and the selectors wanted to look at some different players. David Allen, who had been out of the first three Tests with an injured finger, returned, along with Geoff Pullar, and they also called up Doug Padgett and Tommy Greenhough.

Worse was to follow at the end of the Liverpool match. I was just starting to feel once more at ease with Glamorgan when we heard that the team for the match the next day at Cardiff only included five of the side who had won at Liverpool. Wilf was back, along with Gilbert Parkhouse, Alan Jones and David Evans, and Tony Lewis – his term over at Cambridge – also came in. I, an England Test player the previous week, was one of the ones being dropped.

Perhaps it was meant to be for my own good, to give me time to sort myself out, but my reaction was to write that letter of resignation. By Thursday morning the story was in the national newspapers, with one reporter commenting: 'Glamorgan are a squabbling county and do not deserve to keep Walker.'

John Arlott provided a less sensational view: 'It is easy to sympathise with the immediate reactions of a cricketer who, only a few days ago, was hitting sixes in a Test at Lord's and now finds himself dropped from the first eleven of a county which stands twelfth in the Championship table … Let us hope that he will be able to swallow a little of pride and, balancing six years of sympathy against his dropping – which could yet prove to his advantage – will resolve the disagreement with his county.'

The next few days were hectic with my being tailed by reporters wherever I went. Of the Glamorgan players, only Louis Devereux, a recruit from Worcestershire, and my then flat-mate, Brian Edrich, who was coaching at club level in Wales, went public, expressing sympathy and wishing for some understanding of the kind of pressure I was under.

I had a face-to-face meeting with Wilf. He had been like a father figure to me, a straight-talking man who had done so much to champion me when my Glamorgan future was far from bright and he had probably been my advocate on the England selection committee. We agreed that I would put on hold my resignation and that I would rejoin the team for the next match at Northampton.

While all this was going on, I had the great comfort of a letter from Colin Cowdrey:

Dear Peter

I was very, very sorry to read of your troubles – exaggerated no doubt by our good friends, the Press. May all be restored to order now and very soon the luck will change for you in the Glamorgan side, I am sorry that you were not selected for the Fourth Test match, but please remember that we are keeping an eye on your performances and I hope you keep up your magnificent fielding.

With every good wish.

Yours sincerely,

Colin Cowdrey

It was a gesture that helped to soothe a troubled soul, and Wilf reminded me that there was an MCC 'A' tour of New Zealand in the winter and that I could work my way back into the Test team by doing well on that.

My form improved a little. On my return at Northampton I scored 38 and took seven catches. Then on a dreadful pitch at Ebbw Vale my 28 was the highest score of the match, and in the county's return game against the South Africans at Swansea I made 23 and 26.

But during this match at Swansea the first of the series of the *Empire News* articles appeared. Lurid yellow posters on lamp-posts around Wales screamed out: 'Walker tells all'.

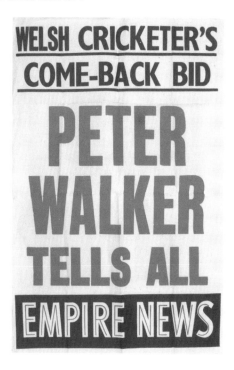

Wilf and I had several meetings. He and Allan Watkins helped me to take a more rational line and regain some perspective. I felt ashamed at my impetuosity. If Allan could soldier on in the twilight of his career with crippling arthritis in both knees, why the hell couldn't I? The two senior men in Welsh cricket talked me through this crisis so that in the end I agreed to hold off a final retirement decision until the end of the season. By this stage the media had lost interest, having moved on to their next feeding station.

The following week at Leicester I made a good 57, but during the match I heard that I had not been selected for the tour of New Zealand, with Don Wilson, the Yorkshire slow left-armer, preferred. It's hard to guess what effect my behaviour had had on the selectors' decision. John Billot in the *Western Mail* thought: 'Selection would have been just the fillip Walker needs for his confidence.' But perhaps, in the words of John Arlott, they thought that I needed 'a nervous rest.'

I did not know it at the time, but my England career was over. I had played three Tests, scored 128 runs in four innings, held five catches and bowled 13 wicketless overs. Playing for England is the cricketing achievement of which I am most proud, coupled with my fighting comeback for Glamorgan the following year and the winning of the Championship in 1969. I had got to the top of cricket's Mount Everest. While up there, the view was magnificent; but I could never have imagined that the journey back to base camp would be so swift or bumpy.

I slipped back into being what John Woodcock, the highly respected cricket correspondent of *The Times*, once described as 'the elongated dilettante that Walker is at heart'. At the time I was not exactly sure if this was an insult or a compliment and thought of writing to John for an explanation. But when I checked it out in my Oxford dictionary – like my father, I had spells of reading a page each night to widen my vocabulary – I immediately recognised that, not for the first time, the man from *The Times* had hit the target.

So, how do I feel 46 years on? There remains a residue of embarrassment that it got as far as it did, because I had made a snap decision when I was not mentally stable enough to make an objective judgement about my cricketing future. However I couldn't then, nor even now with long-distance hindsight, understand why I'd experienced such a massive dip in county form while having a far better than anticipated impact another rung up in England colours. I'd certainly been trying hard enough for Glamorgan, even though the majority of my team-mates thought otherwise, but I'd become too wound up in my inner nightmare. In fact, I've no doubt that, for six weeks or so, I could have been quoted as an even-money favourite to win the Introverted Cricketer Handicap Chase.

CHAPTER 11

THE SUN DOES COME UP AGAIN

By September 1960, at the end of a very topsy-turvy summer, I was glad to put some clear blue water between cricket and myself as I sailed back to a winter in South Africa. I'd been told by Wilf and an understanding committee to use this as a period of reflection and to get my head straight before returning for the start of the next season. I'm so glad that I had second thoughts and that commonsense prevailed over my hasty decision, even if they were at first only to please Wilf, who had announced his retirement as a player. My love of the game, and a sense that I owed it to everyone as well as to myself to put the negative aspects of the 1960 season behind me, drew me back for more.

Although it was not to be the last time I would decide enough was enough, my return to the Glamorgan fold brought me twelve years that included some very high points. A season of great personal achievement in 1961 was very, very satisfying, and it was followed by the twin victories in '64 and '68 over the Australians, both at St. Helen's, Swansea, and, for only the second time in Glamorgan's history, the championship was won in 1969.

I managed at long last to graft some consistency onto my game, thus ensuring that my place in the side was never again in doubt until 1972, my final year on the staff. I came out of the other side of the crisis of 1960 and, from then on, there stretched ahead an awful lot of fun and exploration. I had an enjoyable job for which I was relatively well paid, and for a fortnight in March and September, while travelling from Cape Town to Southampton and back, I was able to sit in the sun on a Union-Castle liner deck, drink a few beers and reflect on the meaning of life. The cherry on the top was that, wherever I was, England or South Africa, it was always summer.

Socially it was the best of times, the worst of times. At the start of the 1961 season, I exchanged speculative glances across the pavilion bar at St. Helen's with a very attractive 18-year-old Swansea blonde. A long-time junior club supporter of Glamorgan, Pat Cross knew more about cricket than most male members and in later years became the first woman to be elected to the Glamorgan committee. Her interest and knowledge of the game certainly filled in those awkwardly gauche moments when neither of us could think of anything much to say to one another. But after I'd invited her to come and see our next match against Lancashire at nearby Neath, our friendship, which lasts to this day, could hardly have got off to a worst start.

The game was played on an uncovered, unpredictable club pitch. We were around 40 for four when I went in to bat. Pat sashayed in through the main gate shortly afterwards. Her arrival was swiftly noted by the visiting close fielders drawing forth a few appreciative "ummms". I just had time to tell them she was my date, not theirs, when I was hit by a ball from England fast bowler Brian Statham which pitched and reared off a length to strike me a fearful blow over the left eye. It felt as if I'd been hit by a hammer!

I fell to my knees. The most concerned person on the field was Brian himself. I put my left glove up to my face, took it down and stared at a pool of blood in its palm. Our physiotherapist John Evans was a familiar figure in Welsh sport, for in the winter he also doubled as Cardiff City Football Club's rub-a-dub man. He came galloping out from the pavilion. Taking one look he said to me, "Oh, it's nothing, just a graze!" The 'graze' needed six stitches and an overnight stay in Neath General Hospital to check if I had concussion. Pat and I were forced to postpone any inter-personal developments until a later date.

Sporting an enormous black eye which made me look like a one-eyed panda bear, I missed the next game but came back for the one after against Yorkshire in Swansea. Before the start, Fred Trueman sauntered into our dressing room – he did this to all teams, indeed so often that his Yorkshire team mates would sometimes take his kit bag into their opponents' dressing room. "Aye, lad," Fred said to me. "I saw Stat blackened yon eye. I'll do the same to t'other one later today," and walked out!

On the county circuit it was reckoned that Fred got 30% of his wickets in the opposing team's dressing room, and I was shortly to add to that statistic. Coming out to bat with 'Fiery' about to take the second new ball, I faced my first delivery. Getting onto the back foot ready for the expected bouncer, Fred proceeded to knock my leg stump out with a perfect in-swinging yorker! "Never bowled a bloody straight ball in my life," was always his stock claim. Slightly exaggerated to be sure – but what a bowler, what a character!

In those carefree days, being a professional cricketer and a bachelor to boot provided one with a wonderful training ground for exploring social opportunities. We breezed into town and spent either three nights – four, if it were a weekend – enjoying the town or city's nightlife. In Wales, too, there was a certain kudos in being a well-known sporting face in the community and, if not on a par with the high-profile Welsh rugby team, most of us enjoyed and maximised this attention to the full. Additionally, a fortnight each way in March and September as a passenger on board Union-Castle mail-boats put me in amongst a great number of nubile females cavorting around the ship's pools. They proved to be irresistible distractions.

But the late 1950s and early '60s was also a cautious age. The contraceptive pill was not readily available and, too shy to go into a chemist where French letters were stored under the counter and usually served by an equally embarrassed girl shop assistant, a young man's main source of supply was more often the local barber's shop. The standard enquiry at the end of Friday's haircut would be… "and something for the weekend sir?" I saw more youths with GI crewcuts walking the streets than ever went to Vietnam!

Having lived since the age of 16 in a male-dominated working environment, I had yet to learn anything of value about women: their likes and foibles and, in particular, the courting rituals they expected from men. But I quickly realised that they could take umbrage, particularly if one shot a sly, inquisitive glance elsewhere while, if they were the subject of a gently sarcastic quip, they lacked any understanding of a male's basic sense of humour, even when it was delivered with a smile. In those days, and perhaps even now, building a relationship was a bit like fishing. The girl stood on the bank holding the rod and baiting the hook while young men swam around eager to enjoy a morsel or two from her cast, even though they were rarely allowed to swallow the bait whole.

That astute French philosopher Simone de Beauvoir summarised it succinctly: 'Men are won with their eyes, women with their ears.'

I suppose that I can justifiably lay claim to being a good listener and a reasonably swift learner. Both were certainly important attributes in my later careers in broadcasting and journalism. Fortunately, my earliest experiences with women – mainly, if not exclusively, on mail-boats – were with females considerably older than myself. Presumably they must have found the untutored gropings of a tall, very fit and not entirely repulsive, young man flattering and worthy of encouragement, not ridicule.

Those two-week trips to and from the United Kingdom had a pattern to them. On the way from South Africa young girls, saddened to leave their steady boyfriends, warmed to a sympathetic ear and a softly, softly approach. On the way back, with six months' experience of a freewheeling, liberal society far removed from their restrictive homeland in South Africa, they were having one final almighty hurrah before settling down with their waiting partners. Either way, for any predatory young male, it was like feeding time at the zoo.

But one could get over-confident. Ashore, at a private party in Johannesburg, I met a very glamorous black-haired beauty. It began with the standard, eyes-meeting-across-a-room scenario and it wasn't long before we manoeuvred our way close enough to chat. We discovered a shared interest in golf so I quickly suggested, "Let's have a game soon," an invitation she readily accepted. A few days later we met at the Kensington Golf Club in Johannesburg. When I arrived, Clarita, exotic name, exotic lady, was already waiting on the first tee.

Sport in South Africa is always competitive and, coming straight to the point, she said, "What are we going to play for?" At the time I had a pretty good game going with a handicap of three and, recognising an opportunity which could lead to a big pay-off after dark, I suggested, "Why don't we play for your honour?" A small smile passed across her lips. "OK; that's fine. We'll play off level, no strokes given." Now it was my turn to grin. This was a cinch. She wanted to lose. Yippee! After a couple of practice swings I teed off first and hit a 250-yard drive straight down the middle.

The ladies' tee was 20 yards in front of the men's. Taking a club out of her bag and without a practice swing, Clarita powered her drive 30 yards past mine! Four down after five holes, I eventually lost the match seven and five. Halfway through the round she confessed to be the reigning South African amateur ladies' champion, with a handicap of plus one! And to rub it in, Kensington was her home course! She had taken me for what I was, a naïve upstart.

Golf wasn't her only forte. In the weeks which followed, we grew closer together. As befitted a former partner of Bobby Irvine, the one-time world professional Latin American ballroom dancing champion, Clarita taught me not only the intricate steps of the then all-the-rage 'cha-cha' dance – but quite a bit more.

However, she wouldn't see me at weekends. One evening I asked her why. Clarita was frank to the point of bluntness. "I travel to Lourenco Marques on the Friday afternoon train and come back late Sunday evening. There I'm the mistress of a Portuguese Army Colonel. He's bought me my flat in Jo'burg and paid to have it furnished so the very least I can do is to bring some pleasure into his life. Have you been to LM?" I nodded, remembering my 24 hours there before joining my first ship. "Well it's an arsehole of a place. Even though I know it won't last, I don't blame him wanting a bit of fun." Clarita was right, it didn't last – me, that is; I've no idea about the Portuguese Colonel.

Back in Britain a brief flame of mine in South Africa wrote to say that she was coming to the UK and could we meet up? The dates she was going to be in London coincided with our match against Middlesex at Lord's. Stella was her name – and stellar by nature too. A former Miss South Africa, she was indeed a beautiful blonde. I suggested that at the end of play she should wait at the player's entrance at the rear of the Lord's pavilion and I'd come down from the first-floor dressing room to meet her. I made this arrangement because at that time, other than the Queen and cleaning ladies, the latter appearing and disappearing almost before the sun rose, no women were allowed into the pavilion.

Manning the pavilion entrance in those days were the formidable Gaby brothers, long-time employees of the owners of the Lord's ground, the Marylebone Cricket Club. Without being vetted, nobody, but nobody, got past the brothers Gaby and certainly not into the Long Room, cricket's holy of holies. Stella duly arrived and, in a split second when the brothers' backs were turned, waltzed in and high-heeled it up the stairs and into the hallowed Long Room. The MCC members in there, those who were still breathing, let out a gasp of horror. The fittest managed to get to the top of the stairs and summoned the brothers to their rescue. At this point I was coming down from the dressing room, only to see Stella being frogmarched off the premises, a Gaby at each elbow. When I caught her up outside, she asked in all wide-eyed innocence, "Have I done anything wrong?" Before I could explain, we were both asked to leave the ground immediately.

Next morning I was summoned to appear in front of the Gabys in their office, severely reprimanded and warned as to my future conduct. For years afterwards they regarded my arrival at HQ with the Glamorgan team with the greatest of suspicion.

But I've got ahead of myself.

Between being left out of the 'A' tour to New Zealand and just before the start of the 1961 summer in Britain, something within me had changed. In cricketing terms I now had a kind of 'been there, seen that, done it' déjà vu mentality. I sensed that I needed something more out of, and to put back into, life, things other than just playing bat and ball. But ahead of the start of a season which turned out to be my best ever, I received an invitation from E.W. 'Jim' Swanton, the doyen of the UK's cricketing scribes, to be part of his team on a month's tour of the West Indies.

On the playing front it was a highly successful trip in that we lost only one of nine matches and that against British Guyana who had in their ranks several international players: Joe Solomon, Basil Butcher, Clyde Walcott (both of the latter getting hundreds), Charlie Stayers and Lance Gibbs.

EW Swanton's team in West Indies, 1961
Back (left to right): Nawab of Pataudi, Bryan 'Bomber' Wells, Harold Rhodes, Ossie Wheatley, Ian McLachlan, Bob Gale, Alan Smith.
Front: Bob Barber, Everton Weekes, Colin Ingleby-Mackenzie, EW Swanton, Ray Lindwall, Peter Walker, Abbas Ali Baig

Without the responsibility of playing for Queen and Country, we were certainly a group of unrestrained party animals. This tour was full of laughter – what tour wouldn't be with a jokester like Colin Ingleby-Mackenzie as captain.

Led by our captain, no invitation to wine, dine and dance was ever refused. As a result of a dusk-to-dawn party at the home of Philip Thompson, a local bon viveur, which was inevitably followed by a particularly unsuccessful day in the field in Port of Spain, Trinidad, Jim Swanton summoned us all to an emergency meeting. It needs to be pointed out that, whereas the team were accommodated in modest hotels or billeted out with local cricket supporters, Jim and his wife Ann always stayed with either the Governor General of the island we were visiting or, at worst, the President of its Cricket Association. In his best army voice our manager called us to attention and said how disappointed he and his hosts were with our performance in the field that day and that we had most definitely to improve next morning. "Mackenzie," said Jim. "As captain, I expect you to set an example. This chap Thompson needs to be avoided so I'm imposing a curfew. I want you all back in the hotel and in bed by 9.30." Quick as a flash and feigning a look of puzzlement, our always last-to-bed-if-at-all captain said, "But Jim, that's only half an hour before the start of play." There were two explosions: Jim's snort of irritation and the whole team's gale of laughter. But our manager, a far more human soul than has often been portrayed, quickly saw the funny side too. From then on our erstwhile party host was always referred to as 'Taboo Thompson'.

The Swanton-led trip to the West Indies was a personal success for me with bat, ball and in the field. It not only bolstered my shaky confidence, particularly after the seesaw happenings of the previous summer, but also restored my almost extinct sense of humour. Jim's trip certainly helped to give me a better start to the new English season.

Although Glamorgan had yet another disappointing season, finishing 14th out of 17, by the end I had achieved not only the double of 1,000 runs and 100 wickets but had also taken 73 catches. The only other man to do the double and take 50 or more catches had been Percy Fender of Surrey and England, way back in 1921 – though he only took 53. Immodestly I could claim to have recorded the finest treble in the history of the game. Certainly, with one-day cricket now dominating the fixture calendar, my record is unlikely to be bettered.

When I look back through *Wisden* and the Glamorgan yearbook covering the 1961 season, what really strikes me is the sheer volume of physical effort and levels of concentration required to end a summer with 1,347 runs in 64 innings, 101 wickets from 998 overs and 73 close-to-the-wicket catches.

In an eight-day period in June, I bowled 50 overs at Trent Bridge against Nottinghamshire (taking four for 83), followed in the next game with another 40 and 27 at Northampton and wound down with 37 more overs at Cardiff against Worcestershire … 154 overs in total. Then there was the batting (at number six) and, added on, hour after hour in the field crouched unblinkingly with full-on concentration at short square-leg.

And the modern cricketer claims he plays too much!

One of my West Indies touring colleagues had been Ossie Wheatley, who that summer took over from Wilf as Glamorgan captain. The fact that, like Wilf, he was a Cambridge University man may have helped his cause, but few would have anticipated that such an archetypal Englishman would fit so smoothly into the Welsh way of life. It didn't seem to phase Ossie one iota, and he swiftly earned the wholehearted respect and support of the team, not only for his undoubted skills as a bowler and tactician. He blossomed in the easy camaraderie of the Glamorgan dressing room and in the eyes and hearts of many strongly nationalistic supporters too.

When his playing days were over, Ossie's all-round leadership qualities made him a natural choice to become Chairman of the Sports Council for Wales. In his six years in the post he was the most powerful and influential man in sporting Wales.

When he arrived in Cardiff in April 1961 we were both homeless and, despite some misgivings, mainly I suspect on his part as he was going to be my captain, we decided to look for accommodation together. We rented a two-bedroomed, first-floor furnished flat at 31 Cathedral Road, not far from the city centre of Cardiff and within a six-hit distance of Sophia Gardens. It was in one of the many gracious 19th century villas in the road and had been subdivided into three self-contained flats.

The main living area retained the original glass-vaulted ceiling of its billiard-room days. While ideal in letting in sunshine and light in the summer, in the winter that followed when I'd returned to South Africa, Ossie nearly froze to death as any heat created went straight through the glass roof!

Indeed, when I returned in early April 1962 I found the blonde-haired Ossie, never the most domesticated of animals and quickly named 'Dai Peroxide' by the Welsh cricketing fraternity, huddled around the grate, twisting rolled-up pages of newspapers to keep the meagre fire alight.

Ossie was the only example I ever came across of a purely coach-created bowling action succeeding at professional level. He got into all the right MCC textbook bowling positions, sideways on, reaching for the sky with his leading arm, standing tall at delivery with a high bowling arm and keeping his wrist behind the ball at release. Although by no means quick, 'Os' had sufficient pace to hurry a batsman into a false stroke. But he was so much more than a bowling robot and had probably the best cricketing brain I've played with or against. He read opposing batsman better than any fortune-teller.

Just one example. He knew that the swashbuckling Hampshire and West Indian opening batsman Roy Marshall didn't rate him. Roy was a destroyer of bowling attacks, but Ossie would purposely bowl a little slower and wider of the off stump than his normal line. Roy, a man with one of the shortest batting fuses in cricket, would let the first couple of overs pass by unmolested but in the end couldn't resist recklessly launching himself at a wide ball and holing out, usually caught behind or occasionally at deep third man from a fierce cut.

Of course the plan didn't work every time, but you needed guts to offer pat-ball – or 'pie throwing', as Australian Rodney Marsh described military medium-paced bowling – to one of the game's most destructive batsmen.

As well as an excellent bowling technique, Ossie had courage in abundance. In the Glamorgan dressing room we were amazed to see his preparations before going out to field. Both ankles would he heavily bandaged and often a knee too. He had bowled for three summers at Cambridge University's ground at Fenner's. "If you'd bowled as long as I did on that flatbed, you'd be strapped up too," he'd ruefully comment. He was too modest to add that his 80 wickets in 1958 remain to this day the University's record for most wickets in their truncated season, a feat which broke A.G. Steel's record of 75 set in 1878. Game after game he had to bowl against the country's leading batsmen, all eager to improve their averages with a run-gorged trip to maul 'the schoolboys' on the batsman's paradise which was a Fenner's pitch.

Ossie was to become a close, albeit during our playing days a slightly distant, friend; close in the sense that we shared and enjoyed many of the same pleasures in life but distant because, as all the best captains have to be, he often kept his own counsel. Despite this, he unwittingly was instrumental in steering me into what turned out to be a 12-year marriage.

During our April 1961 pre-season training in Cardiff he mentioned that he'd heard of a good pub in Newport, eight miles east of Cardiff. He'd recently taken delivery of a snazzy new Triumph TR2 sports car, and he felt like giving it a run. Ossie was not renowned for being the most co-ordinated of creatures – batting at number eleven, one only had to see him face a few balls to recognise this – and on one occasion he failed to see a stray gipsy horse which was quietly crossing a road on Leckwith Common in Cardiff.

But on this occasion he got me safely to 'The Engineers' pub which looked down on the main railway line leading in and out of Newport station. With the cricket season almost upon us and our photographs featuring regularly in Welsh newspapers, it was hardly surprising that our entrance drew some attention. A group of twenty-somethings were having a drink before going off to a private party. One of the girls, a dark-haired, curvaceous creature, obviously primed by the lads in her group, drifted by, pausing long enough for a brief chat before asking us if we'd like to come too.

Two presentable, out-on-the-town young bachelors would hardly be likely to say no. Seventeen months later, Joy Lois Nada Trick and I were married in Newport's St. Woolos Cathedral.

But before then, there was work on the field to be done.

In May, in taking a catch to remove Billy Oakes of Derbyshire off the bowling of Ossie at Chesterfield, I first tried out a technique which I would use again whenever similar situations occurred in the future. It was a poor pitch, one which their wry humorist of an opening bat, Charlie Lee, described as "a whist drive wicket, I don't know whether to play high or low." Billy had made a battling 74 in the home side's first innings by deciding that his best chance of survival would be to charge the bowler and meet the delivery either on the full or half volley. Watching from my customary position at short square-leg, I thought he'd do the same in Derbyshire's second innings.

Setting off up the wicket, particularly to quickish bowlers, was very rare in those days. So before the start of an Ossie over to him and with Billy still not off the mark, I said to my captain that if he adopted the same tactic again, I'd like to try something different too.

Three consecutive seasons as the country's leading fielder with replica Brylcreem trophies.

Second ball, off up the pitch again went Billy. But this time I travelled with him staying in a sideways, crab-like position without losing the level plane of my head which helped me to keep on balance. He got a thin inside edge onto his pad and the ball ricocheted onto the legside almost a third of the way down the pitch. But thanks to my moving with him while he was on the charge, I was still – in relative position to him – at short square-leg when Billy made contact. Diving far to my left, I caught it. It was one of the 697 career catches that gave me the most pleasure.

Something also took place off the playing area in that match which reflected very much the kind of camaraderie which was then an intrinsic part of county cricket. Due to heavy overnight rain there was obviously going to be a long delay to the start of the game. The reporter who covered all our away matches for the *Western Mail* was Basil Easterbrook, an amiable cove. Basil was one of sports' funniest raconteurs and he used to keep us endlessly amused with stories of his winter job covering first division football. From our point of view he was completely trustworthy, for off the field he'd quietly 'miss' seeing things that had nothing to do with our performances between 11.30 am and 6.30 pm.

With little prospect of an immediate start, five of us sat on chairs on the concrete perimeter in front of the quaint Chesterfield pavilion, talking of this and that. Basil, a man who enjoyed his food and fancied himself as a wine buff, told us about a wonderful dessert wine he'd discovered the previous evening. From the island of Madeira, it was called 'The Duke of Clarence'. He rummaged in his briefcase and triumphantly plucked out a three-quarter-full bottle: "And here it is!" Ossie, Tony Lewis, Don Shepherd and I looked at a now clear blue sky and the still saturated outfield and decided that any immediate prospect of play was so remote that it was worth sampling. As we talked cricket, wine and the state of the English game, thrice more the 12th man was sent off to a Chesterfield off-licence for replenishments. Time passed gently by.

Late in the afternoon the umpires returned from a routine pitch and ground inspection and to our horror announced that play would begin in 20 minutes. A mad rush to change into our whites was on, but I admit four of the Glamorgan team who took the field had little recall of what transpired from then until close of play.

Yes, the county game was different then, and the more human and pleasant for it. Indeed, talk to virtually all the players of my generation and, while they envy the salary levels earned these days by county performers, they are glad that they played in their own particular era. Then, some 300 first-class professional players were involved in what was structurally the same game that W.G. Grace had dominated in the latter part of the 19th century; three-day matches played twice a week. Sundays were devoted to benefit or charity games. The whole county scene, players, umpires, scorers, groundsmen, members and paying spectators were all part of a kind of freemasonry of cricket.

I'm old enough to yearn for the good old days in terms of fellowship and fair play. But I'm enough of a realist to know that my feelings are clouded by nostalgia and by a sense of the privilege it was to have played at that time.

CHAPTER 12

THE END OF AN ERA BUT A NEW BEGINNING TOO

In the so-called swinging '60s there were all-embracing changes in the air: in the political landscape, the music scene and the ever-increasing acceptance of the role of women outside the home. In cricket the introduction of the 60-over Gillette Cup in 1963 and the arrival six years later of the 40-over John Player Sunday League transformed the long-standing schedule of two three-day games a week.

In 1962 I was selected to play in the last Gentlemen versus Players match at Lord's, a fixture which dated back to 1806. The following winter cricket finally brought an end to the artificial division between those who played for pay and those who did so under the guise of 'expenses only.' This last match was also a final trial before the selection of the MCC team to go to Australia that winter. For the record the two teams in batting order were:

GENTLEMEN		PLAYERS	
Rev. D.S. Sheppard	(Sussex)	M.J. Stewart	(Surrey)
E. J. Craig	(Cambridge)	J.H. Edrich	(Surrey)
E.R. Dexter (capt)	(Sussex)	P.H. Parfitt	(Middlesex)
M.J.K. Smith	(Warwicks)	T.W. Graveney	(Worcs)
R.M. Prideaux	(Northants)	P.J. Sharpe	(Yorks)
A.R. Lewis	(Glamorgan)	P.M. Walker	(Glamorgan)
R.W. Barber	(Lancs)	F.J. Titmus	(Middlesex)
D.B. Pithey	(Oxford)	F.S. Trueman (capt)	(Yorks)
T.E. Bailey	(Essex)	K.V. Andrew	(Northants)
A.C. Smith	(Warwicks)	N. Gifford	(Worcs)
O.S. Wheatley	(Glamorgan)	D. Shackleton	(Hants)

Players XI. *Back (left to right):* John Edrich, Phil Sharpe, Norman Gifford, Peter Walker, Micky Stewart, Peter Parfitt.
Front: Fred Titmus, Derek Shackleton, Fred Trueman (capt), Tom Graveney, Keith Andrew.

Rain resulted in a drawn match, but not before another 'Truemanism' entered cricket's folklore. It came about thus and, as Welsh entertainer Max Boyce would say, "I know, 'cos I was there."

As neither of my Gentlemen colleagues in the Glamorgan side nor I were in with a realistic shout of making the touring party, we decided to enjoy the experience. For others, particularly batsmen Peter Parfitt and the Reverend David Sheppard, who had made a comeback in county cricket after a long sabbatical taking holy orders, it was a vital match.

Opening for the Gentlemen, David scored a splendid century, so impressive in its execution that the next morning's papers expected him to be named as captain of the party to Australia, although later in the match the selectors announced that they had appointed Ted Dexter to lead the side. It seemed that David Sheppard had done enough to be chosen as a batsman, so now the pressure to top David's century hung heavily on Peter Parfitt's shoulders. Peter was one of the most humorous men in the game but, as he walked out to bat in the Players' first innings, 'Parf' had a grim and deadly serious look about him.

High quality batsmen, and Peter was certainly one of these, are at their most vulnerable until they've played themselves in and reached around 20. He had made a cautious nine when Dexter bowled him a long hop outside the leg stump. Pivoting smoothly on the hook shot, of which he was a prime exponent, Parfitt smashed the ball out of the middle of the bat but straight to backward short-leg where the Reverend was fielding. David only had time to parry the ball upwards and, as he looked down to rub his stinging right palm, the ball dropped back out of the sky and into his hand! Parfitt, caught Sheppard bowled Dexter, 9.

The dressing rooms at Lord's are on the first floor. We could hear Peter's footsteps approaching. The door flew open, followed by his bat, then Peter. He knew that, barring a miracle, he'd blown his chance. The bat had come to rest in the far corner at the feet of our captain, F.S. Trueman. Drawing deeply on his donkey-skin pipe, Fred looked up and said to a still hushed and sympathetic dressing room, "Aye, never mind lad, but when the Reverend puts his hands together he's got a better chance than thee or I."

Happily for Peter he was selected for Australia anyway.

Thirty-seven years later when I was recovering from a major operation, the phone rang. "'Ow are you, lad?" came the unmistakably gruff Yorkshire tones of the man once described by John Arlott as 'England's most famous man'. After momentarily having been taken aback by the identity of the caller, I made the classic mistake of saying, "I'm fine, Fred – how are you?" Twenty-five minutes later I'd done no more than contribute the occasional grunt or two before he finished the totally one-sided conversation with, "Take care lad, I'm thinking of you," and put the phone down. A one-off was Fred.

As was another sporting superstar I met four years later at Lord's. Muhammad Ali was in London, to defend his world heavyweight title against England's Henry Cooper. The West Indies were playing MCC at Lord's, and someone with an eye for a good photo opportunity thought the 'Louisville Lip' ought to pay a visit to the home of cricket.

As a member of the MCC side, waiting my turn to bat, I was sitting in the dressing room when the door swung open and in marched four very large, black American bodyguards, complete with snap-brim hats and ominous bulges under their left armpits. In Hollywood film tradition they 'cased the joint' to make sure there were no undesirables present. We looked a harmless enough bunch so, with a nod of approval in the direction of the door, the main act entered.

Ali was one of those rare sporting animals, smaller in life than he appeared on the screen. He was certainly a shade over six feet tall and beautifully proportioned, but nowhere near as massive as he looked in the ring. Captain Mike Smith took him around his MCC team who were all now standing, if not to attention, then certainly fully alert. Ali came level with me and, as Mike made the introductions, the boxer looked straight through me, his focus seemingly several feet behind my head. It was an unnerving experience. Ali's grip too was unexpectedly gentle. He had small hands for a man of his size and the most limp-wristed handshake I've ever received from a heterosexual male!

He then moved towards the dressing room window, which overlooked the playing area. Pausing at a dressing table and mirror he picked up a brush and ran it through his crinkly hair, saying to his image, "I've got to stay in shape 'cos in my profession you don't stay pruurty for long". He then went out on the MCC team's balcony to watch an over or two being bowled.

To make conversation Mike asked the heavyweight champion of the world, "How long do you think it would take you to master this game?" Ali watched another ball go harmlessly past as the batsman made no effort to play it and said, "I reckon around about three weeks." Then, butterfly-like, he was gone.

The season of 1962 saw me extending my interests in writing and, at the prompting of my father, I wrote up from my diaries my experiences at sea as well as cricketing recollections to date. I also contributed numerous articles on the game for newspapers and magazines like *The Cricketer*. These were the days when batsmen, unprotected as they now are by helmets, chest protectors and thigh pads, had to face fast bowlers on uncovered, unpredictable pitches with them being allowed to bowl as many bouncers an over as they wished. More in jest than expecting to be taken seriously, I wrote a piece in *The Cricketer* proposing that it was high time that, after getting out of the way of an intended head-removing bullet in the shape of a cricket ball, the batsman should be allowed to hurl his bat at the bowler in his follow-through on the basis that, as he'd been trying to hit him, he should be prepared to take something of his own medicine back! Unsurprisingly this was given short shrift by the law-makers at Lord's.

I had a remarkable match that summer against Middlesex at my favourite ground Lord's. In their first innings I bowled 34 overs and took seven for 58, in what would prove to be the best bowling performance of my career. Then I opened the batting against an attack including England's Alan Moss and off-spinner Fred Titmus and ended with 152 not out, which was also the best batting performance of my career. In all, I was on the field for all bar 45 minutes of the three-day game. And all this was sandwiched by two lengthy nights in Raymond's saucy Revue Bar in Soho, rounding off a pretty action-packed 72 hours!

Not Derek Underwood, but still good enough to play for England.

That summer Glamorgan played six games at Cardiff, six at Swansea and one each at Ebbw Vale, Llanelli, Margam, Neath, Newport and Pontypridd. Each had individual characteristics. At the tiny Ebbw Vale ground, stray sheep would sometimes rival in numbers the human spectators on the steep grassy slope square to the wicket. In the 1956 match there against Northampton, Frank Tyson had to shorten his run-up, otherwise he would have had to start it on the adjoining bowling green! At Stradey Park, Llanelli, the tiny pavilion had one solitary shower for which both teams had to queue. At Margam we played alongside the adjoining steelworks, and one year we came off for bad light on what was a cloudless day. A change in wind direction had blown a thick pall of orange smoke across the ground. It was so dense that, from the pavilion end, it was impossible to see what was happening out in the middle!

In my view the game is the poorer as a result of withdrawing from playing matches at out-grounds. Swansea and its surrounds once recruited more members than the capital city, Cardiff, but now has only one county cricket week in the season. As a result, cricket's grass-root development in this very sports-conscious city has inevitably suffered.

In 1962 we played Gloucestershire at Margam on the slowest pitch imaginable. The ball rarely rose above half stump high as we bowled out our opponents for 88. We replied with a 'fighting' 62 which took nearly three hours to accumulate. Out came Gloucestershire again. This time they made 92 during the course of which their captain C.T.M Pugh, coming in at number three, decided in desperation to play a positive shot at every delivery. He waved at, cut at, drove at and heaved cross-batted shots at the ball for 30 minutes before being bowled by Don Shepherd (11 for 51 in the match) for just three runs. On his return to the pavilion, bathed in sweat and, as they used to say in old-time, bare-knuckle boxing, 'with bellows to mend', he was met by that driest of wits, slow left-hand bowler Sam Cook. "See you got rid of that swarm of bees, skip," said Sam. "What swarm of bees are you talking about, Cookie?" asked a puzzled Pugh. "Yon ones you've been trying to swat for the past half hour," his bowler replied.

By the season's end in September, I had had enough of cricket – and so Joy Trick and I decided to get married. I had a feeling that it was time to settle down, learn a trade of some sort and raise a family. At the time, getting hitched seemed the right decision for us both, but I should have heeded some earlier sound advice. During the previous winter out in South Africa, I'd confided to Wilf Isaacs, a squat, perma-tanned Jewish property developer who had become something of a 'guru' to me, that I thought I'd met the girl I wanted to marry. He pursed his lips, raised a warning eyebrow and said, "Remember, Peter, while you're playing a professional sport, the only person you ever live with is yourself."

Over a decade later he was to be proved right.

Two days after our wedding, a full top hat and tails affair at St. Woolos Cathedral in Newport with Don Shepherd as my best man and a reception at the Greyhound, a well known hostelry in the Monmouthshire countryside, Joy and I sailed for South Africa on honeymoon. The Glamorgan year book recorded, 'P. Walker has resigned to take up a business appointment in South Africa but we hope that by the spring he may change his mind.' They were wrong about the business opportunity for none existed at the time, but prophetically right about a change of mind and heart.

Although our marriage was to come to a juddering, painful halt 12 years and two children later, Joy did inadvertently give the kiss of life to my cricketing career to which I thought I'd written finis. She had quickly become pregnant with our daughter Sarah and, while she spent most of her first few months looking down into the toilet bowl of our flat in Sea Point, Cape Town instead of up to enjoy the beauty of Table Mountain, I was having an almost equally miserable time as a quite useless wine and brandy salesman.

I'd landed this job soon after our arrival in South Africa. I can't for the life of me remember why or how, but I do recall that it did meet my desire to live and work in South Africa's most beautiful city. From its headquarters 40 miles inland in Stellenbosch, the heart of the wine growing area, the Anton Rupert organisation was about to launch a new brandy called Richelieu. Its main marketing point was that each bottle contained a measure of French cognac. Quite how much I've no idea, but I was kitted out with a tiny, brandy-coloured Renault Dauphine car, two weeks' training at headquarters, an account at the French bank in downtown Cape Town and given an order book and lengthy list of off-licences and hotel bars in my patch who needed to be called on fortnightly.

It was six desperate months. In order to stock and push our products, sub-human barmen had to be bribed with free bottles of brandy and wine from our portfolio. When I made my calls, even if well before noon, I was ritually expected to join each pub landlord or barman in a tipple. After lunch I wasn't fit to drive, let alone sell. It was a period in my life as depressing as anything I'd experienced in the merchant navy.

In January 1963, my thoughts inevitably began to turn to the oncoming April nets in Cardiff and how I'd miss them. Besides feeling ill during most of her early months of pregnancy, Joy had never before travelled far from her home town of Newport. She desperately missed her friends and in particular her mother, although to her credit she did try to make a decent fist of a new life in a strange country with a relative stranger – me.

On reflection, Joy and I were ill suited. She had been the youngest of four children and, as the baby of the family, had enjoyed something of a cosseted life. When she developed into a stunning-looking, young woman, family protectors were replaced by shoals of enraptured Newport suitors. When I came on the scene with my worldwide travel experience, parents from whom I had inherited a liberal way of thinking, and a high sporting profile in Wales, this heady mixture seduced her away from what would undoubtedly been a more stable and happy future within her own community. Unfortunately, I brought into the relationship all the uncertainties of life with a slightly neurotic, self-centred and restless personality.

During the British winter of 1962/63, but in the beautiful summer of Cape Town, two unhappy people began to discuss what to do next. I wondered if the combination of morning- and home-sickness would be lessened if she were back at home in Newport. "Yes, it would," was her quick answer. Joy's decision helped me to make up my own mind too.

From then on things moved swiftly. A letter to Wilf Wooller asking if Glamorgan still wanted to make use of my services (I was 26 and still in my sporting prime) received a swift reply: 'Come back, you're more than welcome.' I gave in my required three-months' notice at work and, in the middle of June, joined Joy and our expected child who had sailed back two months earlier.

As a temporary home, her parents kindly gave us the top floor of their house at 29 Waterloo Road while I set about making my peace with the Glamorgan team whom I'd turned my back on nine months earlier. After the traumas of 1960 the welcome I got from them could be described as medium in size; but, after a couple of probationary games in the second team and colts XI, in the first week of July I reappeared in Glamorgan colours at Cardiff against Northamptonshire with 26 runs and three for 69 in 27 overs. It made my assimilation back into the team fold a lot easier.

In the two months left of the '63 season, I watched in admiration as Alan Jones, one of Glamorgan's finest ever batsmen and a close pal from our early days on the junior staff together, scored 187* and 105* in the same match against Somerset at Glastonbury as well as being last to bed on two of the three nights we were in town! Then it was back to Swansea where I took five for 41 in 20.2 overs against the West Indies and then up to Old Trafford where I was carried off three times in the match: once after having my chin sliced open from a lifter from England fast-medium bowler Peter Lever, and then being felled fielding at short square-leg in each innings, both times by Lancashire wicket-keeper Geoff 'Chimp' Clayton, possessor of a wicked, unavoidable, flat-batted sweep shot.

It was an eventful summer, and Glamorgan managed to finish second in the table, a mere 20 points behind county champions, Yorkshire.

After it was all over and having returned to the UK to live on an all-the-year-round basis and now with a wife and child to support, I had to find some gainful employment. I spent the winter of 1963/64 trying to cultivate opportunities in print journalism and broadcasting. But there were very few opportunities in either. I ended up writing and producing a holiday brochure for a company called Sunlane, an off-shoot of the well-established Red Dragon Travel Agency, which had an office in Newport as well as Cardiff. A 14-day stay in a four-star hotel in Majorca, including full board and flights, cost all of £45.

I sat in an office on the top floor of the Newport branch writing copy for the brochure, selecting happy holiday photographs and planning print layouts. At the same time I also worked on an instructional book commissioned for the Collins Nutshell series. Immodestly I called it *Winning Cricket*. It wasn't *War and Peace*, but it was a wheel-turning start down a new path in life.

My first sampling of a full British winter was a cold, damp and depressing experience. But the summer of 1964 cheered everyone up, with an early

August centrepiece bringing our first ever victory over the Australians. On the eve of the match at Swansea, Tony Lewis, one of the most gifted and graceful batsmen ever produced by Glamorgan and a fine captain to boot, was having a bad trot. To try to get him back into form he, plus a few of us bowlers, had a special net session at Cardiff Arms Park. Watching proceedings stood the rotund figure of Geoff Ashe, a Glamorgan committeeman. After playing and missing a few times and as he retrieved the balls in the back net behind him, Tony politely asked, "What do you think, Geoff? Any suggestions?" The portly optician, a hugely unsuccessful second team club batsman himself, thought for a moment, then offered, "Tony, you've got two feet and a bat. Use 'em," and walked away. Keep things simple, I suppose, is always good advice!

A couple of weeks before the historic game against the Australians and during a Sunday off in the middle of our county match against Surrey at The Oval, the Glamorgan team had been invited by a Welsh-speaking chaplain at Broadmoor Mental Hospital to play a game against a team comprised of inmates and wardens. It was a strange, surreal experience.

Warders and prisoners wore identical clothes. Every door had to be unlocked and then locked again after passing through, and you kept a wary eye on your immediate neighbour as he cut up his helping of meat at lunch. During the match itself, every time Alan Rees, who had also played for Wales at outside half, hit a boundary, a voice from the edge would yell, "Lovely gravy, Ruby!" Where the nickname 'Ruby' came from no one knows, but it stuck with Alan to the end of his cricket career.

Our visit to Broadmoor was not without other flashes of humour. We had tea outside the small pavilion and one of the opposition, I presumed he was an inmate, told me about their recent sports day. "There was only one event they banned," he said, glancing speculatively towards the 16-foot high perimeter wall. "The pole vault."

Forty-two years on, the embers of memory of our 36-run victory over the Australians in 1964 remain warm. The full details have been well chronicled elsewhere. Alan Rees produced two fine innings of 48 and 47 in Glamorgan's low totals of 197 and 172 while I chipped in with 41 in the first. But the match was a triumph for the Swansea 'spin twins' Don Shepherd and Jim Pressdee. On a pitch giving ample turn if little bounce, between them they accounted for no fewer than 19 of the 20 Australia wickets which fell, nine to Don, ten to Jim, a remarkable achievement. Of the 160.3 overs bowled by Glamorgan in the match, those two sent down 112.3, with Don's 52 in the second innings costing a miserly 71 runs. It had been a remarkable exhibition of stamina and accuracy by the two Swansea neighbours. The only wicket they missed was taken by our other off-spinner, Euros Lewis, but the victory had been masterminded by some typically astute field placing and captaincy by Ossie Wheatley, who rarely missed a trick.

At the end, thousands of spectators raced onto the St. Helen's field to cheer off both sides in what had been a riveting game of cricket, little thinking that history would repeat itself four years later.

Both Euros Lewis and Jim Pressdee could have played for many more years for Glamorgan.

Swarthy-skinned Euros was one of the biggest spinners of a cricket ball I ever came across. As an off-spinner he had a tantalising flight too and, on the uncovered pitches of the time, he could be almost as devastating as Don Shepherd. In and out of the first team between 1961 and '66, he was a far better attacking left-hand batsman than his figures show. Yet despite his all-round talent, he never really blossomed. Was it because of his Celtic temperament and off-the field Bohemian lifestyle? Eventually released by Glamorgan, Euros spent three seasons at Sussex before retiring to drive a bus in his West Wales home town of Llangennech. What a talent wasted.

Jim Pressdee was one who made the best of his abilities. Slow to mature as a cricketer, for three years in the mid-1960s, Jim was the best all-rounder in county cricket. The slowest of slow left-arm bowlers, his 405 wickets at a cost of 22.18 show that not many hard-hitting batsmen of his day ever took him apart. He could also be the most obdurate and perverse of middle order batsmen. Once, in a drawn match against Kent at Maidstone and because he was irritated by the home crowd barracking him for slow play, Jim – on 97 – spurned the chance of a certain century by blocking out a maiden over from that most amiable of part-time bowlers, Brian Luckhurst!

Between 1949 and 1965 Jim's 543 innings for Glamorgan yielded 13,411 runs at 29.16. Throw in 344 often spectacular close-to-the-wicket catches, and it's clear that Jim Pressdee was a key member of the side. But, in the final match of the 1965 season against Essex at Llanelli, Jim typically got involved in a verbal duel which ended his career at the age of 32. The issue which brought this about? Inevitably it involved Wilfred Wooller! Wilf was counting the meagre takings of the day's play in a small room, through which Jim wanted to pass to get to the rear of the pavilion. Somewhat forcibly, Wilf told him to go through the proper adjoining door. Jim refused, promptly resigned and went off to South Africa where he lives to this day. Over such a piffling matter, Glamorgan lost one of their few irreplaceable players!

Under Ossie's shrewd leadership we became doughty battlers in adversity, and circling vultures when scenting victory, and we deserved to finish third in the county championship. The 1965 season saw a huge all-round improvement in Glamorgan's performances as a team, and it included a Tony Lewis innings of 189 against the touring New Zealanders. From the backing-up end I watched the greater part. It had class written all over it.

However, captain Ossie didn't always get it right. Against our neighbours and old rivals Gloucestershire, he declared at 336 for four with Alan Jones and Tony Lewis both getting hundreds. Then, with the ball, Ossie helped to roll over the opposition for a mere 159. However, on a blistering hot June day, his decision to enforce the follow-on misfired badly. The two Browns, David and Tony, both got maiden first-class hundreds and, with a draw inevitable, I ended up first fielding barefoot and then keeping wicket in the same state. It felt like a throwback to my primary schooldays in South Africa.

At the end of August came the most remarkable, explosive spell of bowling I've ever seen. On a bone hard, greenish pitch, in reply to Leicester's 117 all out at their Grace Road ground we struggled to make 185, giving us a lead of 68. Before the Leicester second innings could begin, a shower of rain freshened still further the uncovered surface. We fielders in the slips had our backs to the pavilion as Jeff Jones, then at his quickest, bowled the first ball to the experienced Leicester opener Maurice Hallam. Now Jeff rarely moved the ball in the air – there wasn't time – but this one swung in and lifted sharply to hit Maurice a sickening blow under the heart. On the evidence of that first ball we close fielders immediately retreated five yards. The next, just short of a length, reared too, and our wicketkeeper David Evans just got an upleaping glove to it. We went further back. We could now have held a stage-whispered conversation with the Leicestershire team sitting behind us on their first-floor dressing room balcony.

The pitch had become a viper, dangerous to life and limb. Maurice had a wild flail at the next, got the thinnest of edges and at first slip I caught it one-handed way over my head and still rising. Had it been a few inches higher I swear it would have carried for six onto the player's balcony. No one was happier to return to the pavilion than Maurice, who passed me with a "Well caught, Peter, thank God a tall guy like you was at slip." Peter Marner was next man in – and out: caught Evans bowled Jones. In walked Stanley Jayasinghe of Ceylon. Stanley was a fine, wristy player who in those pre-helmet and body armour days never wore anything more than a thin folded handkerchief as a thigh pad. Square-leg umpire Charles Elliott was in the process of checking the stumps when Stanley arrived at the crease. "Nice suede shoes you've got on there, Charles," remarked Stanley. "Thanks," said Elliott. "I bought these veldskoens in town this morning." "Well, if I were you," said Stanley, "I'd stand back a couple more yards at square leg as I'm probably going to tread on them!" He was braver than that but could do nothing with another Jones flyer which hit him on the glove and ballooned to me 35 yards back at slip.

At one stage Jeff had the remarkable figures of five wickets without conceding a run. He ended up with eight for 11 on quite the most dangerous pitch I've ever seen. Leicester were dismissed for just 40, and we won by an innings and 28!

My daughter Sarah was soon displaying a quick mind, something which was to stand her in good stead when she went to school. During a rare few days off in the summer of '65, she and I lay side by side on our lounge sofa while I read to her from her favourite nursery rhyme book. She already knew it off by heart so, when on purpose I made a mistake, she would quickly correct me! On this occasion, and not finding it the most stimulating of subjects, I must have dropped off in mid-sentence, shifting positions as I did so. I was woken by a whisper in my ear: "Daddy, please move off. I'm only a tiny baby and you're squashing me." Right to this day, Sarah has never been short of a word or an opinion, a characteristic which her beautiful blonde daughter Emily has inherited!

In 1965 too, along came a son Justin to join his sister. His timing was spot on. He was born on 3rd December and on Christmas Day that year my father had his fatal heart attack on Kyalami Golf course on the outskirts of Johannesburg. However, he died knowing that he had a grandson to carry on the line.

Although it was to be a further eight years in finally coming, so different were Joy and I in temperament and interests that a parting of our ways was inevitable. When it did come, I naively believed that the children, by then Sarah was aged ten and Justin two years younger, would not be too badly affected. I fully intended to keep in regular touch and, as my lifestyle of frequently being away for longish spells playing cricket would be familiar to them, I couldn't foresee any major problems. Sadly this did not happen. Joy kept us apart, and we all bear the scars to this day.

Towards the end of the 1965 season, and after a mere eight rather than the customary ten years since being given my county cap, the Glamorgan club committee awarded me a benefit in the following summer. Financially this is the most important season in a player's career for the lump sum gleaned from a combination of collections at games, Sunday benefit matches against club teams and events only loosely connected with cricket like dances and dinners, helped to compensate for the very low salaries then paid to professionals on the English county circuit.

However, my benefit summer proved to be a bad year in terms of the team's results. Third place in 1965 became 14th in 1966 and, with less inclination to support a losing team, our home gates were down, leading in turn to me suffering financially.

It's easy to become pre-occupied in trying to organise a band of volunteers to handle the various outside events which form a major part of the fund-raising side of a benefit, so a loss in form is not an unusual by-product for a beneficiary. Like a desperate double-glazing salesman, beneficiaries hustle their way around amateur cricket clubs trying to drum up their support in staging games against the county side and other events. It is demeaning and often embarrassing to all parties concerned.

Although one tried not to be side-tracked by projects off the field, this proves to be very, very difficult. Unless they are extremely fortunate to have a good chairman and a capable benefit committee to take on most of the administrative load, few cricketers make much of a fist of both roles, playing and canvassing. And of course it remains very important that, day or night, rain or shine, you're seen at every event organised on your behalf.

Volunteer fundraisers start off meaning well but regrettably often don't deliver what they initially promise; mine were no better, no worse than most. But I received a body blow in every sense in a mid-May match against Kent at the appropriately named for me, Gravesend ground.

I went in at number three to face the erratic and extremely quick ex-Oxford fast bowler David Sayer, nicknamed for good reason 'The Slayer'. His first ball to me was a fast, in-swinging yorker which hit me plumb on the right instep. I somersaulted away towards the gully, yelling blue murder;

the pain was excruciating. Taken off to hospital by ambulance, I was told by the duty doctor that my x-rays showed only bruising. A night of agony followed in our team hotel where even the weight of a sheet on my foot was too much to bear.

Then came the long train journey back to Wales via Paddington. I made it using two bats as crutches and next day hobbled into the Royal Gwent Hospital in Newport where further pictures showed I'd broken my instep in five places, one where the ball had actually struck, the other four on the other side as a result of the compression caused by the blow! Heavily plastered, I was out of the game until 8th June.

In fact, I should never have come back so soon. For the remainder of the summer, to run up to the wicket to bowl was pretty painful. But, in a benefit season, to remain in the public eye a player has to get out on the field, even if almost stretchered on and off it.

However, there was a plus side to the injury for as a result of less time bowling my batting improved and in an otherwise difficult season all round, I did manage to make 46 out of 90 all out against Surrey and 95* out of 162 at Taunton, hobbling through to aggregate 1,202 runs for the county. Only Tony Lewis and Alan Jones passed that figure.

But my haul of catches was only 42 and, thanks in good part to the 'Slayer' striking that early blow, my return of a meagre 20 wickets from 232 overs for the county meant that it had by no means been a vintage season.

But one event at Lord's, my favourite ground, did stick in the memory and resulted in an amendment to the laws of the game. Bowling from the Nursery end I delivered a ball from 29 instead of 22 yards which only narrowly missed opening batsman Eric 'Legs' Russell's stumps. Legs was a particular pal of mine and when I tried this delivery, he was well past 100 in Middlesex's second innings. From long experience I knew that he had a mannerism of looking down at the batting crease in the middle of a bowler's run up and giving it several hearty thwacks with his bat, so I decided to take just two strides at the start of mine, and then 'hand grenade' bowl the ball down to the other end.

It duly floated past the surprised umpire at my end. As I'd been well behind him when I released the ball he hadn't known where it had come from. Eric only looked up from his bat-hammering exercise a split second before the ball gently passed him outside the off stump. A fraction straighter and I've no doubt it would have been the end of a beautiful friendship.

At their annual meeting before the start of the next season, the umpires, with the full approval of the custodians of the laws of cricket, the MCC, banned this delivery, declaring it a no-ball if the bowler had failed to give prior notice of his intentions. The umpires rightly maintained that, when standing up near the stumps at the bowler's end, they had no idea as to whether or not it had been legally delivered, a view which carried the day.

CHAPTER 13

TWO RECORDS AND A HISTORIC SEASON

In 1967 Glamorgan County Cricket Club moved from Cardiff Arms Park to Sophia Gardens. The move had been forced on the club through the redevelopment of Cardiff Arms Park rugby ground as the Welsh Rugby Union's international ground. To accommodate Cardiff RFC, who up to then had used the Arms Park as their club ground, the adjoining cricket field had to be sequestrated to provide a new home for what many claimed to be the most famous amateur rugby club in the world.

Sophia Gardens was a natural location for Glamorgan. But first it had to overcome some fierce opposition from a section of the City Council before planning approval was given. For a transitional period the club had to share Sophia Gardens with the cricket section of the Cardiff Athletic Club, but it is now wholly owned by Glamorgan CCC and in 2006 won the right to stage an Ashes Test against Australia in 2009.

Like all new pitches, the one at Sophia Gardens took time to settle down. Frankly for the first few years it was unfit for first-class cricket. I recall one early match where Colin Milburn of Northamptonshire got on tiptoe to play a ball which reared off a length and would have hit him straight in the mouth if he hadn't got his gloves up in front of his face. His smile at his technical skill in having done so was its customary width. However, the next ball of a very similar length hit him on the boot.

From a batsman's point of view playing at Sophia Gardens was like having the Black Spot pressed into your hand by Blind Pugh. Morale amongst the Glamorgan top order could hardly have been lower. In our first year at Sophia Gardens we played Derbyshire who, in ignorance of the unpredictable nature of our pitch, somehow mustered 150 in their first and what turned out to be their only innings. Against their high quality seam attack of Brian Jackson, Harold Rhodes and Derek Morgan we thought we'd done rather well in making 49 and 98 to lose by an innings and three runs!

Despite the growing pains of our home pitch, in 1968 we managed to finish third in the table. This improvement coincided with the arrival of Majid Khan of Pakistan, who went on to play many wonderful innings for Glamorgan. Although he initially spoke hardly at all, he turned out to be the most pleasant and amiable of companions. Majid had been with us for nearly three weeks before, other than "hello" and "good morning," we heard him speak his first sentence. This came at Derby. The Racecourse ground is a venue where the wind, combined with the openness of the ground, has given it a deserved reputation of being the coldest venue in Britain where first-class cricket is played. Before a delayed start of play, we huddled around a brazier in our dressing room.

Majid had sat silently in a corner, listening, as we senior pros discussed the importance of footwork in batting. Suddenly this deep, brown voice stopped us dead. "Footwork is not important." Encouraged that Majid was at last joining in, we challenged him to prove it. So he padded up and we all went outside into the nets. Majid took guard on a green, under-prepared pitch to face the bowling of Jeff Jones, Ossie Wheatley, Don Shepherd and myself.

Majid – we were soon to nickname him 'Bearer' because he belonged to one of the top ten wealthiest families in Pakistan and had many domestic servants back home in Lahore – stood rock still for 20 minutes, going up with the bounce if Jeff pitched short or swaying out of range and whipping the ball square of the wicket on both sides when Ossie, Don or I had a bowl at him. None of us got him out, bowled, lbw or caught in an accredited fielding position. We reckoned Majid would have been around 50 not out had he been batting for real out in the middle. A batting genius, if ever I saw one.

So cold was it at Derby that, when we eventually went out to field, I stood at slip in a balaclava and wearing thick woollen gloves, illegal at the time according to the laws of the game, but the heavily sweatered and overcoated umpires fully sympathised with the players' extreme discomfort, taking a humane view of anyone having to field close to the wicket where a broken finger was a near certainty in the freezing conditions.

Astute Tony Lewis soon found out how to get the best out of the Bearer. He would offer him an ice cream for every 10 runs over 50. Thus incentivised, our star batsman put on quite a bit of weight in that and subsequent seasons.

That summer saw Ossie taking 82 wickets at 12.95 to finish top of the English bowling averages while, to my surprise, I had a haul of five for nine in 3.4 overs as Hampshire took their turn to be baffled by the vagaries of bounce at Sophia Gardens. In that match two remarkable innings by Majid (91) and Tony Lewis (53) on a spiteful pitch had given us what turned out to be a commanding first innings total of 213, enough to result in an extraordinary innings and 16 runs victory over a side which included Barry Richards and Roy Marshall.

But the summer of '68 has gone down in Glamorgan and world sporting history books, because of two matches in August. The first against the Australians at the beginning of the month brought a repeat of our 1964 success over them. This time we won by 79 runs, thanks to splendid batting by Alan Jones (99) and Majid (55) in the first innings and by the two unrelated Davises in the second. Opening bat Roger made 59 while 66 came from Trinidadian Bryan. Coupled with some shrewd captaincy by stand-in skipper and senior pro Don Shepherd, we swept to an even more emphatic victory than four years earlier.

Malcolm Nash, in many of his peers' minds the best new ball bowler in county cricket before a back injury reduced the potency of his late in-swing, had given us a flying start by destroying the Australians' first innings with five for 28 in 15.3 overs. One of the nearly forgotten men from this famous victory is a young Maesteg-born off-spinner Brian 'Bertie' Lewis, who later sadly lost his action and quickly went out of the game. Brian took four for 51 in the first innings and three for 131 in the second. In such a pressure cooker of an atmosphere this was a commendable haul by a young and inexperienced bowler.

After having played something of a walk-on part in '64, I was delighted to get the crucial wicket in '68, though with one of the worst balls of the day. From a genuine long hop I hung on to a fierce return straight drive from Paul Sheahan who, with 137 at the time, looked capable of winning the game for the Australians.

If anything, the crowd's reaction to our victory was even more ecstatic than four years previously. We players were mobbed as we left the field, and it must have taken nearly ten minutes to make it from the playing area and up the 74 steps to the front of the St. Helen's pavilion.

Our joy, and that of our supporters, remains a vivid memory. Aussie captain Barry Jarman, one of three survivors from the '64 defeat, then got the biggest cheer of all from the several thousand strong crowd below when he began his after-match speech from the player's balcony with, "So we've been beaten by Glamorgan; what's new?"

The second memorable occasion in that month of August occurred at five past five on the afternoon of Saturday 31st at St. Helen's, in Glamorgan's county championship match against Nottinghamshire. Cricket history was made when Gary Sobers, unquestionably the game's finest ever all-rounder, struck six sixes in one over off the bowling of Malcolm Nash. This was the first time it had ever been done in a first-class match!

To put the record straight, we were waiting for a Nottinghamshire declaration and the unfortunate Nash was not bowling his usual left-arm, medium-paced swing and seam. With the game drifting towards a declaration, Malcolm had asked Tony Lewis if he could try out being a slow left-hand spinner. In the dressing room Malcolm had often expressed the view that, given the chance, he could be as good a slow bowler as any in the country. Never short of self-confidence and irrespective of the state of the game, he always wanted the ball in his hand. Not for nothing had we nicknamed Malcolm, whose initials were M.A.N. – 'Superman'.

Quite by accident this momentous event was recorded by television and has been shown countless times all over the cricketing world.

In those days, BBC Wales used to cover a number of Glamorgan's home matches. They had just come off air from a live transmission and were on standby to provide an insert, if required, to the *Grandstand* programme. Gary Sobers had not long come to the wicket and, to give a break to the cameramen who worked on rotation on the two cameras, producer/director Johnny Norman told them to stand down.

One of them, a self-confessed 'cricket nut' named John Lewis, asked Norman if he could stay on so he could follow Gary's innings through his viewfinder. The director agreed. Locking off the wide-angled camera and releasing the other two cameramen, over the talkback system Johnny asked commentator Wilf Wooller and scorer Bill Edwards to stay on, too, in case something should happen which would be useful in a highlights programme the following day.

Thanks to that ad hoc decision, history was recorded. The other key men were the engineer in charge of the signal relay dish on top of a mountain overlooking Maesteg, and Derek Griffen, the on-duty videotape editor at headquarters in Cardiff. Derek had absolutely no interest in sport and was of the type who pressed the 'start' button when asked – and did nothing more until told to press 'stop!' But for his work-to-rule attitude and John forgetting to tell him to 'stop', the pictures of what happened next would have remained only in our memories.

As Malcolm Nash ran up to start his over, Sobers, now on 40 and batting at the Mumbles Road end, stood waiting. Bowling spin requires a completely different rotating hand action at release compared to seam-up where the wrist stays upright behind the ball. Malcolm's first delivery was short and outside the leg stump and Gary smashed it away over deep square leg.

The second ball was slightly shorter. It finished over mid-wicket and out of the ground, bouncing off the wall of the *Cricketers'* pub. The stroke took Gary past his fifty.

The third six was technically the best shot of the lot. On a length, it sailed over long-off and back some 15 rows into the member's enclosure. By now, even Malcolm's famous self-confidence had been severely shaken.

The fourth delivery was a rank long hop and was again dismissed with a disdainful full-blooded swipe over fielder Alan Jones at deep square leg. The crowd were now baying for more! Four sixes off four balls, they sensed something momentous was in the offing. Throughout the over I'd been standing at mid-off watching this carnage taking place, thinking to myself, "I know Gary is looking for a declaration. I hope it happens soon for I'm bowling at the other end and, with the short Mumbles Road boundary behind me, I'm due for a battering too."

The fifth delivery was on a length, on off stump. Gary accepted the challenge. The ball flew straight and flat towards Roger Davis standing on the long-off boundary at the pavilion end. Bravely ignoring the cries behind him of "drop it, drop it", Roger caught it at chest height but the ball's sheer velocity knocked him flat on his back and across the boundary rope which lay some ten feet inside a low brick wall. Roger had however managed to hang onto the catch and, after standing up, he nodded to the bowler's end umpire Eddie Phillipson that yes, he had caught it.

Without a moment's hesitation, Gary accepted the fielder's word and started to march off. But the cries from the members behind Roger of "six, six, six" grew louder. Gary paused, and umpire Phillipson conferred with Roger. In his concentration about making the catch, the fielder had been unaware of falling across the boundary rope before regaining his feet back inside the playing area. Under the laws, a player had to stay within this at all times so, with the crowd in the vicinity continuing to voice their view of what had happened, to huge cheers all round, the umpire changed his mind and signalled another six.

Thoroughly rattled, Malcolm decided to revert to his normal seamer's grip and medium-pacer action. But the change back was too drastic and sudden to guarantee accuracy, and he bowled another long hop, the worst ball of the over.

In any case, wherever it had pitched, Gary was going to give it a go! Pivoting on his back foot, he smashed it high and handsome way over the square-leg wall surrounding St. Helen's. Wilf on the commentary mike yelled out in excitement, "He's done it. And my goodness, it's gone way down to

Swansea!" It wasn't quite that far as the Guildhall and town centre were nearly a mile distant, but it was one hell of a blow nevertheless.

To my immense relief, Gary immediately declared at 394 for five and, alongside a beaming Nash, walked off to a standing ovation. As they drew level with me, I overheard the game's most charismatic and accomplished all-rounder ask Malcolm how he could be so cheerful after what had just happened to him? It was typical of Superman to reply, "Well, Gary, we're now together in the world record books, and you couldn't have done it without me!"

There is some dispute about what happened to that last ball. The most popular story is that it was found the next day by a Glamorgan junior member, Richard Lewis, who returned it to the club offices. Whatever the truth, a ball reputed to be the very one is now housed in the museum at Trent Bridge.

Glamorgan 1969 – County Champions
Back (left to right): Eifion Jones, Bryan Davis, Malcolm Nash, Lawrence Williams, Roger Davis, Majid Khan. *Front:* Tony Cordle, Peter Walker, Tony Lewis (capt), Don Shepherd, Alan Jones.

In every sense, Glamorgan's second championship in 1969 was an all-round team effort. The 1948 title had been won by the combined excellence of Allan Watkins, Phil Clift and Wilfred Wooller fielding in a predatory leg trap. The '69 vintage had the same electric-eel agility close to the bat with the prehensile fingers of Roger Davis, Majid Khan, Bryan Davis and myself making the most of our bowler's talents. We took 113 catches between us, maximising the skills of Don Shepherd (81 wickets), Malcolm Nash (80), Tony Cordle (59) and Lawrence Williams and me (56 each).

Lawrence had come out of the South Wales leagues and immediately took valuable wickets – and let's not forget that, in a limited number of matches, we were ably supported by the now semi-retired Ossie Wheatley.

Our batting line-up was led by elegant captain Tony Lewis (1,296 runs) and ultra-consistent Alan Jones (1,581) plus the incomparable Majid Jahangir Khan (1,547). Valuable support from Trinidadian Bryan Davis (1,148) and his namesake Roger (835) gave Glamorgan's bowlers the essential batting platform to work from. Contributions from the middle order from me (892) and mighty telling blows from Barbadian-born but Welsh-raised all-rounder Tony Cordle (480) plus arguably the best wicket-keeper in county cricket, Alan's younger brother Eifion (753 runs, 68 catches and six stumpings) enabled this multi-talented side to become the first team since Lancashire in 1930 to go through a county programme undefeated.

In that memorable season Wilfred Wooller, still actively involved in the BBC Wales commentary box, maintained that for a side to win a championship every player had to contribute at least one individual match-winning performance. And every player did, as I hope that this analysis of the season makes clear.

In the first match we almost lost to Yorkshire, the reigning champions, at Swansea. Our last pair Malcolm Nash and Don Shepherd had to bat out twenty minutes for the draw. Then, with matches against both the universities and two fixtures that were ruined by rain, we reached the end of May joint last in the championship table.

The wheels started turning with a ten-wicket victory over Somerset at Cardiff. While all six Glamorgan bowlers shared the wickets, it was a resolute first innings of 74 on a typically uneven-bounce Sophia Gardens pitch by Roger Davis in an otherwise low-scoring game – the next highest individual total in the match being 44 – which gave us the platform for a win inside two days. Roger, a product of Blundell's School, may not have been the most fluent of batsmen, but he had guts aplenty and you certainly needed those opening the batting on what was sometimes a dangerous Sophia Gardens pitch.

A draw against Lancashire at Swansea was followed by an extraordinary match at Bournemouth where Glamorgan were awarded victory by default. After a lengthy spell of incessant rain, the Hampshire side, under the impression that umpires Lloyd Budd and Peter Wight had abandoned the game, left the ground midway through the third afternoon. But the rain stopped and the clouds lifted. Glamorgan captain Tony Lewis made what he thought would be a routine courtesy call to the umpire's room to say goodbye, only to be told that, despite the fact the game had been meandering towards a stalemate draw, they had not in fact called it off. Laws are laws. So we unpacked our cricket kit, changed and waited. After inspecting the pitch at five o'clock and with just an hour left in the game, the umpires declared that play would start at 5.30.

As the fielding side, we duly trooped out onto a deserted ground. The umpire called 'play', and Tony Cordle ran in and bowled a gentle delivery outside the off stump to an empty crease. As the opposition had failed to turn up, umpires Budd and Wight then awarded us the game and the ten points that went with it!

On our return there was much hilarity in our dressing room as we speculated as to how the news would be received by the Hampshire players when they tuned in to BBC Radio 2 for the close-of-play scores.

Initially the Test and County Cricket Board upheld the umpires' decision but, when Hampshire appealed, common sense prevailed and the game was declared a draw. It had been one of those incidents in which both parties could justifiably plead innocence and frankly, as our pursuit for the title turned into a serious challenge, after the initial joy in being handed ten points on a plate, we were very relieved at the eventual outcome. Had we gone on to win the championship by a margin of ten points or less, it would have cheapened the whole campaign.

At Cardiff, in our next match, we overwhelmed Sussex by an innings and 23. Malcolm Nash and Lawrence Williams bowled them out on a helpful pitch for 79, and we replied with fifties by Roger Davis, Majid Khan and me. Then an explosive 56 not out by Tony Cordle gave our bowlers enough time to bowl the opposition out on a pitch that, by the start of Sussex's second innings, had lost its early venom. Barbadian-born Cordle came to Cardiff to be with his brother, and his first job was with British Rail. For most of his career the *Western Mail* insisted on using a picture of him in his BR shunter's cap. It was about the only thing that could wipe the smile off his face!

We called him 'TC', and I'm not sure to this day if he was aware that for us the initials stood for Top Cat. He was a cricketer who thrived on encouragement, but found failure hard to bear. He was a fast-medium bowler with the priceless gift of producing a wicket-taking ball in amongst some less than deadly deliveries, a hard-hitting tail end batsman and an enthusiastic, if somewhat erratic, fielder. He was also blessed with an infectious singing voice which lightened many a lengthy coach trip to away games. During weekend matches at Swansea we used to take visiting teams to the 'The Fountain' pub in Pontardulais. There we'd team up with members of the world-famous male voice choir who used to call in after their rehearsal session for a few pints and a sing-song. No evening was complete without Tony being asked to give them his version of *Delilah*. Tom Jones never had such a quality backing group as TC did in The Fountain.

We drew against Leicestershire at Colwyn Bay in a match that will always be remembered for Tony Cordle's bowling performance. In Leicestershire's first innings Tony Lewis put him on as fifth change – the last option – and he finished up with figures of 24.4 overs, nine wickets for 49 runs. They were the best bowling figures anywhere in the country that summer. What on earth Leicestershire made of it, I've no idea.

Then, on a pudding of a pitch at Worcester, we beat the home side by 39 runs. This time it was the other Davis, Bryan from Port of Spain, Trinidad, who came good in the second innings, making a quickfire 92 out of our total of 187 for three. Like his namesake Roger, who also had a brother John who played a few games for Glamorgan, Bryan had a brother Charlie who followed Bryan into the West Indian side, in his case with rather more success. Bryan was a typical swashbuckling, free-and-easy opening batsman who found adjusting to slower pitches in county cricket very difficult. Reluctantly moving down to number five in the order, he blossomed against the older ball.

Draws against Somerset at Glastonbury and Lancashire at Old Trafford helped to keep our confidence levels high, and we picked up our winning tempo again at Hastings where we completed the double over Sussex, Don Shepherd taking eight wickets as we won by a comfortable 72 runs.

Throughout my time with Glamorgan there had been a tradition of producing high quality, close-to-the-wicket fielders. The 1948 side had set the standard, and I came in as a young calf in the 1950s, eventually inheriting the role of old bull from Allan Watkins, a role that in time I passed on to Roger Davis. But, when in 1976 he was unexpectedly not retained, the chain was broken.

Roger and I enjoyed a rich harvest from the bowling of the peerless Don Shepherd. It's difficult to express in words the feeling of power and security that 'Shep' gave to his close fielders: power in the sense of being able to put the fear of God into opposing batsmen by our presence standing there almost in their hip pockets and security because the chance of being hit there was minimal.

Such was Don's phenomenal accuracy that Roger and I knew we could afford to be at least half a yard closer than for other bowlers, safe in the knowledge that Don would not stray down the leg side or bowl a full toss!

Roger and I both knew that, if we were hit, it would not be because Don had wavered off line, more that the batsmen had taken a chance and swiped at a good length ball, a stroke which, through anticipation, would have given us a split second to take evasive action.

Don's other attributes were that he bowled a lot quicker than the average slow bowler, much nearer 65 mph than the 55 mph of a more orthodox spinner. This meant batsmen had precious little time to correct any misjudgement. Also, such was Don's physical strength, particularly in the legs that, coupled with his unswerving concentration, he rarely bowled a bad ball. His fitness and stamina meant he could bowl for long spells, and he also had those priceless additional qualities, determination and a bowler's 'heart'. Whatever the state of the game, whatever the kind of pitch he was faced with, Don Shepherd always wanted the ball in his hand. He never gave up.

The next game back in Cardiff, starting on 19th July, was a key one in what was rapidly becoming a two-horse race for the championship, with our opponents Gloucestershire the leaders and indeed favourites. But while Lawrence Williams took five wickets in their second innings, captain Tony Lewis's two innings of 50 and 62 proved to be the key contributions as we won by a massive 208 runs, a defeat after which Gloucestershire never recovered their momentum. There was nothing, on or off the field, which Tony didn't perform gracefully. A talented violinist, well-read, handsome and charming, he was the kind of leader who turned heads and inspired confidence

At Derby, in our next match, centuries by Alan Jones and Roger Davis were important in our win by an innings and 68 runs, but you have to bowl out the opposition twice and in Malcolm Nash (4-32 and 5-56) we had the match-winner. Malcolm hailed from Abergavenny, not then known as a nursery of cricketing excellence, but I doubt if anyone has ever walked onto a field with more self-confidence than 'Superman'. Primarily remembered as a medium-pace, left-arm, over-the-wicket opening bowler, he had a devastatingly late in-swinging delivery which regularly accounted for a high percentage of the top five batsmen in any opposition. As a top class hockey player, with a bat in his hand, anything outside his off stump was thrashed away to the boundary at a blistering speed.

A draw in a rain-affected game against Warwickshire at Swansea followed but, with the winning post in sight, there was no stopping us now. Another Alan Jones century gave the six Glamorgan bowlers used in each innings enough leverage to beat Northamptonshire away by seven wickets.

It would be difficult to find a more pleasant, modest companion than Alan. But with a bat in his hand, what a tenacious battler! He had limitless patience, the soundest of techniques and, for someone who was not the tallest opening bat in history, courage in abundance. His 92 against the full fury of Wes Hall and his fellow West Indians at Swansea in 1963 remains in the memory of all who were there.

Alan very rarely bowled in first-class cricket – but was known to his Glamorgan team-mates as 'Sam'. Why? Well, because he never tired of telling us that, during a winter coaching trip to Brisbane, he had bowled Australian opener Sam Trimble with a ball he claimed had beaten the Australian in the flight and then bounced and turned! As a specialist opening batsman, Alan took over Emrys Davies's role as the rock upon which Glamorgan built many a substantial innings. When he retired in 1983 after 27 distinguished summers he had become the county's highest aggregate scorer, his 34,056 runs passing – yes, you guessed it – Emrys's 26,102.

A draw against Derby at Cardiff saw us off to the Cheltenham Festival for the return against Gloucestershire in a match they had to win to get back on track in the race for the title.

It was not to be, for we produced probably our best all-round team performance of the summer, recording an emphatic innings and 50-run victory. My own contribution – three for 41 in 29 overs in their second innings – may seem modest, but it did stifle their rearguard action as they battled for a face-saving draw. It allowed Malcolm Nash and Don Shepherd at the other end to eat into the rest of the home side's batting. I found the role of containment officer more enjoyable than I normally would have done; on the day it was exactly what the team required.

A rain-ruined match at Trent Bridge featured a third hundred by Alan Jones, and this was followed in the third week of August by one of the most exciting wins of the season, over Middlesex at Swansea.

Chasing 196 to win, we were 158 for seven when Eifion Jones and Malcolm Nash came together. The match ended, with only three balls to spare, when Eifion smashed the ball for a mighty straight six into the rugby stand at the Mumbles end. One blow for sure, but a key one in the circumstances. The quiet man of Glamorgan cricket and Alan's younger brother, Eifion was as near infallible as a wicket-keeper can hope to be. He also brought a steely resolve to a key batting position in any team, number eight, there to support a top order batsman if needed or to shepherd and protect the tail-enders who followed him.

In our first innings at Chelmsford we were 147 for nine, without a single batting point to our name, before Don Shepherd and Lawrence Williams put on 78 for the last wicket. It was remarkable, considering the complete lack of any batting skill either possessed and in view of the fact that the attack they mastered was made up of Keith Boyce, John Lever, David Acfield, Ray East and Robin Hobbs! But, after a sporting declaration by Tony Lewis, which left the home side a mere 199 to win, our first defeat of the season looked a distinct possibility. After Brian Ward had retired early through injury, home captain Brian 'Tonker' Taylor promoted himself to number three and immediately put Essex well in front of the clock. Then it started to rain. The ball rapidly got too wet for the bowlers to grip, and fielding too was increasingly difficult. On the mid-wicket boundary, Tony Cordle borrowed a spectator's umbrella by way of protest while, in between balls, I sought temporary shelter in the press tent, hoping my absence wouldn't be noticed. In search of valuable championship points, Glamorgan needed to stay out on the field – but not Tonker, even with his side at 75 for none and an almost certain win in the offing. Holding his hand up in the middle of an over he announced, in his usual booming sergeant-major voice, "This is becoming a fucking farce" and, motioning to his astonished partner Brian Edmeades, he strode off the field! Our unbeaten record had survived.

After this, we set off in high spirits for Swansea and the immediate return game against the same opposition.

This proved to be the most dramatic game of a dramatic year. The two sides had always got on well off the field. Midway through the game and conscious that we were in the closing stages of a full gallop towards the championship-winning post, Essex captain Brian Taylor said to Tony Lewis, "Give us a decent declaration and we'll go for it all the way down the order." He and his team were as good as their word. Runs flowed, but wickets also fell regularly. The excitement was intense as Roger Davis ran in to bowl the last ball of the match.

Essex wanted two runs to tie with number ten Ray East on 14 and last man John Lever, with strike, on one. JKL was one of the quickest runners between the wickets in the game, a Shergar if you like. He dabbed the last ball through the gully and well to the right of Ossie Wheatley at third man and set off for what looked like an easy two-run canter to bring scores level and give them an extra five points.

By comparison with Lever, Ossie could at best be described as a Clydesdale horse. Ten other Glamorgan cricketers looked on aghast. There was no chance of our winning the match, there were no more points to be had, and the championship would be wide open again.

But cometh the hour, cometh the man. At a full lumbering gallop Ossie, never the supplest of fielders, swooped low, picked up the ball in his right hand and, in almost the same motion, hurled the ball back to wicket-keeper Eifion Jones.

It's often forgotten what a wonderful take our wicketkeeper made as Ossie's throw bounced awkwardly a yard in front of him. But gather it he did and, with a sweep of his gloves, knocked the stumps down with an astonished Lever, having seen who the fielder was and starting to coast home, finishing a yard out of his ground!

The ten of us raced over to congratulate Ossie, a man whose captaincy ahead of Tony Lewis's reign had done so much to mould us into a team with a winning attitude. As we gathered around rejoicing in a 20th century miracle, Ossie put on a look of pained surprise. "Never in doubt, lads. He's not the first to chance his arm to me and perish!"

It would be difficult to over-emphasise the contribution Ossie made to Glamorgan cricket. Following Wilf into the captaincy in the early 1960s was a tough enough order, but the team that Ossie led became more competitive and determined in adversity than many before it. In both victory and defeat Ossie insisted on nothing less than one's best effort, and he led by example.

The penultimate game of the season against Worcestershire at Cardiff proved to be our championship decider. It was one we had to win because our final match was against Surrey at the Oval and that had never been a happy hunting ground for past Glamorgan teams. In the end the Worcester game proved to be a comfortable win by 147 runs on an absolute pot-holed road of a Sophia Gardens pitch.

I remember going into our dressing room after Roger Davis had got out early to find our number three batsman Majid, sitting alone. He had his pads on, bat between his legs, gloved hands resting on the handle. During the most vital game of the season he was fast asleep. "Come on, Bearer," I said, gently shaking him awake. "It's time to bat."

I find it difficult to believe that anyone playing a professional sport can do so without feeling some flicker of nervousness. For a batsman, waiting to be called to duty, these can be very anxious moments indeed. In my early days I'd witnessed little Willie Jones chain-smoking with trembling hands and barely able to speak. Now here was Majid, cat-napping on his bat handle.

I was somewhere between the two. But I did have one giveaway which only I recognised. In moments of real stress I would find myself constantly yawning. This may have given to others the appearance of indifference, but that was far from the truth. The one area in which I can genuinely state that I had no nerves at any time was fielding, where I had complete confidence in my skills. It helped that I knew my team-mates, and crucially the opposition batsmen, had a huge respect for my talents.

Majid said afterwards he had been very nervous knowing how much rested on him to win the game. Whatever his mental state, Majid went out and played the innings of his life. It was certainly the best I've ever seen.

On a lifting, turning strip he hit Worcestershire's very able slow left-hand bowler Dougie Slade for nine fours in four overs en route to 156 majestic runs. It was the innings of the season, one of pure genius in a game where even the likes of Tom Graveney and Basil D'Oliveira had found it hard going. In his eight seasons with Glamorgan, the last as captain, Majid illuminated the game. Inwardly he was fiercely critical of western moral behaviour and standards, but he was nevertheless a splendid team-mate, ready to share a joke, if not a beer, at any time. To stand at the backing-up end, watching him unfurl a series of sublime strokes with effortless ease, felt a privilege.

September 1969. Celebrating Don Shepherd's 2,000th first-class wicket.
Jim Yardley, caught Walker bowled Shepherd.
One of 178 catches I held from the bowling of Glamorgan's greatest.

The championship was ours; no one could catch us now. There were jubilant scenes in front of our dressing room, where well over 1,000 of our supporters congregated chanting and singing. The champagne flowed and flowed.

Unnoticed, I hauled down the very new Glamorgan flag and made off with it as a souvenir. To this day it hangs in my son Daniel's room. My then father-in-law had to stop the car twice on the way back to our Newport home for me to 'chunder' into the gutter. The way I felt for the remainder of that evening – and the next day as well – he could well have left me there too.

Winning the county championship left me as exhausted as a marathon runner in the final stages of a gruelling race as he just manages to cross the line ahead of a closing pack. It's not easily put into words, but within me there soon came a curious feeling of deflation – just at the moment when everyone else seemed to be rejoicing.

As the curtain fell on a quite phenomenal season, which later led to the Glamorgan team being collectively voted BBC Wales Sports Personality of the Year and, with nothing at stake, the final game at The Oval was a draw. I finished off our triumphant season by taking the only two wickets to fall in Surrey's second innings, the last a catch off my own bowling which pleased me greatly.

Under Wilfred Wooller Glamorgan had won its first championship in 1948. Now, in the year of the investiture of the Prince of Wales, the national team of Wales had done it again.

Chapter 14

TOURING'S A DELIGHT – BUT SOMBRE MEMORIES TOO

It was always going to be difficult to follow a season like 1969, but in 1970 we made a valiant attempt to defend our title, eventually finishing 17 points behind Kent. In three successive seasons we had finished third, first and second. It remains the finest three-year period in Glamorgan's championship history.

After the tour of West Indies with Jim Swanton in Spring 1961, I made three more invitation tours: with F.R. Brown's side to East Africa in Autumn 1961, to Pakistan with a Commonwealth team in Spring 1968 and to the West Indies in April 1970 with a post-championship Glamorgan squad. Each a delight, each providing a fund of memories.

Before the overcrowding of official tours squeezed them out, invitation touring sides were quite common. The one to East Africa included players of the calibre of Roy Marshall, Bill Alley, Don Shepherd and Peter Loader. On arrival in Nairobi we were given a reception by the Kenya Kongonis Cricket Club who turned out to be far better at socialising than playing the game. We watched in fascination as a group of our Sikh hosts would close their eyes and tilt their heads upwards before downing a near tumbler full of neat whisky. We thought it was to prepare themselves for the spirit's fiery entry. But we were told no, they were praying to God that it turned to water as it passed their lips!

F.R. Brown's team to East Africa, 1961.
Left to right: Don Shepherd, Bill Alley, Peter Loader, Colin Ingleby-Mackenzie, Peter Walker, Freddie Brown, Roy Marshall, Richard Jefferson, Laurie Johnson, Bob Gale, John Hall, John Mortimore.

The Sikh brigade was matched tumbler by tumbler by our captain Freddie Brown – except that, throughout the tour and although past his 50th birthday, the former England skipper never seemed to close his eyes! The actual cricket was not too taxing but, when we played a game on the island of Zanzibar, I got an insight into the kind of inner hatred of batsmen great fast bowlers have as part of their genetic makeup. The small ground had a concrete strip in the middle, over which was laid a coconut mat. The groundsman had tightened this to the tension of a kettledrum skin. Peter Loader ran up to bowl the first ball of the match. It was of modest pace, a loosener just outside the off stump. But the ball 'took off' and, still rising, cleared wicket-keeper Laurie Johnson's head 20 yards back and hit the boundary board behind him having bounced only twice! Peter's eyes gleamed in anticipation. The next ball, more at his normal pace, nearly removed the poor, unsuspecting Arab batsman's head and went soaring away for four more byes. At the completion of the over the batsman on the receiving end dropped to his knees, presumably to thank Allah for having preserved him, Freddie Brown had to remove the ball almost forcibly from Loader's hand.

The Commonwealth tour to Pakistan was organised by the journalist Alex Bannister and pitted us against sterner opposition. Alex, whose stock reply to any question would usually be prefaced with "Well, old son", was a contemporary of E.M. Wellings of the now defunct *London Evening News*. Alex and his acerbic colleague, who wore a permanent look on his face as if he had a shirt pocket full of rotting seaweed, were good pals and were known in the press box as 'Arsenic and Old Son'.

Alex spent the first week of the tour arguing about our hotel bills, and it wasn't until the arrival of the experienced former Australian skipper Richie Benaud, a campaign veteran from leading an Australian team around Pakistan, that things settled down. In Karachi, our bill came to something over seven million rupees. Before calling a meeting with the hotel management, Richie warned us, "You must keep smiling at them, however much you know you're being stitched up." He suggested for future reference that we should stay on and observe how he approached the task of reducing the huge bill.

Slowly and with great deliberation, line by line, he went through it, smiling and mouthing pleasantries all the time, getting agreement on things such as "Twenty steaks at 800 rupees each? Well those steaks were wonderful, a real credit to the hotel and the chef. But as there were so many, don't you feel that perhaps 400 rupees each would be better for both of us?" This 'compromise' suggestion was delivered with a smile. The hotel management responded with similar expressions of pleasure, gratitude and eventual agreement.

After well over an hour of discussion, the final agreed bill came to three million rupees. Honour and face on both sides had been maintained and, with much handshaking all round and entreaties for us to return again in the future, we left.

A consummate politician, negotiator and captain was our Richie, as well as a mighty handy cricketer in his pomp.

Alex had gathered together a more than useful side, and we played three so-called Tests against the full Pakistan team. The first at Multan was held in the middle of a medieval fort which a few days earlier had staged a camel carnival.

The outfield had solidified camel pats everywhere and, after partially clearing most of them, a matting pitch was rolled out on a wheelbarrow and anchored down in the middle. We changed in a tent right alongside an open latrine, dug especially for our use. It had plenty of visitors and included the Northampton opening batsman Roger Prideaux who virtually camped alongside it for the duration of the match.

Five times a day the game would be halted for prayers, surprisingly often at the very point when it looked like our more-than-useful bowling attack of Keith Boyce, Peter Marner, David Allen, Don Shepherd, Mushtaq and me were on the point of making a breakthrough! We made history in Pakistan's first innings when Don got an lbw appeal against the legendary Hanif Mohammad upheld by the local umpire. We reckoned that it was the first time in twelve years that Hanif had been given out this way in a home match and, to no one's surprise, the guilty umpire failed to reappear for the remaining three days of the game.

In the second 'Test' at Lahore, Richie made a most generous declaration. Asif Iqbal made a fine hundred, and they only wanted 54 to win in 50 minutes when Hanif, coming in low down the order because of what we'd been told was a severe knee injury, arrived at the crease. Richie set an ultra-defensive field. The minutes ticked by and, with a draw suddenly looking possible, the crowd – excited by Asif's earlier innings – became restive and took to barracking their captain, Hanif. Before the last over began, Richie called us around him, not to talk tactics but merely to say, "Listen, when the game's over, for God's sake, leg it back to the pavilion as fast as you can, don't hang around out here." I was stationed at mid-off with my back to the pavilion.

Pakistan's greatest batsman then blocked out the final over. The game was drawn, but the crowd were incensed and were after Hanif's blood. After he'd carefully pushed the last ball back to the bowler, I immediately turned as ordered and raced off towards the pavilion. With 20 yards to go, I was passed, not by Hanif's runner, but by the man himself, 'crippling' knee injury and all. He knew what was about to happen and didn't want to be around to be garrotted.

The crowd broke through the security fencing as if it wasn't there and charged after us, laying siege to both teams' dressing rooms, chanting and threatening to burn the place down. It was two hours before the police finally dispersed them and we were able to retreat to the safety of our hotel.

In Karachi we looked on the point of gaining an unexpected victory when, with 45 minutes to go, we were told to leave the field, get our tour blazers on and, together with the similarly attired Pakistan team, stand in a line on the boundary edge to meet a minor official of the local cricket league. It wasted 20 minutes and was enough for the home side to emerge with what their newspapers described as 'a creditable draw'.

As the results were relatively unimportant, the trip itself was voted a great success and much enjoyed by all us visitors.

Winning the championship in 1969 opened up a chance for Glamorgan to make a three-week, pre-1970 tour of the West Indies. With my travel agency experience to fall back on, during the winter of 1969/70 I had the idea that we should try to get some warmth into our winter bones rather than freeze to death in the April pre-season nets at the Neath Indoor School. With the help of Peter Corrigan, a newspaper pal of mine who was then working in a large Cardiff advertising agency, we managed to get sponsorship for a six-match itinerary from Rizla, the makers of roll-your-own cigarette papers who had a factory just outside Cardiff.

They kitted out 15 of us (including our coach Phil Clift who acted as tour manager and Bryan Davis, awaiting us back home in Trinidad) with smart blazers, grey slacks and the newly fashionable large coffin-type cricket bags. Rizla also paid our airfares. In all it cost them just £5,000. We stayed either in modest hotels or privately with residents on each of the islands we visited: Bermuda, St. Kitts, Dominica, Grenada and Trinidad.

However, the 1969 county champions didn't do much to distinguish themselves, as we only won one of the six matches played and that against a Trinidad under-21 side, thanks largely to a dubious lbw decision given in Ossie Wheatley's favour after he'd been the only one who'd appealed.

The former Glamorgan captain also played an important part in quite the biggest hit I've ever seen on a cricket field. It came about in Bermuda during our first game of the tour. It was played on a matting pitch. Ossie ran in to bowl to a huge, powerfully built West Indian called Lloyd James. Lloyd had an unusual stance for a batsman, bolt upright, feet wide apart with his bat raised high over his shoulder in true American baseball fashion.

Ossie had twice stopped in his run up to check he was ready. I was down at deep square leg a yard inside the boundary when, on the rise, Lloyd laid into a good length ball. I believe the crack of willow on leather must have been heard all over Bermuda. Up and up the ball went before seeming to change course and head out to sea. It passed me overhead, still climbing! We fielders stood in amazement and some even waved goodbye to the ball as the commentator for the local radio station yelled into his mike, "Keep it on the island, Lloyd." We never found the ball but reckoned it must have carried nearly 150 yards from the pitch. Talk about a home run; the blow was worth twelve, not six.

Apart from the results, the West Indies trip was exactly what we needed in preparation for the defence of our county championship title.

Despite moving down the batting order in 1970 to number six I still managed 1,049 runs, took 60 wickets and held 39 catches. Against Derbyshire at Swansea I held eight catches in the match, a total that only Wally Hammond has exceeded.

It would have been around this time that I first saw a batsman employ the reverse sweep, an ugly but, when successful, particularly effective counter against accurate spin bowlers.

I was bowling at the effervescent Mushtaq Mohammad of Pakistan and Northamptonshire in a county match at Sophia Gardens. After trying to tempt him with a succession of deliveries wide outside his off-stump, to my own and everyone's amazement he suddenly thrust his front foot down the pitch, rolled his wrists over and backhanded the next ball past an astonished fielder in the gully for four runs!

After this, there was a great deal of amiable backchat between Mushtaq and me, and it started again when my turn came to bat. Now it was Mushtaq with the ball in his hand and, when I got down to his end, he suggested I should try to do the same as he had earlier. I told him, "I don't trust you, Mushy. You'll probably bowl me a flat, top-spinning yorker and knock my middle stump out."

"No, no, no," he said with a smile. "When you next face me, the third ball I bowl to you will be a leg-spinner, wide outside the off stump. Just see if you can do it. It's easy. Trust me!"

Sure enough, the third ball was as promised. Copying Mushtaq's method, I had a go. Off-balance I totally missed the ball – but not the smile which spread across Mushtaq's face!

The following year, 1971, was a poor one all round as the club slipped to 15th in the table. I got two hundreds, against Lancashire and Hampshire, and ended with 1,120 runs, 39 wickets and 37 catches. During the season I'd been commissioned by *The Guardian* to write a number of player profiles. One of the men I'd chosen to interview was Gary Sobers, then still playing for Nottinghamshire. In 1968 I'd been up close to the supremely talented West Indian when he'd hit those six sixes at St. Helen's. In 1971 I had to suffer myself as the world's greatest ever cricketer belted Glamorgan around Swansea for 151 not out.

When we were playing at Lord's against Middlesex, during the luncheon break a knock came on our dressing room door. A small, elderly man put his head around and asked if he could have a word with Peter Walker. A team-mate pointed in my direction. The old man shuffled over to me and stretched out his hand. "I just want you to know how much I enjoyed your piece with Gary Sobers," he said. "It's the best article I've read about a modern player. Congratulations." He smiled and turned away to leave before I could say more than a "thank you" or think of a more suitable response. After the door had closed, one of the younger Glamorgan players asked, "Who was that? Did you know him?" Did I know him! He definitely needed no introduction to someone who, since a small boy, had immersed himself in the writings and history of the game. The 'little old man' was Neville Cardus, arguably the 20th century's most descriptive and cultured chronicler of the game. I felt as if I'd scored a chanceless hundred.

But my over-riding memory of 1971 is of a near-fatal tragedy on the field of play. Roger Davis had come into the Glamorgan side in 1964 and over the next two seasons I gradually handed over the mantle of short square leg to him, the fielding position which I'd made my own nearly a decade earlier. Roger did not let me down, nor Glamorgan's reputation for producing, rather like the mythical 'Welsh rugby outside half factory,' a regular stream of high-quality, close-to-the-wicket fielders. He was fit to be ranked with the best of them. Rather as I had looked for inspiration to Allan Watkins at the start of my career, fearless and agile Roger regarded me as his mentor. He and I would spend hours practising diving and catching exercises to improve our skills and agility. But not even these were enough to prevent him from receiving a fearful blow which almost cost him his life.

The game was Glamorgan versus Warwickshire at Sophia Gardens, Cardiff. It was Saturday 29th May, the first day of the match. Shortly before tea and with the second new ball Malcolm Nash, that most accurate of medium-paced bowlers, bowled an in-swinger to Warwickshire's opening batsman, Neal Abberley. Neal was particularly strong on the leg side with a short-arm jabbing stroke which close-in fielders found impossible to anticipate. Aiming towards midwicket, he absolutely middled the ball. Roger, no more than four yards away, had only time to half-turn his head to the right before he was felled by a sickening, full-on blow to the left temple.

It was obviously a serious injury. We all, Neal included, rushed to Roger's prostrate body. He was unconscious. Then the colour gradually started to drain from his face; he started to twitch and turn blue. His breathing came in short, stifled gasps. Unqualified as medics, none of us had any idea what to do to help. But thankfully, amongst the small group of spectators present was a doctor, Colin Lewis. Swiftly recognising the severity of the injury from his seat in the members' enclosure, he had immediately run out onto the field. He turned Roger on his back, put his finger down the cricketer's throat and pulled his tongue back into position so it no longer blocked his windpipe. Roger's life was undoubtedly saved by the doctor's swift reaction and by the kiss of life he administered thereafter.

The umpires wisely decided to take an early tea interval, and it was about fifteen minutes before the doctor allowed Roger to be moved and stretchered from the field into a waiting ambulance. We, his team-mates, sat in silence in the dressing room. None of us wanted to go back onto the field. Then, unexpectedly out of a grey but thinly clouded sky, it started to rain gently. Not heavily, just a light drizzle, but it kept us off the field for around half an hour by which time we'd recovered some composure.

A message came through from St. David's Hospital, less than a mile away from the ground, that Roger had suffered a hair-line fracture of the skull and had had to have a blood clot on his brain surgically drained and removed. He had regained consciousness but was in a serious condition.

We were obliged to go back onto the field. Short square leg was a key position to a bowler of Malcolm Nash's type and, as someone who'd done my time in what was known as 'Boot Hill' and survived, I volunteered – somewhat reluctantly, I admit – to go back into my old position. But Tony Cordle beat me to it. Seeing a motorcyclist alongside the pavilion he nipped over and asked if he could borrow his helmet and, suitably protected, went and stood at short square leg – albeit at least twice as far back as Roger's normal station. So far as I'm aware, it was the first time in county cricket's history that a helmet had been worn by a fielder. The laws may not have permitted it at the time but, after what had happened, I suspect that no umpire would have stopped Tony from wearing it.

Roger eventually did recover, and he declared himself well enough to make a comeback towards the end of August, despite having problems with his balance and speech. He played in the last three games of the season, batting at number seven, but he was not allowed to field close to the bat.

Roger played for another five summers, having his best season with the bat in 1975. But at the end of the following summer and after a 13-year career which brought him 7,367 runs, 241 wickets and 208 catches, the committee decided not to retain him, a decision which cost him a benefit and some measure of financial security. The game can be heartless as well as painful. Roger nearly gave his life to it.

There is one other cricketing memory which, even to this day, is etched into my soul. I played in an era when the worst accusation that could be made was that one cheated by not 'walking' after knowingly edging the ball. In August 1971, at the Grace Road ground in Leicester, we were caught on a real flier of a pitch. I came in at number seven, with the score on 8 for five, and we were soon 11 for eight. I somehow managed to hang on in there to reach 10, turning out to be the only Glamorgan batsman to get into double figures, when Terry Spencer, a valiant, hard-trying fast-medium bowler produced a lifting delivery just outside my off stump, to which I got the faintest of edges. There was a strong gale blowing behind Terry's back and wicket-keeper Roger Tolchard and the slips, clearly hearing the edge, went up for the catch. Upwind, however, neither Terry nor the umpire had heard anything, and there certainly hadn't been a noticeable deflection from the bat. Both looked at me still standing in my crease. I looked back. "Not out," said the umpire.

As they passed me at the end of that over, I couldn't bring myself to look at the Leicester slip cordon nor in particular Tolchard, but I knew they'd mentally branded me a cheat. To my enormous relief I was bowled by Australian Graham McKenzie in the next over but that score of 24 all out remains as Glamorgan's second lowest total of all time and the most uncomfortable personal memory of my time as a professional cricketer.

The following summer, 1972, turned out to be my last with Glamorgan, as I provided a diminishing return for my employers. I had become increasingly involved with media work with BBC Wales as well as becoming a rugby columnist in the winters with several national newspapers.

In that season, erratic team selection severely limited my opportunities. Wilf Wooller's old adage, 'Glamorgan are in a transitional stage', was now certainly true. Aged 36 I was in and out of the side and in 19 matches mustered a mere 370 runs, 29 wickets and 27 catches. Glamorgan finished a lowly 13th in the table, winning but one solitary match, that against Hampshire at Portsmouth. Due to Tony Lewis having aggravated a long-standing and what turned out to be a career-shortening knee injury, I captained the side in a three-day county match for the one and only time.

However, it's important to be lucky as well as skilful, and shortly before the end of that season the BBC2 John Player Sunday League cameras came to Sophia Gardens to cover one of our limited over games. Frank Bough was its regular presenter and, on a day when much of the play was disrupted by rain, I was asked to fill in as an interviewee. In those days there were few videotaped library programmes that could be wheeled out to fill the dead time; live broadcasting meant just that. Warts and all, it was most certainly live!

I'd met Frank on a couple of occasions, and we'd got on really well. He and David Coleman were the BBC's top sports presenters. In Cardiff we chatted on and off for the better part of the scheduled four-hour transmission. When at the end of the season Frank told Bill Taylor, the producer of the Sunday League cricket programmes, that he wanted to cut down on his heavy workload next summer, he suggested that I was the man to fill his shoes.

Remembering the stint I'd done for him in the rain at Cardiff and my by now substantial winter experience in working with BBC Wales as an outside broadcast television presenter and reporter, Bill needed little persuasion. It was to be the beginning of a fruitful partnership with him and with his eventual successor, Bob Duncan, that lasted for 18 years.

In September 1972 the Glamorgan cricket committee decided to offer me a match-only contract for the following season, and it clinched my decision to retire from the game. So far as I was concerned, the sticking point was that they were not prepared to pay me for the time and effort I would have to spend practising and keeping fit so that, should the call come, I would be in some sort of physical shape, if not form. I cited as an example how impossible Ted Dexter had found a similar situation at Sussex. If someone as talented and athletic as Ted couldn't retain fitness and form, how could I be expected to do so?

I also suspected that, because I was Glamorgan's representative on the Professional Cricketers' Association Executive committee, I was regarded as something of a troublemaker. As a senior player in my later years with the county, I was certainly among the first to speak my own and my colleagues' minds on matters affecting our playing conditions and livelihoods.

This was at the beginnings of the growth in 'player power' and might well have been one of the reasons the committee wanted me out of the way. Looking back, I feel no shame in being in a vanguard which helped to bring about changes in what had been a feudal system of master and servant for over a hundred years.

Back in the mid-1960s Fred Rumsey, of Somerset and England, had spent most of his last two summers in the game holding meetings in opposition dressing rooms, spelling out how the county committees were financially short-changing us players. At that time there was no standardised minimum wage, no long-term contracts, no injury insurance and no pension provisions, and there were draconian restrictions on players who wanted to change counties. Thanks to the pressure exerted by the PCA, particularly in the 1970s and '80s, these are now all issues that have been resolved in the player's favour.

In 1974, and two years after retiring as a player, came another call to arms when I became Chairman of the Association. With the threat of a players' strike hanging over the Test and County Cricket Board, I was proud to be part of a PCA negotiating group which included Jack Bannister, Mike Brearley and PCA accountant and financial advisor, Harold Goldblatt, as we blackmailed the TCCB with a strike threat into agreeing to make the PCA a 0.075% annual donation (then £3,500) from their total income from the game to enable us to provide proper injury insurance cover for our members.

When in 2001 I finally bowed out of active involvement with the Association, this had risen to £300,000 and it's since doubled! The PCA is now a well-organised, well-funded operation, offering current and recent past players many benefits including exceptional insurance cover, training courses for a career after cricket, and legal and accounting advice. It can also act as an agent for players negotiating new contracts and salary levels with their club. Now, from the armchair luxury of a Vice-Presidency of the Association, old lags such as myself find it hardly credible what's been achieved on behalf of professional cricketers in such a relatively short space of time.

Despite these commitments, as a free spirit I would hardly describe myself as a typical trade unionist at heart. But my experiences in the merchant navy had shown the importance of solidarity so I had no problems with becoming a willing convert and participant in support of the PCA's objectives.

Between 1999 and 2001 I also chaired a new Association off-shoot, the Professional Cricketers' Association Management Company (PCAM), the brainchild of Harold Goldblatt.

Harold was an immense presence throughout the first 35 years of the PCA, his advice and wise counsel proving invaluable in the Association's early, uncertain days. In 1983 it was Harold who persuaded the TCCB to return 50% of the monies they levied equally on clubs and their players who failed to bowl a prescribed 18 overs per hour. This went directly into a Cricketers' Association Charity which Harold set up to look after cricketers and their dependents who had fallen on hard times, including many of an older generation who were active before the formation of the Association. This money, wisely invested by Harold, formed the bedrock of the Charity's ability to give financial aid to those in distress. Since the mid-1980s I have been proud to be a Trustee.

Harking back, I still harbour some minor regrets at my outspokenness during my playing days, suspecting that it prematurely ended my Glamorgan career in 1972, when the county handed me my P45. As is the case with the majority of cricketers, when their time is up, the parting between club and player is rarely sweet or amicable. I believed then, and still do now, that I should have been retained. I was lean, fit and agile and, what's more, with Tony Lewis standing down as captain at the end of that summer, I think I should have been passed the captain's torch. If Wilfred Wooller, another all-rounder, had somehow survived the privations of a Japanese POW camp and managed to play on until he was 47, I'm sure I would not have found it a physically impossible task at the age of 37.

Don Shepherd was pensioned off at the same time as me and, as a result of this loss of experience, the short-sighted Glamorgan committee managed to plunge the club into a deep downward spiral from which it took well over 15 years to resurface.

Even though that's now long done and dusted, the fact that I was denied the chance to shepherd the new generation of Glamorgan youngsters into a more successful future remains a sad memory.

But perhaps I should be grateful to the committee for they did me a favour, my retirement coinciding as it did with the BBC television offer to present their network Sunday League coverage.

But right to my last day for the county on September 1st 1972 I retained a professional pride in my catching skills. My last wicket for Glamorgan was a caught-and-bowled off Norman Featherstone of Middlesex, the one-time primary school boy whom I'd coached in Johannesburg and who coincidentally finished his playing days at Glamorgan.

The time really had arrived for me to sever my playing links and to march towards new horizons.

CHAPTER 15

LIFE IN THE FAST LANE

The habits, interests and knowledge ingrained in me during 18 years as a professional cricketer didn't just evaporate. So, after a season of reflection, licking my wounds and believing that I could contribute something to the club's future, in the winter of 1973/74 I decided to stand for election to the Glamorgan cricket committee. In order to be eligible, I had to enrol as an ordinary club member. I duly did so.

However, what followed convinced me that neither I nor Glamorgan had anything to offer one another in the foreseeable future. Getting the required proposer and seconder for the Newport area, where Joy and I lived, was straightforward enough, and I went to the regional meeting pretty confident of being elected. After all, wouldn't a first-class career of roughly 17,000 runs, 800 wickets and 700 catches carry the day?

Nine Glamorgan members turned up, including the up-for-re-election committeeman. Handicapped by a clubfoot and an arm permanently damaged by an accident at work, he had never played cricket above a lowly club level.

I lost to him by five votes to four! Worthy though he may well have been, the Newport area's decision told me that it really was time to cut what was left of cricket's umbilical cord and immerse myself totally in writing and broadcasting.

My association with BBC Wales actually stretched back to the mid-1960s. I'd been interviewed a number of times for the *Good Morning Wales* magazine radio show, the regional equivalent of Radio 4's *Today* programme. By a strange coincidence it mirrored my time as a professional cricketer for it too was to last 18 years.

An opportunity came up to audition for the role of presenter of a proposed new television series called *Sports Line-up*. Cliff Morgan, the former Wales and British Lions outside-half, was then doubling up as Sports Organiser for BBC Wales and presenter of their sporting output and had understandably grabbed the chance to move to London as deputy editor of *Grandstand*, BBC1's blue-riband Saturday afternoon sports programme.

This was in the very early days of regional television, and over 300 hopefuls applied. An eventual short list of four was chosen by cv rather than interview. I was one of them. We duly pitched up for a screen test. It was in two parts, conducting an interview in the studio and then two minutes of sight-reading a news bulletin. This was a real test as helpful studio props such as Autocue, which turns presenters into speaking dummies, were not yet available in the provinces. The interview section saw the almost certain elimination of two of the contestants, who rambled and stumbled their way through the three minute allotted time without gleaning much from their interviewees. This left a photogenic young man and me as the front runners.

We went in reverse order for the news-reading section, with me third and my main challenger last. Each of the bulletins put in front of us was different. I got through mine with only one or two stumbles. Reading something 'cold turkey' and getting the right inflections, never mind getting one's tongue around some almost unpronounceable Welsh place names associated with some of the stories, believe me, is no easy task. I walked out of the studio, thinking that I'd probably blown my chance.

The favourite for the post gave a faultless performance for a minute and a half – the job was surely his – until he came to a story that a drowning man had been rescued by lifeguards at Abersoch beach. My rival then sight-read, "He was only revived when lifeguards administered artificial insemination."

On that one slip of the tongue, I got the job!

Live broadcasting is littered with such gaffes; we've all made them. One which did the rounds for many months within Broadcasting House in Cardiff involved a female newsreader who announced that a plane from RAF in Valley, Anglesey had developed engine trouble over the Irish Sea and the pilot had "ejaculated to safety"!

One of my more memorable stumbles came some years later when, as producer and presenter of a 15-minute, late-evening radio news show called *Round-up*, which had a total budget, including my presenter's fee of £12, I had written a link reporting the death of Walter Glynn, one of Wales' best known singers. My idea was that at the end of the programme we would listen to half a minute or so of Walter in full voice.

I duly started an LP disc of his with the fader closed. It was timed to end three seconds before the hour and the beginning of the next programme. Having made a suitably sombre introduction, I eased open the fader and segued into the disc. But I'd misread the studio clock to my great embarrassment; all we had time for was Walter's final high C singing, "Goodbye ..."

I much preferred radio to television; it was more immediate and fewer things could go wrong. It was less technically fussy and therefore far less demanding, as it did not have the additional requirement of pictures to support words. In any case, I've always believed that producing a radio report or comprehensive feature which painted a vivid word-picture in a listener's mind required greater creativeness on the part of both producer and reporter than anything similar with moving images.

But presenting on television was far more nerve-racking. I shall never forget introducing my first *Sports Line-up* programme from the BBC Wales television studios, an old church building in Stacey Road, Cardiff. The suburb is named 'Splott', and my debut felt very much like it too. TV lights are exceptionally bright, hot and unforgiving and, before coming to terms with this environment, one feels rather like being a rabbit in the headlights of a car – transfixed.

Producer Dewi Griffiths gave me an easy opening link. These were the days when everything had to be either memorised or else read head-down from a script. All I had to say was, "Good evening and welcome to this first edition in the new series of *Sports Line-up*. First, today's soccer results," and off we went to an out-of-vision reader. With the palms of my hands flat on the table in front of me, I successfully got through this simple introduction. But when I lifted them up, there were two pools of sweat on the desktop. I remember thinking that facing Frank Tyson on a lively pitch was nowhere near as frightening!

Of course, in time it got easier and, although I gradually broadened my range, it was difficult to escape the sporting label. I wasn't ungrateful for this as it had given me my break into broadcasting, but I enjoyed expanding into news, current affairs and the arts.

In the twilight of my cricketing career, I had done several winter stints as a contract producer on *Good Morning Wales*. For years the programme was introduced by Vincent Kane, comfortably the best heavyweight broadcaster the region has produced. He had a marvellously powerful and authoritative voice with a presence and intelligence to match. But largely because he invariably knew far more about any given subject than the researchers and producers who were supposed to brief him, Vincent was virtually impossible to control. *GMW* was his fiefdom, and he could be a particularly difficult handful for the programme's female contributors. When he was eventually persuaded to share the presentation role with the very able Noreen Bray, at first he gave her a mighty hard time until, recognising that she was complementary to him and not challenging in her own right, he grudgingly came onside.

But reporting remained my own pleasure. I found the structuring of an in-depth item within a fixed time slot particularly satisfying. As a freelance broadcaster, a working week was as long as the items you were commissioned to cover. On occasions it could run to over 80 hours. One such event was the disaster which struck at a quarter past nine on Friday 21st October 1966.

A short Press Association message came through that a coal tip, four miles south of Merthyr Tydfil near the tiny mining village of Aberfan, had slipped.

With the other BBC Wales reporters I'd been hanging around in the Stacey Road newsroom on what had started off as a quiet news day, waiting to be sent off to cover something newsworthy.

Our editor was Alan Protheroe who, following the way he managed events in the next 72 hours, found his career fast-tracked upwards, to become eventually Assistant Director-General of the BBC.

Protheroe had a nose for a strong news story. After about ten minutes, when nothing more had come in, he telephoned Eric Warrilow a Merthyr-based freelance cameraman and told him to pop down and have a look at what was going on. At the same time he despatched up the valley from Cardiff two of his senior reporters, Brian Hoey and the bilingual Arfon Roberts. While the three were still en route came a second PA flash: 'The village school has been flattened by a twelve foot high tip slide; there are children inside.'

Destabilized by a fortnight of incessant rain, an avalanche of coal slurry had crushed to death 28 adults and 116 primary school children.

Every reporter in the newsroom capable of using a tape recorder was sent off. I was one of them. An emergency Radio Wales appeal went out for anyone who had a shovel to report to the scene. Although this was quickly rescinded, it was too late; hundreds came.

As we reporters battled our way through to near where the school had been, the scene was chaotic. Miners coming off shift from Rhondda valley coal pits and beyond were hustled to the front where their experience and skills counted for so much more than the efforts of untrained civilians. These miners dug, raked and scraped the slurry onto corrugated iron sheets. Until they literally dropped from exhaustion, to be helped away and replaced by fresh men, others propelled the sludge away from the site. After recovering, the miners went back to their own pits and next shift. But once that was over, most returned to Aberfan to rejoin the rescue operation again.

I felt like an observant ghoul. Putting my tape recorder down on a terraced house step, I joined the amateurs who were scraping the thick black slurry from the corrugated sheeting and thence off site. It was back-breaking, heart-breaking, futile work. Never had I felt so impotent nor less inclined to report on a story. All shared the valley community's feeling of overwhelming despair.

As darkness fell, emergency arc lighting threw a ghastly light over a scene of frantic desperation. Every now and then a whistle would blow and silence would fall, listening for what all prayed would be the sound of a child's voice.

There were very few.

A few weeks later, driving past Aberfan along the high road on the opposite side of the valley from which had been delivered the black wall of death, I stopped, got out of the car and looked across to where clearing-up work was still going on. The black finger, which had wiped out a generation of the village, was still there, a monument to evil. It looked like an arrow from the quiver of the devil who had taken deadly aim on the school and ignored most of the terraced houses on either side.

I have never been of a particular religious bent. I turned away, thinking that, if this was 'an act of God,' it was not a God I wished to have anything to do with.

*

Down the years I worked with a number of idiosyncratic news cameramen. An off-beat approach to life seemed to be a requirement of the job.

Based in Swansea, Harry Hynam – with Sid Rowe, his quiet but efficient soundman always alongside him – had been a tail gunner in the war. Harry was desperate to get rid of his expensive Arriflex 16mm camera in order to claim the insurance which would enable him to retire He would frequently leave his camera outside on a pub pavement while he went indoors to enjoy his essential lunchtime pint of Guinness. To his chagrin, it was always there when he returned! For a cub reporter, working with Harry was a very intimidating experience. "Oh Jesus, they've sent me down another bloody amateur," would be his morose welcome, but he was the fastest man in the west when it came to being ready for action. Almost before his car engine had stopped turning over, Harry would be out, camera hoisted onto his shoulder, barking, "Right, I'm running," totally ignoring the fact that the reporter still hadn't thought of his opening line or of a suitable location to film.

In my very early days, and to gain some experience in logging a record of the goals at a Welsh Cup football match, the producer of *Sports Line-up* sent me to the Lovells Athletic ground in Newport. On a freezing Saturday afternoon in January, Harry had been wheeled up from Swansea to film the game. The cameraman professed to hate all sports, and his mood was not improved when we were shown the rickety temporary scaffolding which had been especially erected for us. Harry spent most of the afternoon, turning round to bollock either Sid or me for moving about on the rostrum and causing it to shake.

The score was 9-1 to Lovells but, because of Harry's frequent lectures, we never got a single goal – and 800 feet of expensive film had been exposed!

Years later, having by this time established a good working relationship with Harry, I was sent out to report on the first daffodils of spring. It was to be our lead item in the *Wales Today* evening news programme. A group of senior news executives from BBC Television Centre in London was due to make a very rare visit to Cardiff to see our news gathering operation. Anxious to impress, our producer David Morris-Jones had sent a memo to all reporters and cameramen that it was essential that they brought back something of the highest quality to create the right impression.

At Broadcasting House in Cardiff, the top brass gathered around film editor Peter Mayby as he opened Harry's tin of processed footage. Out fell the cameraman's 'dope sheet,' a detailed record of what he'd filmed. In large, bold letters Harry had simply written across it, 'This is NO showpiece!'

Eric Warrilow was another World War II survivor. Eric only had one good eye but was absolutely fearless in a job which often required considerable risk-taking. Before the start of one cricket season I took Eric to cover a Glamorgan training session at the Neath indoor school. In the 1960s Jeff Jones was quick enough to open the bowling for England. Eric watched for a few balls and then said, "Peter, there's only one place to film this, from head-on where the ball lands."

Now, although Jeff was unquestionably pacy, accuracy was never his strong suite. Eric went off down to the empty batting end and lay full length, face down near a good length with his £20,000 film camera pointing towards Jeff, who waited at the end of his run up. "What do I do, Peter?" asked Jeff. "For God's sake, make sure you bang it in short so that it clears Eric," I said anxiously. The cameraman gave a wave to indicate his camera was turning over. Then, true to form, Jeff got his radar wrong and over-pitched the ball.

Eric must have seen this object rapidly getting bigger and bigger in his viewfinder as at 90 mph it whistled just over his head, thwacking against the rear concrete wall and rebounding past Eric halfway back up the net towards Jeff. Without a word, the ashen-faced cameraman got to his feet, picked up his camera and said, " I think I've got enough of that" and took refuge in the safety of the dressing room.

Jack 'Robbie' Robinson was a pipe-smoking cameraman for whom nothing was worth a rush. He once locked off his camera at right angles to a trampoline event, pressed the start button and turned away to light and enjoy his pipe. He never once altered the shot and when I suggested this might be an idea, he said, "No need young man, I've got it all within the frame." Well, he had – almost. When the 400 feet of film came out of processing and into the editing suite, even at 24 frames a second all one could see was a blur shooting out of the top of frame and disappearing at the bottom on its return. It was so fast that even a freeze-frame could only pick up an out-of-focus image of the human equivalent of a flying shuttle in a cotton jenny!

Robbie and his soundman Sam Lewis travelled around in a large campervan. One blustery day we were filming a story on top of Penarth cliffs near Cardiff. In need of a fresh light for his pipe, Robbie went to shelter behind his van. He returned half a minute later to find his expensive 16mm camera had been blown off the cliff and was in pieces some 100 feet down on the rocky beach. But what really upset Robbie was that the force of the wind had blown out his pipe!

Jock Sinclair was a Castella cigarman himself. A Scot with a very, very short fuse. Whatever the weather, whatever the season, he wore Jesus-type, open-toed sandals. We went to film an 81-year-old lady who the weekend before had holed in one at Pontypridd Golf Club. Jock's idea was that she should try to do it again for the camera. The golf club is on top of a mountain and it was a cold, hard-blowing, rainy mid-winter's day.

Jock insisted that I get the old dear out on the tee and be ready to go before he and his amiable soundman John Fowkes would venture out from their big Volvo Estate. I did so, gave him the thumbs up and out leapt Jock – straight into a foot of standing water! In almost the same bound he jumped back into the vehicle and refused to have anything more to do with the story.

David Jones was another mercurial character. He was one of the few news cameramen I worked with who had the creative talent worthy of feature programmes. His fuse, if anything, was even shorter than Jock's! David would fire well-meaning sound recordists almost as quickly as Majid in my cricketing days could devour ice creams. If David didn't think a shot which his reporter asked for would work, he would either refuse to shoot it or do so with such bad grace that the rest of the assignment was very hard-going. Most of the time David would be right, but it did make for a rumbustious relationship and he rowed on a regular basis with virtually everyone he ever worked with.

Strange folk are cameramen. So too were some of the sub-editors who created the programme's scripts and oversaw the editing. Clive Clissold was an inveterate practical jokester, but he had his uses too – as when I received a letter summoning me for jury service. In those freelance days there was no such thing as payment for time off, and I couldn't afford not to be working. Clive suggested a way out of which I remain not very proud.

"Write to the Clerk to the Court," advised Clive. "Thank him for your call-up for jury service and tell him that you're all for repatriating every convicted Indian, African, West Indian and Chinaman to their own countries. Don't forget to add that so far as burglars are concerned you believe the Saudi Arabian treatment of cutting off a hand for the first offence and the other one too if they repeat the crime, is absolutely right. Finish by saying how much you're looking forward to being on a jury so you can make sure British justice can be seen to be done."

I followed Clive's advice and, sure enough, back came a reply thanking me for my interest but but standing me down. To this day it has kept me out of the courts, but I have a sneaking feeling that on my Home Office file I am identified as a dangerous racist bigot, not to be turned loose in a jury in any circumstances. It's probably too late now to put the record straight.

They were happy, exciting days in the BBC Wales newsroom, and I still miss the buzz of being part of the creation of a daily programme.

One of the perks of working for the BBC.
Interviewing Max Boyce at a St. Pierre Chepstow golf tournament. Ian Botham looks on.

Within the pool of BBC Wales freelancers, as I was rising up the ladder both in terms of seniority and in range of skills, I was also making the odd inroad into network programmes. The BBC then, and I suspect even now, is very much a metropolitan-driven organisation. People working 'out in the sticks' were at best thought barely competent; while if you lived west of Reading, well, you were presumed to be covered in woad! Getting a toehold in a programme produced and transmitted from London not only looked wonderful on your cv but also provided a huge hike in earnings.

In the winter of 1977 I was invited up to Lime Grove studios in London to share in the presentation of a Friday night sports slot in the popular early evening magazine programme, *Nationwide*. Three of us were involved: Ron Pickering, the athletics coach whose most famous pupil was Lynn Davies the Olympic long jump champion, Desmond Lynam, then already a big name in radio sport, and me. Looking back, I now realise that it was an audition to provide cover for the BBC's two main sports linkmen, David Coleman and Frank Bough.

In terms of presentation skills, Des was light years ahead of both Ron and me, and he went on to become one of the best-known and best-loved faces on British television. But I happened to be on duty to do the first inter-continental satellite interview with Kerry Packer, the Australian multi-millionaire who that year had recruited most of cricket's finest players to take part in a tournament he called World Series Cricket. The repercussions were to have a dramatic effect both on the game's structure and players' on-the-field behaviour which has lasted to this day.

During my stint with the programme, I got inveigled into taking part in the *Nationwide Show Jumping Stakes* at the Horse of the Year show at Olympia. The programme's Cardiff-based researcher Dave Simmonds seduced me into taking part with the offer of a hundred guineas. All freelancers have a fee at which they can be bought, and mine was certainly well inside that price range. For this I was to be filmed being tutored by Debbie Johnsey, one of Britain's finest show jumpers who lived on her parents' farm near Chepstow. I'd last been on a horse – well, actually it was a seaside donkey – as a teenager on the sands at Weston-super-Mare.

After three weeks training, *Nationwide* presenters from all regions of the United Kingdom were to meet up at Olympia for a live, prime-time BBC1 televised competition.

It proved to be the most painful three weeks of my life.

When I first met Debbie, she looked up and down at my 6'4" and said, "Good God, I can't let you ride my pony Champ. Your feet would touch the ground. But we do have something in the stables which should be OK." She disappeared. Ten minutes later the clip-clop of massive hooves got nearer and nearer. Around the corner came the biggest horse I'd ever seen – he looked about seven feet tall at the shoulder! "Meet King," said Debbie. "He's an Irish steeplechaser we bought at the Limerick sales a couple of weeks ago. He'll be just right for you."

The horse and I looked warily at each other. My first leg up into the saddle launched me straight over King's back to land in a heap the other side. As the pair of us went around and around the Johnsey indoor schooling shed, my knees were soon rubbed raw against the saddle. King barely broke into more than a fastish walk as he stepped over a series of crossed poles just above ground level. With his breeding, background and training, the steeplechaser was too proud to pretend to jump, particularly with me bumping along on his back. Every now and then he'd stop dead in front of the poles which more often than not led to me doing a less than graceful somersault between and over his ears. Prostrate, I'd look up at him and he down on me. I swear that bloody horse often winked. He knew who was in charge, and it most certainly wasn't me.

At Olympia I had a bad attack of first-night nerves. Many of the *Nationwide* regional hacks who'd been dragooned into taking part, all excepting Jimmy Hill of footballing fame who was also an accomplished show jumper, felt as I did. At the morning rehearsal we were asked by Raymond Brookes-Ward, then the BBC's show jumping commentator, to do a trial lap over the lowest of fences. When King and I had finished Raymond said, "Peter, for your own safety, we'll keep to the crossed poles."

Just before the off, Debbie – equally concerned about my committing hara-kiri live on TV – anxiously suggested, "Peter, let me have a go on King in the warm-up ring. That should settle him down." Never mind him, I thought; I was the one who needed the reassurance! She got a leg up into the saddle and expertly 'popped' King over a couple of five-foot high fences before smoothly sliding off to wish me luck.

Horses are supposed to have an IQ of around 40 which, in human terms, puts them in the relegation zone of football's Conference League. Although there was about six stone difference in Debbie's and my weights, when I suddenly reappeared on King's back, he initially seemed not to notice or, for that matter, care. Now centre stage, where he no doubt felt he belonged and in front of a sell-out audience, King smoothly trotted up to, and then stepped over, the first six obstacles with me on his back hanging on grimly.

But then the damned horse spotted a couple of seven-foot-high fences being erected at the side of the arena for the next event. Recognising something which he was used to getting his teeth into, King's ears pricked up. He broke into a fast trot and then a canter. Now with both hands on one side of the reins and to gales of spectator laughter, I managed to haul his head around so he could no longer see to carry me off to a certain fatal accident. We trampled on a couple of the remaining crossed poles but finished the course still together if in last place. We were awarded a red rosette and a jockey's whip for having the misplaced courage to turn up.

On my bowlegged return to Cardiff and for having conned me into a fate close to death, I had plans to apply the whip severely and often to the behind of Dave Simmonds.

With my feet literally back on the ground and on familiar territory, when Peter West was away fronting the BBC's television coverage of Wimbledon, I stood in for him introducing Test matches. During a badly rain-affected game against Pakistan at Headingley, for two hours I interviewed virtually every man and woman in the ground who looked vaguely Pakistani without knowing any of their names nor often what they were saying.

But it was as the regular front man for BBC 2's *John Player Sunday League* cricket coverage that I became a recognisable face on national TV. Thanks to the recommendation of Frank Bough, my relationship with the programme lasted from 1973 into the early 1990s when Sky gained the contract and understandably wished to put their own presenter and commentary team in place. In its latter stages, the BBC's programme had changed from attracting a steady audience of over two million to becoming a truncated insert into *Sunday Grandstand*, which had a markedly negative effect on viewing figures.

Cricket-lovers deserted in droves. Some years later I was told that the BBC had had more letters of complaint about this cricketing cutback than about any other programme they had ever transmitted.

While the BBC had a virtual monopoly of cricket's television coverage, commentators John Arlott, Jim Laker and I shared a somewhat jaundiced view of the value of this Sunday afternoon cricketing fad. Although we recognised that the instant fix of 40 overs a side, with a guaranteed result, had substantial spectator appeal, John in particular only did Sunday League commentary because his broadcast contract demanded it. He nearly always handled the first 20 overs of each innings so he could be in his car and on the way back home to Hampshire almost before the 21st over of the second innings had been completed!

John also had a fear of heights, and he refused point black to climb a ladder so the BBC had to spend a small fortune building proper staircases at each venue.

Down the years he and I spent a great deal of time together, particularly in the early days of the Professional Cricketers' Association of which he'd been immensely proud to be asked to be founder President. Winter committee meetings over extended and extensive lunches at the Liberal Club in London usually ended with the 17-strong executive in a pleasant, alcoholic haze.

On summer Sundays, John rarely lunched with the production crew preferring, if the weather was kind, to sit outside, open his aircraft-captain-sized briefcase and draw out two bottles of claret to go with some strong-smelling cheese and biscuits. John had an immense knowledge of fine wines, in particular claret, and also wrote the definitive history of Krug champagne. To do his research, he was transported in the Krug family helicopter from his home in Hampshire to southern France and back.

John was a world authority on ceramics too and had a complete set of first editions of Thomas Hardy and a similar set of the writings of Pierce Egan, the father of sporting journalism in early 19th century England. Added to this, John also wrote some elegant poetry, had done a spell as a BBC poetry producer (the first to give air time to Dylan Thomas) and, of course, his bookshelves housed a full set of *Wisden Cricketers' Almanack*. But wine was always his first love.

After a particularly heavy night at Alresford, his last home in England before retiring to Alderney in the Channel Islands, over dinner I watched him single-handedly see off three bottles of claret with scarcely any change in his normal, deep Hampshire burr. I asked, "Just out of interest John, how many bottles of claret do you reckon you drink in a year?" He reflected on this for a few moments. "Arrr, I usually manage around three bottles a day." He paused, allowing this to sink in. Then, with a mischievous look in his eye, he added, "And I do like a drop of white, too."

I worked out that, from 1948 when he had his first sip of wine in South Africa, this meant that well over 1,000 bottles a year of claret alone sluiced through his veins – with heaven knows how much white to follow either before or after!

John once confided in me that his Test match radio contract stipulated that he never broadcasted after the tea interval. Why? "Because in front of a mike I report what I see. It comes in through the eyes and goes out of my mouth without leaving a memory. To shape my piece for a newspaper, I need to sit, look and think objectively about the game in order to be able to write constructively about it."

It was John who had suggested to me that there was a book in the 18-minute-or-so tea-time interviews I used to do on Sundays with a variety of cricketers and celebrity fans including people like Willie Rushton, Eric Clapton and Roy Hattersley. It eventually emerged as my second book, *Cricket Conversations*. Later came a re-working of *Winning Cricket*, called *The All-Rounder*.

I felt privileged to do the last television interview with John – after his final *John Player* commentary stint at Edgbaston in 1980. A chat with John without a glass or three of wine was unthinkable. So, before we began what was our usual tea-time conversation slot, I managed to scrounge from the Warwickshire committee room half a bottle of vin ordinaire, a 1976 Chateauneuf du Pape. John wrinkled his nose at its arrival but, while we chatted, he was gracious enough to take an occasional sip. At the end he scrawled a note on the label. 'Stolen from me, furnished by Peter Walker – John Arlott.' A few dregs still remain. It's one of my most precious mementoes of a very special man.

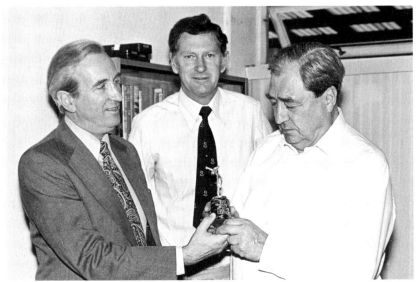

After doing the last television interview with John Arlott at Edgbaston in 1980, watching as he receives a replica of the John Player League trophy from the sponsors of the League.

Jim Laker took a lot more getting to know. He was essentially a private man but, once he had sized you up and if he liked what he saw and heard, he was delightful company with a sense of humour as dry as anything in John's 2,000-bottle cellar. I'd played against Jim during his twilight days with Surrey and, right at the end of his career, with Essex too, but I wouldn't say more than a dozen words had passed between us in that period.

When I replaced Frank Bough on Sundays, Jim was somewhat wary of me. With typical Yorkshire bluntness he swiftly taught me a lesson in broadcasting etiquette, which a lot of sporting commentators and radio interviewers these days would do well to take on board.

It came at the start of one of my earliest appearances fronting the BBC2 Sunday cricket programme. The match was at Tewkesbury; in those days producers made a conscious effort to cover games at locations far removed from accredited first-class grounds. As always, we went on air five minutes before the game's starting time of two o'clock. I'd mentally prepared what I thought was a marvellously descriptive piece about the area, the Civil War battle that had taken place in the vicinity and of course a few glowing lines on the magnificent Tewkesbury Abbey. I was still in full flow as the umpires came out and, with time running out before the start, the director cut up captions of the two teams which I then expounded on man by man. By the time I'd finished, the bowler was about to run in and bowl the first ball so I ended with the customary handover: "And now for commentary, here's Jim Laker." I sat back smugly, pleased with my opening until Jim responded: "Thank you, Peter, you've said it all."

He did not speak another word for fully fifteen minutes.

152

On his headphones the director pleaded with him but no, to make his point Jim stayed totally silent. Make it, he most certainly had. I had learnt a hard lesson: never, ever steal the main man's thunder. But things did, of course, improve and thereafter Jim was immensely kind to me.

What an attack Surrey had in the 1950s: Lock, Laker, Bedser and Loader, four high-quality England performers. No wonder they won seven county championships in a row. Years later when both of us were long retired, Jim told me that he and Tony Lock had never really got on well. I suspect the introverted, Yorkshire-born Laker found Lock, an exuberant southerner, rather too impetuous and somewhat empty-headed for his taste.

One Sunday evening we drove back to Jim's home in Putney. He'd recently had all his cricketing memorabilia stolen, including the balls with which he took 19 of the 20 wickets to fall in England's 1956 victory over Australia at Old Trafford. It was a loss he took with a typically phlegmatic shrug. We got around to discussing that match. Tony Lock had got the one wicket he didn't, and Jim looked at me with the hint of a grin. "When you next see Locky, if you want to see him blow his top, ask him how we shared the wickets at Old Trafford."

Jim would not be everyone's first choice as a dinner companion, but he has a special place in my memory. As does a memorable climax to the 1976 season.

When the final Sunday of the John Player season arrived, Sussex and Somerset were joint first in the table, with 40 points each, but, if neither of them won, they could be overtaken by Kent, Essex or Leicestershire, who were all on 36 points. Sussex were at Edgbaston, Somerset at Cardiff, Kent at Maidstone, Essex at Leyton and Leicestershire at The Oval. This posed a huge dilemma for our new cricket producer, Bob Duncan. Boxing, not cricket, was Bob's forte, and he relied heavily on Jim and me for guidance as to which matches we should cover.

Jim was a keen betting man on the horses. Looking at the other matches, he reckoned that Sussex had the form edge so we opted for Edgbaston as our main match, with single camera coverage and a commentator placed at both Maidstone and Cardiff. Replica trophies at each would be standing by. In case we'd guessed wrong, Bob had chartered a helicopter to be on stand by at the BBC Pebble Mill studios half a mile from Edgbaston, ready to whisk the real trophy and me to either of the other two venues if the outcome of their games looked like warranting it – and, of course, providing we could make it in time.

Even on a quiet day, in the control van called a 'Scanner', producer/director Bob used to get very excited, and his voice level rose steadily throughout this particular afternoon. Midway through the second innings at Edgbaston it became apparent we were at the wrong venue for Warwickshire were en route to pulling off a surprise victory over Sussex. However, the games at Cardiff and Maidstone hung in the balance.

Bob yelled into my earpiece, "Get airborne and await instructions." Together with a representative of the John Player organisation and carrying the real trophy, we hot-footed it off to nearby Pebble Mill. The plan then was that Bob would monitor Cardiff and Maidstone and direct us via the helicopter's radio to the likely winning venue.

Bob dutifully kept us informed on progress. It seemed as if Kent had the edge in their game while the Glamorgan–Somerset match looked like going right to the wire. I suggested to the pilot that, as it was now almost 6 pm with matches scheduled to finish by seven, we should hover over Reading which, in flying time, was roughly equidistant between the two grounds. We did – but then ten minutes later the chopper's radio went down!

Back at Edgbaston, excitable Bob must have levitated at this point! There was no time left to weigh up the options; we had a 50-50 chance of being right either way. Above the engine roar I shouted at the pilot, "Let's go for Maidstone." We raced east. As we swooped low over the ground and with only five minutes of programme time left, the players were starting to leave the field, the crowd surging all around them. Had Kent won? Had Middlesex? From the air it was impossible to tell.

"Put it down there." I shrieked, pointing to the middle of the square which had already been roped off by the protective Maidstone groundstaff. To the pilot's eternal credit he ignored Civil Aviation rules on low-level flying over built-up areas and dropped the helicopter out of the sky and down onto the freshly used pitch.

Engine still running, I grabbed the trophy, threw open the door and, together with the puffing JP man trailing behind, legged it towards the pavilion. It was three minutes to seven, just two minutes before the scheduled end of our transmission. As I ran, I yelled to the spectators, "Who's won?" I was given an extra yard of speed when, to cheers all round came back the reply, "We have. Kent are the champions."

I just had time to thrust the trophy into the hands of the John Player representative and he to shovel it on into the arms of the Kent captain. I turned to the camera on the pavilion steps and said something like, "What an end to the season. We and Kent have just made it," before we went off the air!

As we calmed down, news came through that Glamorgan had beaten Somerset in Cardiff by just one run. Our luck had held.

Then I made a landline phone call to Bob, still locked in the Scanner at Edgbaston where I've no doubt steam must still have been coming out of his ears. Because of the radio failure, he would have been completely unaware as to our whereabouts until his camera at Maidstone had picked up our descent. Although hoarse, he managed to croak out a memorable comment: "Well, remember, Peter, every great producer needs a little bit of luck."

So there I was, 250 miles from home and no transport to get back to Wales. The helicopter was banned from flying after dark and was nearly out of fuel anyway. My last abiding memory of the day was the pilot trying to explain to the groundsman that his couple of tons of helicopter wouldn't have done any lasting damage to his precious square!

In the winter I returned to life within BBC Wales, coupled with weekend match-reporting on Welsh club rugby for a variety of Fleet Street newspapers including the *Sunday Telegraph* and the *Mail on Sunday* for whom I also did a general sporting column. One year I was elected Chairman of the Welsh Rugby Writers' Association, an honour of which I was very proud.

There were other sadder and more profound moments, such as covering the funeral of Merthyr boxer Johnny Owen, killed in a Los Angeles ring as he challenged world bantamweight champion Lupe Pinto of Mexico. He lingered in a coma for three weeks before eventually dying

Two years earlier at Pontypool's Leisure Centre, I'd seen Johnny's first professional fight where he'd come in as a late substitute to beat on points the then Welsh bantamweight champion George Sutton. From then on, I reported on all his contests in Wales as he became British and then European bantamweight champion before that one contest too many in California.

For his funeral, thousands lined the streets of Johnny's hometown and the three-mile route to Dowlais cemetery where this shy, likeable matchstick-thin young man was eventually laid to rest.

Hugh McIlvanney, one of Britain's finest sports writers, had been at ringside. I'm sure that Johnny, stretchered from the ring to die without regaining consciousness, would have appreciated Hugh's epitaph in the *Observer*: 'Johnny Owen's tragedy was that he was articulate in a violent language.'

Oh to have the talent to be able to conjure up a valediction as moving as that!

For over a century the iron foundry town of Merthyr produced a regular supply of equally hard but out-of-the-ring gentle men like Howard Winstone and Eddie Thomas. At the funeral of Eddie, a one-time British and Commonwealth welterweight champion and manager of world champions Ken Buchanan and Winstone, one of his several brothers spoke to the packed Welsh chapel. He recounted how, in their small, terraced family home, money was always tight and that clothes from Eddie, the oldest, were handed down from brother to brother until, in a pretty threadbare state, they reached him, the youngest. Looking down at the coffin placed in front of the pulpit he said, "Eddie, I was proud to inherit your clothes but one thing that never fitted me then – or now – were your shoes."

Recalling this tribute from a simple man of the valleys still brings a lump to my throat.

CHAPTER 16

UPHEAVALS APLENTY

My unpredictable lifestyle stretched to the limit the comfort zones of a traditional home life. Since the age of 16 I had been a roamer and a loner, conditioned to fending for myself, giving as and when required and anticipating little in return. I certainly enjoyed people's company – but I was always glad to move on.

The tensions this created in Newport were, in retrospect, largely of my own doing. While I was devoted to my daughter Sarah and son Justin, I grew steadily more distanced from my wife Joy. Back at home, amongst the people she had grown up with, she was understandably more comfortable in returning to what she was at heart, a small-town girl. In contrast, my own youth had been spent in households where wide-ranging conversation, debate and, of course, music were an intrinsic part of everyday life.

Although Joy and I jogged along for 12 years, we were headed nowhere. For us both, life together had become stale and sterile; our paths had originally crossed at the wrong time. When I eventually did leave, I naively believed we could part with the minimum of fuss and the children would soon come to terms with having an absent father; after all, that's what I'd been during my cricketing days – a week at home followed by sometimes up to two weeks playing away. With its unsocial hours this working schedule continued when my blossoming career in broadcasting replaced cricket.

My departure did not change my role as the family's only breadwinner, nor would it for the next 25 years. When Joy and I broke up, I bought her and the children a detached house in Ridgeway, one of Newport's best suburbs, and paid the mortgage until it was finally cleared 20 years later.

Joy was very bitter at the split and, although we had been granted joint custody, a long-term wedge was created between the children and me. It took over a decade before Sarah, Justin and I were able to begin what was a slow and sometimes painful process of reconnection and reconciliation. Throughout this time, my life – by force of necessity of having to fund two homes – had to change up a couple of gears. My working hours became even more unreasonably long.

In the early 1970s and in the twilight of my cricketing career, I'd spotted a very attractive lady watching us play at Worcester. Susan Davies turned out to be the girl friend of Rodney Cass, one of the opposition's cricketers. After the end of the day's play we met briefly in the clubhouse bar and hit it off. Her relationship with Rodney was cooling on both sides. Sue was an air stewardess with British Overseas Airways, and I found myself identifying with her lifestyle, so similar to my own. Her job had taken her all over the world, spending two to three weeks away followed by a week or more at home near London. She was the kind of lady who would go off exploring the various countries where the cabin crew had a 'slip' – a few days off. Sitting around a hotel pool drinking the local 'jungle juice' and gossiping was not her scene.

Sue became an important part of my life. As my marriage to Joy finally crumbled in 1972, Sue's quiet, unconditional, non-pressurised support became more and more important to me.

After my departure from Newport and following a decent period of reflection, she moved west to join me in Cardiff. We bought and redecorated a small, dilapidated, mid-terrace house in Llandaff village, a suburb of Cardiff. During this period Sue continued to commute to and from Heathrow until completing ten years of flying, when she finally decided to clip her own wings. Sue was well read, well travelled, independently in control of her life and comfortable with managing her own affairs. She had the wit to recognise that the Walker male line was not always easy to live with and needed to inhale plenty of its own air for its own good. Darby and Joan, we most certainly never were.

In 1978, along came our son Daniel. As a very small baby he quite unwittingly engineered the first chink in the suit of armour Joy had encased around Sarah and Justin. Up to then their visits to meet me had been very rare and never once, until some time after Dan's arrival, did they meet Sue. Dan proved to be a useful diversion by helping to fill in those awkward moments when conversation flagged.

While my offspring have long gone their separate adult ways, they are all now on very friendly terms, thanks largely to Sue's calm and gentle encouragement and her early refusal to put pressure on the two older offspring to accept the new arrival.

In 2000. Celebrating Peter's 65th birthday, wife Susan's 60th and Daniel's 1st class honours degree from Leeds University. *Left to right:* Ali (Tim's partner), Tim, Illian (Tim's son), Dan, Sarah, Justin, Kelly (Justin's partner), Peter and Sue.

A reconciliation with Glamorgan took place when I was co-opted onto the club's 12-man cricket committee – along with Roger Davis, from the 1969 championship side, and Jack Bannister, then a Pontypridd resident but a one-time Warwickshire opening bowler and a leading light in the Professional Cricketers' Association. Together with chairman Hugh Davies, who had played for Glamorgan in the 1950s, we were the only ones who had hands-on, first-class cricket-playing experience. Not unnaturally we presumed we would be able to make some useful contributions.

However, with a change in chairman, came a change of policy and, as part of a plan to reduce the size of all the club's committees, we three alone were thanked and shown the door. Such is life.

During the latter part of my cricket career I had steadily built up a domestic property portfolio in Newport by raising a bank loan from the first investment house that I'd purchased with the bulk of my benefit money. The rental income from these properties, plus a growing contribution from my BBC freelance work and other journalistic commissions, gave Sue, Dan and me a comfortable lifestyle and also protected those I'd left behind in Newport.

Dealing with difficult tenants, reluctant interviewees and peculiar producers was hard graft, involving long hours in often highly stressful situations but, looking back, I believe that I thrived on the buzz that I got from working with energetic, creative BBC people committed to meeting daily deadlines within the public service broadcasting ethos.

But spending 18 years before this particular mast did take its toll mentally as well as physically, diminishing the originality of the ideas I put up for consideration to programme commissioners. Late in 1984, David Parry-Jones, a broadcasting colleague, and I were separately called up to see Gareth Price, the Controller of BBC Wales. In essence he said that it was time for programmes and us to move on – in our case, it was more a question of move out. But, with uncalled-for generosity in what can be a surprisingly heartless profession, Gareth said that, in recognition of the length of service we had both given the 'Beeb' and to allow us time to find other vineyards in which to labour, he would extend our freelance contracts to the end of 1985.

Thrown together in such circumstances David, a vastly experienced news reader, general reporter and rugby commentator, and I discussed at great length our shared dilemma. We were appreciative of the Controller's largesse – for what pair of 50+-year-olds could have reasonably expected 12 months' notice? What could we do? Even if I so wished, I was probably too old to find a full-time post in cricket. For his part, David might have eked out a modest living, writing a few articles and a book or two, but nothing either of us had in the pipeline would be sufficient to maintain the lifestyle we'd worked hard to achieve.

It didn't take us long to come to the conclusion that what we did know a great deal about – and, in our view, were certainly still young enough to play a major role in, either in front of or behind the camera – was television.

Because of the nature of regional broadcasting, freelance performers needed to be multi-skilled. David and I had acquired extensive experience both presenting and producing programmes. In my case, I'd even been on a short course at Television Centre in London to learn news studio camera directing. Between us, and through our different professional and social contacts, we were also on first-name terms with virtually all the business, political and sporting movers and shakers in Wales.

Fortuitously too, a window of opportunity had just been opened by Prime Minister Margaret Thatcher, who had broken the vice-like grip of the trade unions on radio and television. Her legislation had thrown open 25% of available airtime on BBC and ITV to programmes supplied by independent individuals and production companies. Until then these outlets had been hogtied by the widespread restrictive trade union practices which also affected the print media. This kind of closed shop could no longer be justified in law.

Our path, therefore, was clear. Sue and I had moved from our original small, terraced dwelling to a more spacious, semi-detached home in Llandaff, Cardiff. Early in 1985 I convened a meeting in our house for a brain-storming session on how to take advantage of this new scenario. Together with close friends and BBC working colleagues, Patrick Hannan, then BBC Wales' political and industrial correspondent, Beti George, a prominent Welsh language broadcaster, and Bruce Rawlings, studio director of the nightly *Wales Today* news programme, we sat around our dining-room table, discussing the possibilities. There was much speculation as well as initial scepticism about just how much opportunity the reluctant broadcasting organisations would give to outsiders. But, thanks to our one-year's paid notice from BBC Wales, David and I had little to lose. We had to test the temperature outside Broadcasting House, Cardiff.

But what to call ourselves? We initially chose Avalon Television – but this name had already been taken by a retail shopping group. So, keen to retain our Welsh identity, we settled on Merlin Film and Video Limited. Later this was shortened to the much more dynamic Merlin Television. As only David and I could have a public profile, the roles of the others would be to contribute ideas, write scripts, do translations into Welsh where required and suggest contact names who might be interested in making what rapidly became known as 'corporate videos'. As sleeping partners, Pat, Beti and Bruce agreed to chip in £50 each for a minority shareholding.

Within two years Merlin had become the largest and most successful independent production company in Wales, moving beyond the provision of programmes to the BBC, HTV and S4C into the much more lucrative and fertile fields of corporate programming, television commercial production and media training.

Our colleagues' individual investments had been transformed into substantial four-figure sums as Merlin turned out to give a far larger and more assured return than the stock market!

But first we had to find Merlin a proper home. I bought a small, two-bedroom, mid-terrace house at 4 William Street, Pontcanna, Cardiff. It had one largish room downstairs and one telephone, around which we used to hover, praying for it to ring! The two bedrooms upstairs were used as our edit suite and a tape storage area. Bruce already owned a small, transportable low-band editing set-up and sub-broadcast standard camera which he offered to hire out to us for what at the time seemed an exorbitant £100 per day. He was also prepared, subject to his BBC commitments, to direct our location filming, again for a fee.

This worked well until, a few months into our venture, we found out that the ambitious Bruce had also set up his own production company and was actually tendering against Merlin for corporate work! A parting of the ways was swift and inevitable.

To replace Bruce we managed to lure into joining us a young Irishman named Dave McClean, who was then working as a video-tape editor in BBC Wales' news department. Initially he came on an ad hoc basis but, as commissions started to trickle in, he joined our staff full-time. Up to then our staff consisted of just David Parry-Jones and me. Dave Mac brought unexpected creativity as a cameraman as well as inventive editing skills and a wonderful ear for appropriate background music. However, like many Irishmen, he had a restless spirit and, after five years with us, he decided to return to his homeland.

Luckily, well before he left, an unemployed, footloose young man called Dean Smith came knocking on our door. He had some limited experience as a DJ, and would we employ him as a sound recordist? What clinched it is that he offered to work for £25 a week!

Dean Smith became the hub of Merlin. He grew into being a quite brilliant all-rounder. When Dave McClean departed, he took over as our cameraman and video-tape editor, combining and indeed exceeding anything that had gone before him, in the process greatly improving the quality of our end-product. Dean soon developed two other key attributes, becoming an absolute wizard in maintaining and repairing what eventually became a highly complicated array of electronic equipment. And, with precious little by way of artistic temperament, he was a delight to work with. Nothing was too much trouble for Dean who would spend literally all night in the edit suite, fiddling around with different electronic effects, experimenting with music backgrounds, doing essential maintenance of the kit and snatching pockets of sleep based on need – of which in his case there appeared to be little.

Dean was truly indispensable. Without him Merlin would have been far less successful and certainly less profitable. If only we could have persuaded him to remain a bachelor! But we put temptation in his way by employing the very attractive Emma Birch as a receptionist and researcher. She went on to become his wife and mother of his ever-expanding family.

One of the better appointments in our still tiny company's existence came very early on. We soon realised that we needed a full-time telephonist and receptionist who, if needed, would be able to come out on location filming to record the logging notes which are essential guides in the later editing process. I contacted a local secretarial college. Did they have anyone they thought might be suitable? Of course they did.

The doorbell eventually rang, and we opened it to see an attractive twenty-something blonde. Both David and I were new to the staff-interviewing role but we liked her manner and speaking voice. However, when we asked if she would have any problem about staying overnight if she came out on a shoot, she thought for a moment and then said no, that wouldn't be a problem as she knew of someone who could keep an eye on her daughter. This somewhat threw DPJ and myself. We both thought a young unmarried mother with a small child was a recipe for disaster. I asked, "And how old is she?" "Oh, she's 17, and honestly she's well able to look after herself," came the swift reply.

Joan Bird-Meyers turned out to be nearer 40 than 20. So much for DPJ's and my judgment of age! Despite her occasional forgetfulness and somewhat idiosyncratic spelling – for German was her first language – Joan proved to be a top-class all-round asset with never a complaint about the erratic working hours nor the tasks we asked of her.

When ten years later I eventually left Merlin to become Director of Development for the newly created Cricket Board of Wales, she soon followed me through the door at Sophia Gardens, to become a key member of the staff at Glamorgan County Cricket Club.

Whenever we had a shoot needing specialist skills, like all independent companies we used to hire in experienced, freelance operatives. So the last but one of our permanent staff became Chris Jones, a Welsh speaker from

Merlin outside its first proper home, 1 Pontcanna Place, Pontcanna, Cardiff.
Left to right: Dean Smith, Carol Williams, Chris Jones, Peter Walker, David Parry-Jones, Paul McCarthy, Joan Bird-Meyers, Eddie Sinclair, Dave McClean.

Aberaeron who shadowed Dean. He eventually found a niche in S4C where he became one of their regular weathermen.

Merlin's first commission was a promotional video for a Cardiff architect, who was trying to attract Japanese money into a major redevelopment of the former home of the Rolls family of Rolls Royce engine fame.

It was a vast country estate near Monmouth, which in its prime had been merely a weekend retreat! We made an eight-minute promo and we charged £800 all up, wondering if we'd overpriced ourselves. We were soon to find that, in this new, volatile and still relatively exclusive market place, £1,000 a finished minute was really the going rate!

In the year of our notice from the BBC and thanks to some vigorous marketing of our new company by David and me and by working in our spare time when not required by the BBC, we turned over £94,000. It confirmed in our minds that, when they finally called time on us, and given a following wind with no major dip in the country's economic climate, we were onto, if not a gold mine, then certainly a passable living.

We soon outgrew the little terraced house and moved directly across the road into a derelict former bakery at 1 Pontcanna Place which we converted into proper offices with a small studio where the ovens had once been. Commissions, if not flooding in, were sufficient to keep us above the waterline. DPJ and I had a new spring in our step as, no longer bound by the BBC sacrosanct mantra of 'balance', we revelled in being able to produce one-eyed, biased programmes showing off our clients' best features. As the corporate area was far more profitable than the broadcast sector, we channelled most of our energies in this direction. Backed by the editing skills of Dave McClean and Dean Smith, I became adept at fast-turnaround productions loaded with eye-catching visual effects. But it was the more considered approach of DPJ which really established our fledgling production company's bona fides in the broadcast sector.

We entered David's *Snowdon, the Accessible Wilderness* into the Chicago Video Festival, then the largest of its kind in the world. The film beautifully portrayed the stunning scenery of North Wales, and it carried off the Gold Award in a category where there were 1,500 entries. Shortly afterwards the 20-minute programme did the same at the New York Festival.

News of David's successes put Merlin at the hub of the now rapidly expanding independent sector, not only in Wales but in England too. As a result of the twin successes in America, we gained valuable street cred with the big local players: the Welsh Development Agency, South Wales Electricity (try making a video about electricity, which is invisible), Allied Steel and Wire, the Wales Tourist Board, several local councils and area health authorities. This ensured Merlin's rapid growth.

As we evolved, we moved up-market technically by acquiring virtually all the increasingly essential broadcast-quality recording and editing equipment. Unlike our main competitors, we could advertise these facilities as being 'in-house'. Two further moves took us first to the former Rentokil Offices just off Cowbridge Road East in Cardiff (a few wry jokes did the rounds on this relocation), then to The Wharf in the rapidly developing Cardiff Bay area. That took Merlin about as far as David and I could realistically hope for.

There were many high points in the ten years that Merlin Television was under our direct control. I was Managing Director while DPJ filled the Production Director role To head up our marketing drive, we recruited the hyperactive young Paul McCarthy from HTV. Paul had trained as a BBC Wales videotape news editor, but his entrepreneurial energies were frustrated by the monotonous nature of the job. He was certainly a hustler of a salesman with an approach very different from DPJ and me. But we dovetailed beautifully and together effectively blanketed the market.

During this period I seemed to land most of Merlin's big outside broadcast contracts.

These took me, sometimes accompanied by our in-house crew of Dave McClean and Dean Smith plus general handymen Chris Jones and occasional freelance cameraman Eddie Sinclair, all over the world. Doing a preview for BBC1 of the 1988 Winter Olympics in Calgary, Canada, in temperatures of minus 20 degrees Centigrade all our recording gear froze. Acting like a mother hen by holding the various bits under his woollen fleece to thaw them out, Dean Smith somehow brought it back to life, only for me as presenter/producer/director to be unable to speak my lines because my lips were frozen stiff!

On the bobsleigh trail, we followed the British team to St Moritz. The tiny Swiss mountain village boasted no fewer than five 5-star hotels. Our sponsors, Allied Steel and Wire, who supported and equipped the British team, booked us into the Kulm Hotel; its rate of £250 bed only, per person, per night, was then a vast sum.

Into the bar one evening strode a dozen wealthy American women. There was no snow in Colorado so they'd decided to check things out in Europe. An inevitable hanger-on around the British bobsleigh team tried to chat up one of the more attractive Yanks. She was obviously completely uninterested and rejected her potential suitor's suggestion that they have dinner together with the most withering put-down I've ever heard. "No thanks, pal," she said. "You look like a guy with a low sperm count!"

Off we then went to Koenigsee in the Bavarian Alps where Hitler had his Eagle's Nest hideout. Here the Army team were representing Great Britain in the European championships. The event comprised four trips down a twisting, steep 1,500m track with a 360-degree turn midway down called a Kreisel.

The four-man bob teams were made up of highly trained, powerful athletes. On solid ice and from a standing start, they can explosively push their 600-kilogram sledge 50 metres in less than five seconds and then jump aboard with split-second synchronisation. The total time taken to complete a run was under a minute. We only had one camera to cover the British involvement for BBC1's *Grandstand* programme and had done a deal to buy-in the multi-camera German outside broadcast unit's output for our main coverage. We decided to do close-ups of the Brits at the start of their first run. We'd then hot-foot it a little way down the steep hill to where the bob was picking up speed during their second run, pick up their performance around the Kreisel bend on their third and be waiting for them at the finish line at the bottom on their fourth and final run.

On the first, the brakeman at the rear of the bob failed to get in at the end of the 50-metre push start. Second time down, one of the runners on the bob came loose and GB1 limped down to the finish in a time nearly double that of East Germany, the eventual winners. On the third descent our lads capsized coming out of the Kreisel and went banging down against the sides of the icy track all the way to the finishing line 700 metres away!

Smartly turned out in matching GB bobsleigh team kit, provided by our sponsors, we waited anxiously at the finish for their fourth and final run. Alongside us stood a tall, aristocratic-looking Austrian, complete with monocle and full-length camel-hair overcoat. On a huge screen, the outside broadcast cameras tracked the British team from the start. This time all went well.

All four got on board at the end of their explosive shove, rapidly picked up speed down the long straight, got through the Kreisel and hurtled towards the finish. But, as they crossed the line, the brakeman – like all the crew bar the driver he had his head down to minimise any wind drag – misheard the call "brake" from the driver as "great", for they had at last got down the run in one piece. So on and on the British bobsleigh careered and flew across a road, scattering spectators on all sides before coming to a halt in a neighbouring field. The tall Austrian turned to us and, with a Nazi-type curl of his lip said, "And you von zee war?" before turning on his heel and marching off. He didn't actually click his heels together, but we knew what he meant.

In Hong Kong, Melbourne, Johannesburg, Cardiff and Kiel we recorded the World Squash circuit for Sky television, and for three summers Merlin had the contract to cover a number of Glamorgan cricket matches for BBC Wales. Here I tried to combine the roles of producer and commentator. It was rather like being a high-wire walker with vertigo.

Then early in 1989, and very much out of the blue, came a takeover bid from Trilion, a large London-based independent production company. Following on from the £29 million sale of their Trocadero studios in Leicester Square, they were on the acquisition trail. With the relaxing of constrictions on who could provide programmes for broadcast television, their research had identified Edinburgh and Cardiff as the UK's two most likely growth areas. In the independent sector, Trilion were already big, big players. One of their companies, Cheerleader, was then responsible for the launching of the popular Channel 4 American football series, and they also had massive London studios in Limehouse, Canary Wharf and near the old Wembley Stadium. To say that we were flattered by their interest would be a huge understatement.

Trilion's Managing Director Ian Reed and his Finance Director Alfred Smith came to Cardiff to take DPJ and me out to lunch. Ian said that they'd seen some of our stuff on Sky and enjoyed it. If we could agree a price, how would we like to become part of the Trilion empire? And how we would!

At the time Trilion were also interested in three other Cardiff media companies, all of which were based in the former Coal Stock Exchange building in the Bay area. They were Stylus, an electronic graphics specialist, Echo, an audio-dubbing facility, and Team Television, a post-production house. Coincidentally a few months earlier, in order to increase our editing capabilities greatly, we had invested £15,000 to buy a third share in Team.

This opportunity had arisen because some 18 months earlier Team's staff had engineered a management buyout of the Welsh language channel S4C's facilities arm, then called Mentrau, and needed more capital. As an independent, they had got off to a phenomenal start, hugely increasing their turnover. However, a sticking point in the negotiations with Trilion was that they did not have audited accounts dating back far enough to give an accurate picture of their financial position, and it later transpired that the Londoners were also uneasy about the people then running Team. We had calculated that, on a payout based on their figures, Merlin's one-third share of the company was worth around £750,000!

In the end, Echo too failed to pass the due-diligence financial criteria. So we became the first of the Cardiff-based companies that Trilion bought. A year later Ian Reed decided to acquire Stylus as well. The market dramatically weakened over the next two years, and their debts proved to be enormous, with astronomically high running costs too. Eventually these were to prove major factors in taking Trilion into liquidation.

Before these problems surfaced, out of the blue my old captain Tony Lewis, who had excellent connections in India after leading an England cricket team there, rang to say that he had an Indian business acquaintance who might have a proposition for Merlin. His name was Lokesh Sharma, a close friend of Indian cricket legend Kapil Dev.

Lokesh had obtained the television rights to India's 1989 tour of the West Indies, and he needed a TV production company to do what the BBC and ABC in Australia had failed to do in the past, to relay pictures from a Test series in the Caribbean. Indeed, in those days even the individual West Indian islands were unable to see pictures originating in other parts of the Caribbean!

To this day I break out in the proverbial cold sweat when I think of what we took on. Because there was no pre-production money available, I had to forego the normally essential exploratory technical recce of the island grounds and to rely on my memories from playing visits there nearly 30 years earlier! To save costs, Lokesh had also done deals to utilise what turned out to be each island's antiquated outside broadcast cameras and recording and editing facilities, together with the necessary personnel to man them.

Doordarshan, the Indian equivalent of the BBC, contracted Lokesh to provide coverage of all four Tests. Fortunately we were not expected to provide live pictures – that was far too ambitious and expensive – but we were committed to producing an hour-long edited highlights package each evening and sending it by satellite back to India. It was a Herculean task.

This was just, but only just, possible from the islands which had a television service. In the case of Guyana, where the first Test of four was scheduled, they had none! Ahead of travelling out from the UK, I'd decided I couldn't risk having to work with local outside broadcast television directors who might not have any idea as to how to handle multiple camera coverage, so I hired Johnny Norman, a former BBC Wales colleague of mine who was an experienced outside broadcast sports television director. Lokesh had managed to do a deal with Bernard Pantin, Head of Programmes at Trinidad and Tobago Television, the nearest television service, to hire his scanner, equipment and technical crew, load them onto a chartered boat and sail them the short distance to Georgetown on mainland South America, where we would meet them.

Off the coast of Venezuela, the small coaster carrying our equipment and crew nearly ran aground and, when it eventually made it up the Essequibo river to the Guyanese capital, our vessel was promptly impounded by customs officers who demanded a one-million US dollar bond before they'd release our gear. They also said that the only man who had the key to the dock gates had gone 'up country' and wasn't expected back until after the Test was over!

Fortunately, the President of the Guyanese Cricket Association was also a general in the army. It was quite amazing how quickly he managed to arrange not only to have our gear released from bondage without charge but also for a spare key to be miraculously found for the gate! However, getting our equipment to the ground wasn't the end of our problems. To be sure, there was scaffolding at both ends, but it was of a primitive, rickety nature totally unsuitable for television cameras which needed to be rock steady. Nor was there any sign of a staircase or ladders to climb up to the 30 feet above the ground platforms at either end. But the General snapped out some orders to a sergeant, turned to me and said in that immortal West Indian phrase: "No problem."

Experience had already shown that, when you hear those two words in the West Indies, your heart sinks, for you know you're in deep and serious trouble. However, so help me, the next morning there at each end of the ground, and behind the bowlers' arms too, which was a real bonus, were splendid hardwood staircases which would stand any test of time. They were large, solid and beautifully put together by a bunch of squaddies, who must have laboured through the night.

The scaffolding platforms had also been stabilised so we were up and running – that is, providing we didn't get a power failure from our primitive Trinidadian back-up generator.

At Georgetown the former Indian Test batsman Mohinder 'Jimmy' Amarnath flew in with Lokesh. Jimmy was billed to share commentary and also act as summariser. I use the word 'share' in its widest sense for, lovely guy though Jimmy was, whatever the incident his sole comment on being asked his opinion turned out to be, "It was a lovely shot." But, praise the Lord and Lokesh, we were also joined by Tony Lewis as our main commentator. This took a huge load off my shoulders.

Now I had to plan how to get the master tapes from Georgetown to the nearest satellite uplink in Trinidad. I edited the cassettes at close of play, lying across the rear window ledge of the small scanner van and giving the videotape editor the 'ins' and 'outs' of the required sequences from my logging sheets. These I'd had to write as well as doing some commentating. The final obstacle was zigzagging the 20+ miles over the deeply potholed main road from Georgetown to its primitive airport where, with engine running, we had a small charter aircraft waiting to fly the tapes and me to Trinidad, a journey of about 40 minutes, in order to hit our satellite booking time at midnight. From there the pictures would be sent back to India via one of only four satellite transmitting and receiving stations in the whole Caribbean, the others being Antigua, Barbados and Jamaica.

If a three-and-a-half-day deluge hadn't saved us in Georgetown I don't think we'd have had a hope in hell of meeting our deadlines. The rain also saved the Indian team from what I'm sure would have proved to be a crushing defeat. During a brief period of play on the first day, drizzling rain, not hard enough to take the players immediately off the field, dripped through the front part of the roof of our scanner and onto the always temperamental electronic gear. It promptly blew a gasket.

At one stage director John Norman, operating from the van's driving seat, was left with one functioning camera out of five. But, as an ex-BBC engineer with time done in Nigeria, John was a great belt-and-braces man. While repairs were undertaken, somehow he got two cameras' worth of coverage out of one.

John and I shared a huge sense of relief that the Test had been washed out, thus relieving us of having to deliver four more edited highlights packages. But things didn't improve even after we'd left Guyana.

Arriving in Bridgetown, Barbados the afternoon before the second Test was due to begin, a check of the island's broadcast facilities cheered us both up. But then, on day one, the local technicians went on strike because, rather than risk using a local director, I insisted on Johnny Norman being the man to direct the cameras. John had cut his teeth during a two-year attachment from the Beeb to set up a television service in Nigeria so he wasn't too fazed by this initial setback. Fortunately, he had a wonderful sense of humour – and needed it by the bucketful during our six-week trip around the Caribbean.

We eventually managed to placate the Barbados TV crew, but by then several overs of the Test had gone and India were one wicket down for 14 runs! Additionally, our scorer had failed to turn up, and the local commentator also refused to get involved, miffed that he hadn't been given top billing.

While John punched the buttons in the aged, small Toyota scanner van behind the pavilion, I was pressed into doing the commentary. Not only was I without a scorer but also, thanks to a concrete pillar smack in the way, I was unable to see more than half of the scoreboard. It didn't help either that I recognised hardly any of the Indian players, but somehow we staggered through that day and the subsequent three before India slid to the first of three Tests defeats in a row.

The experiences in Barbados proved to be a suitable hors d'oeuvre for the remainder of our voyage of discovery around the 'Windies'. From then on, everything that could go wrong went wrong. Mind you, the problems weren't confined to the Caribbean, for when I returned to the UK for a week between the third and fourth Tests, I found the Trilion option to buy Team Television (and our valuable share) had finally foundered.

Back in the West Indies, using whatever local television-editing facilities were available, each evening I battled to produce the 60-minute highlight package to meet our late-night booking via a satellite uplink. Because of the time difference between the islands and India, this was usually around midnight Caribbean time. Achieving this was stressful beyond belief. We were recording onto old, multi-used low band tape – after VHS, the lowest form of videotape life. To compound the problem, the Caribbean worked in the markedly inferior American NTSC video format. The pictures were full of speckled dropout, while the sound quality could at best be described as poor. The local videotape editors allocated to me during the first two Tests could be fast and inaccurate – or slow and inaccurate.

Each day our ragbag of a finished product would be up-linked from the nearest TV headquarters to a satellite over the Atlantic and beamed from there down to the Goonhilly receiving station in south-west England. There it was converted into the PAL format, as used in India. This brought a further degradation in picture quality before it was beamed up again to another satellite over the Indian Ocean. Down it then went into a ground receiving station four miles from the New Delhi headquarters of Doordarshan, rounding off a signal journey of some 15,000 miles!

Although it's hard to believe, the pictures did somehow arrive at the other end – if occasionally in black and white. But in the four miles of underground cable between the satellite receiving station and the transmission suite in New Delhi, the sound was either absent altogether or mangled to the point of being incomprehensible!

Despite all this, throughout our tribulations in Guyana and Barbados, and indeed during the rest of the tour, Lokesh astonishingly rarely lost his cool, even when eight of his nine sponsors withdrew their support as India suffered defeat after defeat in their nine-match tour.

When we got to Port-of-Spain for the third Test, things definitely improved. If their equipment was 15 or so years old, the level of professionalism of the local crew raised John's and my spirits. The Trinidad and Tobago Television studios were within easy walking distance of the Queens Park Oval. At TTT, I met Daryl, a first-class VT editor who never seemed to tire and was fast and accurate on the buttons too. His favourite expression, yelled out in a loud voice when a batsman was dismissed, was, "Next contestant!"

During our stay in Port-of-Spain Daryl became my best and most valued ally. With the agreement of Bernard Pantin of TTT, we were able to take him with us for the remainder of our trip. Without him, as Private Frazer in *Dad's Army* would have said, we would have been "doooomed!"

Every day, in each Test, we faced at least one major logistical problem, as severe a test of character as anything being suffered by India out on the field. But somehow we battled through and survived. That is until the very last day of the tour at Sabina Park, Jamaica, where, in the fourth and final Test, the West Indies, two-nil up with one drawn, were once again giving the Indians a pasting. Behind a section of the boundary boards flourished neatly planted rows of marijuana, the crowd helping themselves as and when they felt in need of a puff.

Cameramen working downwind nearby at ground level had to be on half-hour rotas. Any longer than that and their pictures would start to go soft focus and they had difficulty in following the ball!

However, the television facilities in Kingston were the best in the Caribbean, and for the first four days all went reasonably well, certainly by comparison with what had gone before. I took up a position in a proper edit suite in the Jamaica Broadcasting headquarters. Here I had the luxury of pictures from the outside broadcast unit being beamed from the ground via a transmitting dish, located on the top of a nearby hill, and thence directly into JBC's studios.

By the hotel poolside on the fifth and final morning, John and I sat together in silent contemplation, worn out by the unending daily battle, until I tempted fate by saying, "John, I don't know how to thank you for all you've done. Virtually every day you've had a major technical catastrophe on your hands and every day, if not finding a complete solution, you've somehow got around it and kept us recording." The Windies only needed another 27 to win with nine wickets in hand. Everything that could go wrong had gone wrong but, from this point in, I was sure that nothing else could happen.

As usual in the Caribbean, such optimism was guaranteed to put the mockers on even the most rock-solid plans. With six runs wanted for victory, back at base my screens suddenly flickered and went blank. I got on the phone to the scanner and yelled, "What the hell's going on this time, John? We're going to miss the winning runs!" Back came his voice, tired and full of resignation. "Peter, you know that transmitting dish we have on the top of the pavilion to send you back the pictures? Well, a gust of wind blew it off the roof. Believe it or not, just as we were retrieving it, a beer lorry reversed straight over the dish and smashed it into a thousand pieces!"

Take it from me, our six weeks in the Caribbean was no sun-drenched beach holiday.

Later that same year Trilion ran into some terminal bad luck. They had bought us at the peak of the independent production company boom where 14 times gross profit was the norm for media takeovers. But within 24 months, rather as happened with many of the dotcom companies, the balloon not only lost much of its air, it burst asunder. With Stylus's 'help', Trillion too imploded.

So, led by Paul McCarthy, showing a business and negotiating savvy way beyond his years, we bought ourselves back from Trilion's receiver, including all our sophisticated equipment and office accommodation, for a paltry £40,000. We started again from scratch.

Thereafter, the most memorable event I got involved in was an S4C-commissioned, hour-long programme in the run-up to the first free South African elections in April 1994. It was entitled 'Mae'r wlad hon yn eiddo i ti a mi'. (This land is your land, this land is my land.) Together with Dean Smith, soundman Eddie Sinclair and our presenter, Welsh speaker Emyr Daniel, with initial research in South Africa undertaken by Beata Lipman, a former BBC Wales colleague, we set off to the land of my upbringing.

In the three weeks we were there we garnered a collection of differing views, ranging from enthusiastic optimism on the part of those Africans and Indians who had never before been recognised as citizens, let alone been allowed to vote, to whites angry that their gravy train of 350 years was about to be shunted into a siding. But, despite fears for their own and their families' personal safety, a surprising number of the whites were determined to make the best of it because "I'm a third generation white South African and this is my home."

Our most revealing moment came at what is known as a 'bush pub'. This particular one midway between Pretoria and Johannesburg was a pretty basic thatched roof on stilts in the middle of nowhere. Besides Castle lager beer, it dispensed bile and hostility. Organised by Beata, we were en route to try to get an interview with Eugene Terreblanche, the leader of the far-right Afrikaner party, later to be jailed for his part in the shooting of a number of black Africans in the vicinity of the Sun City casino.

After driving three miles down a sandy road, the pub appeared on our left. I decided to ask if we were literally on the right track, for there was no guarantee

Merlin on location. Sun City, South Africa.
Left to right: Peter Walker, Dean Smith and Eddie Sinclair

that Terreblanche would meet us, let alone talk. There were some dozen men and a few women leaning against the open-air bar. As I approached they oozed suspicion and hostility of such intensity one could almost touch it.

Dusting off my rudimentary schoolboy Afrikaans, I explained that we were a television crew from Wales, not England – always a good opening gambit, this, when confronted by any group who were mentally still fighting the Boer War in 1900 – and that we were hoping to interview Commandant Terreblanche. They lightened up at my attempt to speak their language and visibly thawed, particularly when I invited them all to have a drink while they phoned ahead to see if Terreblanche would see us.

As their confidence in us grew, I thought to myself, "A few quick interviews with this bunch should be interesting! I can just imagine what they think about the prospect of living under black rule." I explained what we'd like to do and that, although Emyr would ask his questions in English, if they so wished, I was happy to record their replies in Afrikaans and, when we did the editing, we'd sub-title these in Welsh.

Some decided they had good enough English to respond but, when a typically bull-necked, thickset man stood in front of our camera, he launched off in a tirade in Afrikaans against 'uitlanders' (foreigners) and in particular the overseas media, who were misrepresenting his country and in the process destroying his way of life.

Emyr was standing alongside cameraman Dean so our interviewee was looking virtually straight at the camera lens. Sound recordist Eddie, too, had no idea of what our interviewee was saying. I did. His final words were chilling: "Die erste kaffir dat sy kop or my grond sit, sal ek hom dood skiet!" (The first black who puts his head over my land, I'll shoot him dead!)

Midway through this sentence he had reached into his jacket pocket, pulled out a revolver and, to emphasise what he meant, pointed it directly at the lens!

Both Emyr and Dean must have thought they were about to be shot but, to their credit, stood their ground and Dean kept the camera rolling. Slowly, ever so slowly the gun was returned to its holster, unfired.

On our return to Wales I edited what I felt was a fair and balanced representation of life in the about-to-be irrevocably changed South Africa. Events in the twelve years since those elections have confounded virtually all the sceptics and banished our bush-pub drinkers even deeper into their historical hinterland.

But a year on from making that programme, David and I had become older and more tired in television terms. Soon, instead of Paul being on our side of the table, he was negotiating hard from the other to take over Merlin for himself. He knew, we knew, that he had us over the proverbial barrel, but we eventually struck a deal which gave benefits to us all.

So, in October 1995, a mere ten years since DPJ and I, an anxious pair of freelance journalists, had sat around my dining room table with our soon-to-be ex-colleagues from the BBC, we finally took our leave of what had been an exciting, unnerving at times, but always fascinating decade.

CHAPTER 17

ANOTHER DETOUR

Now I was going to enjoy the rest of life in retirement and work at getting my golfing handicap down below six. But three months later fate decreed otherwise. I needed some information about my cricketing past and called in to the Glamorgan offices in Sophia Gardens, where Mike Fatkin is one of the best Chief Executives in the country. While waiting for him to finish a phone call, my reporter's roving eye lighted on an A4 sheet of paper on his desk which had as its heading, 'Application form for the post of Director of Development for the Cricket Board of Wales'.

I had read in the press that the England and Wales Cricket Board was in the process of establishing 38 county boards, including one covering the whole of Wales. Their aim? To foster and develop amateur cricket with particular emphasis placed on creating opportunities for schoolboys and girls. Successive governments' indifference to team games meant that opportunities to play the UK's national summer game – and others too – had been severely limited. Secondary school playing fields, in particular, had been sold off, mainly for housing estates. Over a period of twenty-five years, through reducing facilities and specifically by downgrading the importance of team games in favour of non-targeted PE, the state education system has to plead guilty to causing a sporting famine throughout Britain.

I picked up the paper – Mike was on an extended call – and read down the job specification. I found myself mentally ticking off each requirement with a 'Yes, I can do that, and that, and yes, that too.' The position required the Director to lobby for, and obtain funding from, the private sector as well as local authorities, to raise the general awareness of cricket and promote its reintroduction in schools in their area.

It was common knowledge that, throughout the United Kingdom, a substantial number of adult cricket clubs needed to be cajoled into creating playing and coaching opportunities for boys and girls under the age of 19. The Director would also be responsible for establishing and running education programmes for coaches and setting up and administering fixtures for elite squads at age levels 11 to 17.

Besides a track record in playing or administering cricket, a business background would be considered an advantage.

When Mike came off the phone, I asked about the closing date. "End of this week," he said. "I might have a go at this," I replied. Things moved quickly thereafter. I made the short list and was offered the job on a three-year contract, thus extending my working life and once again putting serious golf improvement on the back burner.

The ECB would provide some start-up funding, and each of the 38 Boards had to submit a detailed business plan to one of its offshoots, the Cricket Foundation. Over three years it had been allocated £7 million for junior development. There were only two months to go before submissions had to be in. Creating a detailed business plan from scratch to such a mighty tight deadline led to the busiest six weeks of my life.

The first requirement was a whistle-stop, self-educational tour around Wales. Right from the start I was determined that the Cricket Board of Wales would be just that, not merely concentrating on the densely populated South Wales area where two-thirds of Wales' population of three million live. I had meetings with virtually every sports development officer in the 22 county councils, their heads of department and the heads of education too, hammering home the message of the social, physical and behavioural benefits of their supporting team games in general and junior cricket in particular.

Eventually, after 16-hour days spent travelling, talking, gathering information, analysing, writing and re-writing, the CBW's Business Plan was finished. On the final day for acceptance, 15 copies dropped onto the desks of the Cricket Foundation's offices at Lord's.

On the practical level, I was able to hit the ground running because Tom Cartwright, the former Warwickshire, Somerset, Glamorgan and England all-rounder had, for more than a decade, been the National Coach of the Welsh Cricket Association, the governing body of amateur cricket in Wales. Tom had already set up and overseen seven volunteer regional development committees and a wide ranging programme of Coach Education courses, in addition to being virtually the sole selector and manager of the Under 16 and 17 national teams, the only ones existent at the time.

So Tom had done all the preliminary spadework and saved me from what would have been a massive task. Indeed it would not be an exaggeration to say that, starting from scratch, it would have taken me all of my three-year term to create and bed in a suitable system. My first task, therefore, was to concentrate on doing some widespread additional seeding and nurturing.

With Tom Cartwright, National Coach of Wales. One of the old school who believes in the importance of correct technique, hours of practice and playing in a sporting manner.

If junior cricket in Wales is now in good shape, with a growing number of senior clubs running junior sections and giving opportunities to the most talented youngsters in their senior league teams, much of the credit for this belongs to Tom Cartwright whose commitment to, nay obsession with, the game of cricket will have an influence way beyond both of our lifetimes.

But Tom and I both knew from the start, that our horizons would be limited by what slice of the available cake came our way. Did it help that my old cricketing compatriot and flat-mate, Ossie Wheatley, chaired the Foundation? Tom too had played with him during his days at Warwickshire, and they had a great respect for each other. When considering the 38 bids for funding, I've no doubt Ossie remained totally impartial but, when the news came through that we had been granted £105,000 in year one, the fifth highest amount awarded, I felt that we could go places and would be able to take the game into most sporting nooks and crannies in Wales. I recognised, too, that Ossie's appreciation of the vast distances and peculiarities associated with living and working in Wales had played a key part in the evaluation of the amount we had received.

With former captain, team- and flat-mate, Ossie Wheatley, Chairman of the Cricket Foundation. Handing over a cheque to fund the Cricket Board of Wales' development of junior cricket.

However, despite Tom's and my efforts, and those of my successors, Mark Frost and Geoff Holmes, ex-Glamorgan players both, youth cricket still remains something of a non-runner in state secondary schools although it does retain an important toehold in the independent sector at Monmouth, Llandovery and Brecon.

During my period in office, the 1999 World Cup was played in Britain. In Cardiff the Australians were billeted with us for their two-week preparation period ahead of a competition they were to go on and win. All competing national teams were contractually bound to hold a coaching session for local youngsters in their training area. I circulated all the 200 cricket clubs in Wales, inviting them to send a maximum of three junior members to our two-hour session at Sophia Gardens.

The faces of those Aussie superstars, when they found 300 eager youngsters waiting for them, should have been captured on film! However, they were collectively brilliant, none more so than Shane Warne. The Australians divided themselves into pairs and took up stations in a huge circle around the Sophia Gardens outfield. Groups of ten youngsters then spent fifteen minutes with each pair before moving on around the circle.

I walked around on the inside, monitoring how things were going. Warne was showing an enraptured group of youngsters the various grips and the action needed to bowl leg-spinners and googlies. He then sent one lad down 22 yards away to act as wicket-keeper. Taking no more than two strides and talking throughout, explaining what he was doing, Warne then bowled three leg-breaks which the keeper took comfortably. Then, as he walked back, he winked and whispered to the others at his end, "Watch this". He then bowled a perfect googly which the keeper read as another leg-break and missed by yards! There was much hilarity amongst those at Warne's end, but he immediately went down to the bemused youngster, put an arm around him, picked up the ball and, taking a pen from his track suit, signed it before stuffing it into the lad's pocket as a souvenir.

The scheduled two-hour session lasted nearly three, for to a man the Australians stayed on and signed every book, scrap of paper, bat, glove and pad that was thrust in front of them. When it comes to contesting the Ashes, Australians may be single-minded and ruthless competitors, but that day in Cardiff they demonstrated the true heart and spirit of cricket.

They were three very happy, very busy, very tiring years. The cash from the Foundation – plus substantial financial support from two influential figures in the Sports Council of Wales, Graham Davies and Mark Frost, the latter a one-time Surrey and Glamorgan opening bowler who later succeeded me at the CBW – enabled us to appoint full-time cricket development officers in North Wales (John Huband) and Mid-Wales (Bill Higginson). The Cardiff and Vale of Glamorgan areas were already well served by Malcolm Price, a former headmaster whose demonic energy levels and commitment to junior cricket was matched only by our National Coach.

But, due to some restrictions on how we could spend the Foundation's money, there remained three 'black holes' in our development programme coverage: in the far west of Wales, in the Swansea area and in the county of Gwent. I was able to convince the management committee of the newly constituted CBW and the Sports Council for Wales that we had three prime winter assets right on our own doorstep: Glamorgan first-team regulars, Steve Watkin, Tony Cottey and Steve James. With the approval of Mike Fatkin, who also became Secretary to the CBW, Steve Watkin who lived near Maesteg took over responsibility for Swansea, Tony Cottey whose home was not far from

Llanelli handled the enormous patch in the west taking in Carmarthenshire, Ceredigion and Pembrokeshire while Cardiff-based Steve James concentrated his efforts in the county of Gwent.

I reckoned, particularly in the early days of CBW, that having high-profile, first-class cricketers going into schools would prove inspirational to youngsters and help to draw them into our net.

By their enthusiastic efforts the three professionals proved this to be true. Since then, all have moved on but, looking back, they, together with Messrs Higginson, Huband and Price, spread the gospel by establishing CBW's presence in junior cricket development in the north, south, east and west of Wales.

The CBW Board members, drawn from all parts of Wales, had an able and efficient treasurer in Graham Crimp, who kept me from being too headstrong as well as fending off my regular claims for new tyres because of the vast mileage I was clocking up! Also invaluable was the penetrating, often acerbic, analysis of what I was up to, or planning to do, from Dr. Richard Kemp of University College, Aberystwyth.

It was hinted that some of the heated correspondence between Richard and me has been lodged in the National Library of Wales for future historians to smile over – but this may be just a rumour.

At the end of my three-year contract I was asked if I would stay on for a further year by David Morgan, then a very supportive CBW chairman who also chaired Glamorgan CCC before moving on to become chairman of the ECB itself. But I felt I'd virtually run my course and turned it down. With a

Spreading the gospel. School group in Rhondda, Cynon Taff, one of the first Welsh local authorities to recognise and support the promoting of cricket in their schools.

clear conscience, I took the view that it was inappropriate for a 63-year-old man to be in charge of youth cricket. In any case, after my departure, the ever-reliable and apparently ageless Tom Cartwright would still be there to provide continuity, which he did until he retired in 2002.

In my three years as Director, I believe that I did increase awareness of the joys and benefits of supporting junior cricket in each of the 22 Welsh local authorities, a response which has lasted to this day.

It was time for the 'evangelist' to move on. But well before that, and at a dinner where I was guest speaker, I gained an all-important three-year sponsorship deal for our national teams from age 11 right through to 17. This came about, following an impassioned speech about deprived kids in the Rhondda valley who had cricketing talent but no horizons to aim at. After I sat down, my table companions, senior executives from CarnaudMetalbox, the huge Neath-based sheet metal factory, immediately volunteered to help in any way I wanted. Thanks to them we became the smartest, best turned out, best behaved teams in UK junior cricket, and we played like champions too.

During my time at CBW, I'd been approached to become involved in a new golfing development at Hensol, some eight miles west of Cardiff's city centre. Two pals of mine, golf professional Peter Johnson and Dave Haller, a highly respected Olympic swimming coach, urged me to join them in a new golf and leisure venture which, over time, they believed would become the best in Wales.

Peter had obtained a lease, with the option to buy down the line, sufficient farming land to build two 18-hole golf courses. By the time the pair approached me, they had received planning permission for the first phase: a driving range and a nine-hole course. I hummed and hawed, instinct telling me that collectively we didn't have enough financial clout to make a go of it. But in the end, and much against commercial logic, friendship won me over. Soon after committing myself, and thinking I might persuade him to invest, I decided to approach the father of my former Merlin colleague, Paul McCarthy, about taking a financial stake in the project.

Mike McCarthy, or 'Boss' as he was known to his family – and to me – was a hugely successful property developer. I walked him around the still virgin fields, with grass up to his waist. A blunt, no bullshit operator, Mike got back into my car. There was no need to ask for his support. "Peter," he immediately said. "I have two business rules in life. I never put money into anything that eats or grows!"

Despite this rejection, we pressed ahead. The range started to make a few bob but, without proper funding, the course Peter eventually had to design was never going to attract serious golfers. I then had a mini-brainwave. Why not talk to the man who lived in a lovely house at the end of the fields bordering our land about coming on board? Creator of three large out-of-town department stores, Gerald Leeke certainly had the financial wherewithal to make our dream come true. A more than decent club cricketer in his day, I knew him reasonably well. During my time with Merlin we'd done a number of television commercials for his stores, and he'd also underwritten our journeys around the world when following the world squash championships which were televised by Sky.

It took many months to persuade the cautious accountant Gerald to take the bait, but finally he did. Throwing men, money and energy at the development, he almost overnight transformed the Vale of Glamorgan Golf and Country Club so that by 2008, two years ahead of the Ryder Cup coming to Wales, it will undoubtedly be one of the UK's finest leisure complexes.

Understandably Gerald eventually wished to buy out founder directors, Peter, Dave and me, together with the other original shareholders, Ginny Golding and John Saunders. It was typical of the man that at the time he gained 100% control of the Vale, Gerald threw in life membership for us all and our direct families while, on the golfing side, Gerald kept Dave and me on board as directors with Peter remaining as Director of Golf until he too moved on to develop his own golfing project near the top of Caerphilly mountain.

Thanks to Gerald's vision and drive the Vale of Glamorgan currently has two 18-hole championship courses, the Welsh National and The Lake, a well-stocked pro-shop complete with experienced teaching professionals, a splendid 145-bed hotel and an almost football-sized £3 million Astroturf indoor training Academy. So impressive is this facility that not only do the Welsh rugby and football squads make this and the hotel their winter home, but the 2005 British Lions too took up residence ahead of their departure to New Zealand – even though it didn't do them much good!

A state-of-the-art leisure centre, with 5,000 members and a golf driving range with a bar, lounge and restaurant, complete the current picture. The further acquisition of surrounding land, including the former Hensol Castle hospital, will enable the development of a spa and upmarket health centre and offer wooded walks and fishing in the large adjoining lake. All this is due to come on stream well ahead of the 2010 Ryder Cup at nearby Celtic Manor.

In the future, quality time-share villas alongside the Lake course's 10th hole will be able to absorb any overspill from the hotel, while lining the road into the complex the stone-built former hospital wards are to be converted into apartments.

I wouldn't be surprised if, by the time the overall development is finished, it will be worth something in the region of £300 million. From the very small acorn they inherited from us founders, Gerald and his eldest son Stephen, now Managing Director, are in the process of creating a legacy of which they, and Wales, can be justifiably proud.

Was being in at the start of this now massive project to be my final 'hurrah' in life?

Well actually, it so nearly was.

A month and a half after retiring from the Cricket Board of Wales job, I played a round of golf with my former BBC boss, Onllwyn Brace, one-time Head of Sport at BBC Wales. The following day my wife Sue and I were due to fly to Pisa for a five-day holiday which included performances of two Puccini operas, *La Bohème* and *Turandot*. It was a mighty hot day and, at the end of our 18 holes, I had two pints of ice-cold lager.

That night my stomach started to rumble, loud enough to waken Sue. First thing next morning I popped down to see our GP who prodded me and said, "I don't think it's anything serious, but take these enema pills. I'm sure they'll clear it out." Nothing happened. I still had a bit of a stomach ache as we drove to Gatwick, boarded the plane, landed at Pisa, drove to our hotel 30 miles from the city and went for a walk to the top of a nearby mountain village. At a small restaurant, sitting outside under an awning, we had a pleasant lunch. Having eaten, I felt a little better.

It was the last food I was to take on board for 15 days.

Waking the next morning, my stomach was a little distended, but I wasn't in much pain, just a feeling of slight discomfort. The evening outdoor performance of *La Bohème* was spectacular and took my mind off my ills, but on the 45-minute return coach trip I had to loosen my trousers for my stomach had further increased in girth. I now looked about four months pregnant.

That night I couldn't bear to have even a sheet rest on it. At my suggestion, the next day Sue went off to do a spot of sight-seeing while I stayed in the hotel room. When she got back things certainly hadn't improved so she called a doctor. He too thought I needed an enema and prescribed one. But again, no result.

Off we went to that night's performance of *Turandot*. I made it to the end of the first act but now, in serious discomfort, I left to lie down on a wooden bench in a square outside the theatre, staying there until soon after 11 o'clock when the performance was over. This time the coach ride back to our hotel was a real ordeal.

Near midnight Sue and I were dropped off at an all-night surgery. Another doctor examined me. He'd spent a number of years in New York and spoke good English. Despite looking like a middleweight boxer who'd had too many losing fights, his diagnosis was familiar. "We see a lot of this sort of thing around here among visitors. Here, you take this enema, that'll fix it."

Whatever he prescribed also drew a blank. The next day matters worsened still further. The pain now was ever present, and I didn't leave my hotel room at all until departure time. The coach ride back to Pisa airport for our return trip to the UK is something I shall never forget. It stopped for an hour's sight-seeing at a town called Lucca, Puccini's birthplace. In the dusty coach parking area I went and lay down on the exposed, gnarled roots of a large tree. By comparison these were comfortable with what was going on inside me.

It was past midnight when we arrived back in Cardiff and, after a sleepless night, I was first in the queue the following morning at the doctor's surgery. He took one look at the size of my bloated stomach and said, "This isn't what I saw five days ago; we'd better get you straight to hospital."

Llandough Hospital is roughly three miles from Cardiff's city centre. The next five days were taken up with a series of inconclusive tests. I was allowed out for the weekend but had to return on Monday, when I was spun around in a body scanner, made a few more visits to the x-ray department and had numerous blood tests and regular ward visits from the Registrar. In the end he came clean. "Mr Walker, you've got so much by way of faeces inside you that we can't get any decent x-ray pictures. I'm going to give you an enema; that'll shift it." I felt like I was greeting an old friend.

Whatever it was the hospital concocted could have put a man on the moon! Six visits to the loo later my insides must have been as clean as a jaybird. I was relieved too for, like a pricked balloon, my swollen stomach had also deflated. After another visit to the radiography department and a scan, I returned to the ward and started to gather up my things, preparing to leave.

Then the matron came up and said, "Mr. Walker, your x-rays are back. Could you just pop down the corridor and see the Registrar?" I knocked on his door and entered.

He came straight to the point. "Mr. Walker, I'm afraid I have some bad news. You have colon cancer."

How did I feel? Funnily enough, relatively phlegmatic. Perhaps it was nature's way of cushioning the shock. The Registrar went on to say that the cancerous growth was near the end of the intestine leading to the anus, and I would need an operation within the next few days. He added that surgeon Andrew Ratcliffe would come to talk me through it the next morning. A phone call to break the news to Sue rapidly brought her and son Daniel to my bedside. They seemed to be more concerned than I was. All the usual encouraging platitudes were exchanged between us: "We'll fight this together", "They must have got it before it was inoperable" and "You'll be back home soon."

Families always do their best in such circumstances, but they cannot share or take away the cancer. I was allowed home for the night and then it was back to Llandough to await Mr. Ratcliffe's visit.

While I was awaiting the outcome of my tests, I had been put in an 18-strong, all-male ward. It was full of diverse characters. If hospitals weren't such citadels of suffering, ours would have made a wonderful setting for a television sitcom. There was an elderly Pakistani who refused to eat the insipid hospital food, claiming the staff were trying to poison him. So each night his five sons would come in, carrying a variety of takeaway dishes which they shared with their father behind the drawn curtains around his bed. Wafts of spicy curry aromas nearly drove the rest of us – on jelly and blancmange – mad with desire.

An amateur astronomer on the other side of the ward, with waving arms à la Patrick Moore, gave us detailed lectures on the relevance of a full eclipse of the sun, which took place while I was in Llandough.

Around two o'clock one morning, a chap four beds down from me, who was on a couple of intravenous drips, suddenly flipped. He wanted to go home to Lydney. As he tried to heave himself out of bed the two female night-duty nurses battled to restrain him. I was the most able-bodied amongst the rest of the patients, all of whom had been woken by this commotion, so I trotted down to the man's bedside to try to calm him down and get him to stay put.

To take his mind off his determination to leave, I lay down alongside him and asked him to tell me about his problems The tactic succeeded for he dropped back onto his pillow and started off on his life story, saying at regular intervals that he wasn't going to stay in hospital as they wouldn't tell him why he was here. Like the Pakistani on the other side of the ward, he was convinced the hospital staff were out to kill him!

During his ramblings the senior nurse came around on my side and whispered in my ear that her colleague had gone to get male nursing help and a strong sedative to calm the patient down. In the semi-darkness of the ward my 'bedmate' rambled on. I stayed at his side and, to keep his mind on his story, I offered the odd grunt of sympathy. Back came the junior nurse, syringe in hand, and, creeping up around the bed, he plunged it into my left buttock, squeezing its contents into me. "No, it's not me," I hissed, pointing at the form next to mine. "It's him you want to knock out."

It was the last thing I remember for it was broad daylight when I finally surfaced from the sedative-induced coma. The difficult patient had disappeared, leaving me with a hangover of king-sized proportions!

Three hours before my operation I recall sitting by myself in the visitors' lounge at the end of our ward and looking out over green fields towards the distant town of Barry. Thoughts like, "Will I get off the slab? What if I don't wake up? And if I do, what sort of life lies ahead? Would it be full of pain and a long, lingering death?" But a strange kind of peace drifted over me. If it was indeed to be the end, what regrets did I have? Other than I wished that I had not been the source of the grief I'd inflicted on Sarah and Justin, the two children by my first marriage, it had been an unusual, complex and varied sort of a life. I concluded that, if my life membership was about to be rescinded, so be it.

The operation was scheduled for five in the afternoon. At three, surgeon Andrew Ratcliffe came into the ward, partly I suspect to make sure I hadn't done a runner. Back in the lounge I'd decided to make two important phone calls before being taken off to the operating theatre. One to Tony Parfitt, my valued financial advisor for over thirty years, the other to Philip Howell-Richardson, a lawyer pal. Both were executors of my will.

The nursing staff were petrified of Mr. Ratcliffe. I was told later that in the operating theatre he could become something of a monster if the staff weren't doing their jobs to his satisfaction. To patients he certainly was brusque, lacking the kind of caring bedside manner normally portrayed in TV soap operas. But he had a first-rate reputation as a surgeon, which was good enough for me as I didn't expect to be talking to him much once he got out his scalpel. Anyway, he came around the side of my bed, grunted a "hello" and sat down to tell me what he was hoping to achieve by the operation. I then told him about the two vital phone calls I wished to make. He turned to the matron hovering behind him. "What time are you giving Mr. Walker his pre-med pills?" he asked.

I was aware that these were to put the patient into a relaxed and calm frame of mind before an operation. "At a quarter to four, Mr. Ratcliffe," came the reply. Turning back to me he said, without a flicker of a smile, "Well, if I were you, I wouldn't make any important calls after four o'clock because you won't know what you're saying." Then he was gone – as was I when the pills kicked in, shortly after the appointed hour.

However, I do vaguely recall that, as I was loaded onto a trolley and wheeled off to the operating theatre, my fellow ward inmates gave me a round of applause. Had I a cricket bat with me or a cap on my head, I'm sure I would have raised both in acknowledgement of their support.

"Come on, wake up, Mr. Walker, you're back where you belong." Reluctantly opening my eyes, I glanced around. The surroundings were familiar, so too were the three nurses gathered around my bed. Only my position in the ward had changed; I had been moved next to the night nurse's desk so she could keep a post-operative eye on me. As I became more compos mentis I looked left and right. There were various tubes coming from a number of parts of my body, but I was not in any discomfort – at least not then. But a few hours later, as the anaesthetic gradually wore off, I developed a searing lower-back pain aggravated, I'm sure, by the firm, rippled rubber mattress placed underneath post-operation patients to promote circulation and prevent bedsores.

Regular shots of self-administered morphine certainly helped, but for the next four days, if a knacker's van had pulled up outside our ward, I swear that I would have somehow levered myself upright and hitched a lift.

My recovery wasn't helped by a chatty night nurse. She came from the valley town of Tonyrefail and throughout the night was constantly on the phone to a female confidante, discussing in lurid, intimate detail how she was juggling three men in her life: a randy husband and two equally demanding and seemingly highly sexed lovers, none of whom was apparently aware of the other two! A few days after my operation and around four in the morning, desperate for some sleep, I suggested she include me in her conversations as I felt she was in need of some independent counselling. Unsurprisingly my kind offer was turned down, and for my part I certainly wasn't in any sort of a position to offer her anything by way of her usual distractions.

However, a day or so later, I was transported by ambulance to the less exhausting and emotionally charged surroundings at the BUPA hospital on the other side of Cardiff. I badly needed the rest and recuperation. Slowly my body came to terms with the missing six or so inches of colon, but there was still one final bit of post-operative pain to experience. Like all bowel cancer patients I'd had a catheter inserted in my penis to allow me to pass urine. After a week, the time came to have it removed so the nurse in charge told me to sit in a hot tub and it would gently float out of its own accord. Of course it didn't, even when I gave it a couple of gentle, but very painful, tugs to try to help it on its way. She looked in to see me wrestling with this very embarrassing state of affairs. "Having a bit of a problem are we?" she said and, reaching down into the water, she suddenly gave it one mighty, freeing heave. I swear my feet touched the ceiling, and the yell of animalistic pain must have been heard the other side of the Bristol Channel! I was mighty pleased when I eventually got home – far away from my BUPA 'carer' and from the emotional roller-coaster of life in Llandough hospital.

CHAPTER 18
THERE'S MORE TO LIFE

Under the sympathetic eye and the listening ear of oncologist Mr Tim Maughan, a saint on earth if ever there was one, there followed six months of chemotherapy. This remarkable man's cancer clinic at Velindre Hospital in Cardiff gives hope to those without it, comfort to those who sense their remaining days on earth are few and confidence to those who eventually survive. I am lucky to be one of the latter.

Chemo is a wide conglomerate of drugs, mixed together in various proportions depending on the location of the cancer. Although it's been the standard post-cancer treatment for many years, the medical profession are still not completely sure as to why it works in some cases but not in others. Before I left Llandough, Andrew Ratcliffe had said to me, "It's a sort of insurance policy. It not only kills off malignant cells but others as well. So you may find your immune system takes a hell of a battering." On this, for him a rather cheerful note, we said our goodbyes. I owe him a great debt of gratitude, not only for his skills as a surgeon but for his quirkish sense of humour which mirrored my own.

My own treatment consisted of carrying around in a bag strapped to my waist a load of this potentially lethal cocktail, which drip-fed, via something called a 'pic line', into a vein less than half an inch from my heart. The tiny tube, or pic, is inserted into a main vein in an arm just above the elbow. Within a matter of seconds it has travelled along the vein to stop just short of penetrating your heart. That's providing the highly trained nursing staff have measured the distance correctly!

This ingestion of chemo lasted for a week, followed by a week off. The 'on' weeks were inhibiting, but I was one of the lucky ones. I kept what hair I had left and, other than a feeling of great tiredness, sailed through the treatment. The 'off' weeks cheered me up for I was able to return to the golf range, renewing my eternal quest for golf's holy grail, the perfect swing.

However, sitting in the Velindre Hospital waiting room to see Tim Maughan for my monthly check-up was a sombre experience. Looking around, the image of being in a line leading to a Nazi gas chamber was a recurring thought. To overcome this, Tim was unfailingly encouraging, so much so that the expressions on the faces of those emerging from his presence nearly always radiated new hope.

What perked me up too was that I could go back to making a few bob at after-dinner speaking at cricket clubs, Rotary and Round Table meetings, charity events, golf clubs and, once even, the Lord Mayor's annual banquet at the Guildhall in London. Over the years I had either personally experienced or plagiarised a raft of repeatable-in-mixed-company anecdotes, an essential if your captive audience to drop off.

Onllwyn Brace and my former Merlin co-director David Parry-Jones had also started a project called the Wales Video Library or Living Obituaries, as we privately called it. They went around doing extensive, in-depth interviews with people who had something to say about their lives in, or affecting, Wales. I felt privileged to be one of their subjects but equally flattered to be asked to do a number of those interviews. Over 230 men and women of Wales have bared their souls. The unedited tapes are stored in the National Library of Wales in Aberystwyth, to provide invaluable research material for future historians.

While at the Cricket Board of Wales I'd added an additional arrow to my quiver by becoming a so-called tour leader for the Tewkesbury-based Gullivers Sports Travel company. During my annual leave, and still to this day, I head up parties of between 20 and 70 England supporters who follow their team around the world on their winter tours. Other old cricketing lags like me who fill this role have included Norman Cowans, Jim Cumbes, Mike Denness, Mike Gatting, Norman Graham, Warren Hegg, Alan Oakman, Clive Radley and Derek Underwood.

The real work, covering flight bookings, land transport, transfers, hotel accommodation and match bookings is the responsibility of Clare Powell, Phil Dumbelton and the mainly female Gullivers staff, in particular Rachel Barber and Geraldine Norris. They are all supremely gifted organisers. We former players' role is to talk with their tour parties about the day's play and about cricket generally. In addition I also arrange cricket forums in the evening where the likes of Ali Bacher, Jack Bannister, Henry Blofeld, Pat Murphy and my fellow tour leaders, plus occasionally members of the England touring party, expound on the game and answer questions.

Gullivers have taken me to every major cricket playing country in the world. An astonishingly diverse range of people go on these tours, all sorts from High Court judges to redundant park labourers.

On my first trip, to South Africa in 1995, we had as clients a Japanese Professor of Mathematics at Manchester University and his daughter. He spoke not a word of English and recorded every ball in his self-created, Japanese-notated scorebook. The Prof always wore a Beau Geste type of cap with a flap protecting his neck and gave a short, high-pitched maniacal cackle and loopy-looking return smile, even when just greeted with a mere "good morning". Every match day his solicitous daughter brought to the ground a dozen or so small plastic cartons of presumably Japanese food and would occasionally leave her father's side to sidle up to me and ask in-depth, complex questions such as "Does this bowler have a computer data base on this batsman?" or "What is the difference when the bowler rubs the ball on the back or front of his trousers?"

I had a sneaking feeling that they must have got on the wrong plane in Manchester but, on landing in South Africa, decided to make the best of it there rather than re-route to Tokyo!

I also led a group of 20 supporters to Pakistan, a 'dry' country in every sense of the word. However, as foreigners we soon discovered that, providing we signed a provincial government form stating that we were alcoholics, we could get a limited supply of the only beer produced in the country. It was called Murree and its main constituent seemed to be helium gas. The local gin wasn't much better either.

Members of that group included Britain's first nuclear submarine commander, two BP executives who were like Bill and Ben of flowerpot fame, a chain-smoking and proud lesbian, a man who was a former head of NatWest Bank's training division with a wicked sense of humour, another who claimed to be a retired Durham miner but who turned out never to have been at the coal face, having worked above ground in administration all his life, and a small man who, day after day, wore nothing but a singlet and the briefest of day-glow lycra shorts. He was nicknamed 'Wiggie' because his slicked down hair looked as if it had been glued on.

On this same trip – and on many others too – came someone known to us all as 'The Invisible Man'. I've never met anyone with such an encyclopaedic memory of cricketing personalities and facts. He delighted in approaching anyone who claimed similar wide-ranging knowledge of the game and baffling them with the most obscure questions, to which I suspect only he and *Wisden Cricketers' Almanack* knew the answers.

Oh yes, he was known as The Invisible Man because he rarely appeared at more than the first and last days of a five-day Test match, no one knowing where he went between.

Most trips have a small group of dedicated scorers. They usually sit together in a line, scorebooks on knees, recording every ball bowled. At the lunch and tea intervals they'll compare individual scores and totals which very occasionally don't agree. Often the problem comes over the type of extras that have been signalled by the umpires. These debates can sometimes get a little heated and last the duration of the game's intervals.

In such company I sometimes feel my role is superfluous, for most of them appear to know far more about the game than I do! But they provide an interesting, if different, perspective on a game in which I've been deeply immersed for nearly five decades.

Nor has the umbilical cord that ties me to cricket been completely severed – for, along with a group of eight other former professional cricketers, I operate as one of the England and Wales Board's Pitch Liaison Officers, PLOs for short. We prowl around the grounds where first-class cricket is played, sitting in judgment on the quality of pitches provided. The job's been described as a horticultural variation on 'watching paint dry', but it's much more than that and, over a period of five years, I believe it has led to a marked improvement in the quality of first-class pitches throughout the country.

During my five years as a PLO, I haven't come across a single strip which I felt was unfit for first-class cricket. The penalties are a severe deterrent to any county found guilty of wilfully producing such a surface. In my playing days, when pitches were uncovered, home sides quite openly prepared pitches which favoured their own bowling attacks. For example, when we went to Derbyshire, we expected to see a green pitch often indistinguishable from the rest of the square; it suited down to the ground men such as Les Jackson,

Harold 'Dusty' Rhodes and Alan Ward. When they came to us, they expected, and met, a Swansea dustbowl where Don Shepherd in particular was a match winner.

My view is that today's pitches are by and large too bland, producing equally bland batsmen who are long on crease occupancy but short on a variety of batting techniques and skills. Nowadays, there is even biodegradable glue available which sticks the surface together; a useful add-on if the pitch has been previously used. It provides precious little assistance to bowlers but gives a huge comfort zone to any half-decent batsman. I belong to the school which believes a game of cricket should always be a contest between bat and ball.

I also believe that the influx of overseas and Kolpak players into our game has become a cricketing albatross. Initially it was an excellent idea, with the cream of the world's cricketers appearing, men like Viv Richards, Gordon Greenidge, Mike Procter, Barry Richards, Alan Donald, Andy Roberts, Gary Sobers and Allan Border. Home-grown players used to draw inspiration from playing alongside the best in the world. But now, due to the ever-increasing international programme, they have been replaced by players who are minor even in their own domestic patch, and this has severely retarded the development of home-grown talent.

In my view there is a relatively simple solution. Adopt the American Football 'Draft' system. In outline it would operate like this:

ECB circulates all the world's cricketing nations, saying that any overseas player wishing to play county cricket has to register with them, not with individual counties. A pre-condition will be that they must make themselves available for a full English season and declare their interest by 31st December each year. From the respondents, the ECB selects 18 names, comprising six each of batsmen, bowlers and all-rounders, with a reserve list of six more.

The ECB fixes and controls, on a single-season contract basis, one payment rate for all, thus saving the counties from the present auction which drains money out of the English game.

The side that finishes bottom of Division 2 has first pick; next from bottom then follows and so on until the side that topped division 1 has the last choice. The overseas players will not have a choice of where they ply their trade. If a county wishes to pass on its first choice, it will have the chance to look again at what's left of the list at the end of selection process. But there will be no obligation to do so.

This will ensure that British-born and domiciled players will have more opportunities. The game here will no longer be, as it is at present, a big earner for outsiders. But as what to do about Kolpak players? Unfortunately that's a matter for the lawyers of the land!

The camaraderie that exists amongst those who have played the game professionally at first-class level could well be compared to a masonic brotherhood. Throughout the world, where the game of cricket exists, you'll run into a friend, the stories will flow and there'll be much laughter shared at past indiscretions and failures as well as recalled triumphs.

Sons Daniel and Justin with their old man. Nowadays all are better golfers than cricketers!

Can it really be sixty years since that barefoot primary schoolboy in Johannesburg charged into the nets and tried to bowl as fast as he could? That lad has experienced an extraordinary roller-coaster of a ride through life. It's often been thrilling, sometimes depressing but on balance immensely fulfilling. Sure, with a more roundhead rather than cavalier approach to his cricketing career, he could perhaps have done more at international level – but then many others could say the same too.

To have, albeit briefly, stood at the top of cricket's Everest, metaphorically shoulder-to-shoulder with the game's equivalents of Hillary and Tensing, was reward enough.

But in addition there were other things in life which were to arouse his curiosity and act as channels for all that restless energy. There was royalty to meet, historic performers in other sports to shake hands with, men and women of influence to learn from, and breath-catching moments: like a full moon rising behind the hills surrounding Port Alfred on the Eastern Cape, or the beautiful sounds of the Ex Cathedra choir which never fail to soothe current fears or troubles.

But all these blessings go back to that 16-year-old's desire to become a professional cricketer. The game has been, and continues to be, the hub of his life, bringing pleasure – and very occasionally pain too.

But that's the story of life for most us. In his case it's been great fun.

A BRIEF STATISTICAL DIGEST

Peter Michael Walker

Born: 17 February 1936

BATTING AND FIELDING IN ALL FIRST–CLASS CRICKET

Year	Matches	Inns	NO	Runs	HS	Average	Ct
1956	7	11	4	65	15*	9.28	2
1956/7 South Africa	1	2	–	10	8	5.00	2
1957	20	33	1	603	60	18.84	24
1957/8 South Africa	3	6	–	75	27	12.50	6
1958	30	50	6	1052	104*	23.90	34
1959	31	53	7	1564	113	34.00	65
1960	32	55	2	900	68	16.98	69
1960/1 West Indies	3	5	–	204	67	40.80	3
1961	35	64	10	1347	112*	24.94	73
1962	34	61	9	1528	152*	29.38	48
1962/3 South Africa	3	6	–	96	60	16.00	4
1963	18	29	6	510	45	22.17	18
1964	31	52	6	1057	100	22.97	41
1965	30	46	6	1307	99	32.67	54
1966	27	50	6	1213	95*	27.56	42
1967	28	46	7	1149	103*	29.46	38
1967/8 Pakistan	7	9	4	325	112	65.00	6
1968	27	48	8	1032	121*	25.80	33
1969	27	38	10	925	73	33.03	29
1969/70 West Indies	2	4	1	149	48	49.66	3
1970	27	49	6	1049	114	24.39	39
1971	27	45	2	1120	120	26.04	37
1972	19	26	9	370	61*	21.76	27
TOTAL	**469**	**788**	**110**	**17650**	**152***	**26.03**	**697**

He hit 13 centuries and 92 fifties.

His highest innings was:

152*	Glamorgan v Middlesex	Lord's	1962

BATTING AND FIELDING IN TEST CRICKET

Year	Matches	Inns	NO	Runs	HS	Average	Ct
1960	3	4	–	128	52	32.00	5

BATTING AND FIELDING IN ONE–DAY CRICKET

Years	Matches	Inns	NO	Runs	HS	Average	Ct
1964–72	72	68	7	1218	79	19.96	32

BOWLING IN ALL FIRST–CLASS CRICKET

Year	Overs	Maidens	Runs	Wickets	Average
1956	20	10	36	1	36.00
1956/7 South Africa	*4*	*–*	*32*	*–*	*–*
1957	357.3	94	871	36	24.19
1957/8 South Africa	*45*	*10*	*156*	*6*	*26.00*
1958	479.1	125	1276	36	35.44
1959	815	192	2226	80	27.82
1960	633.2	179	1643	57	28.82
1960/1 West Indies	*90*	*15*	*260*	*10*	*26.00*
1961	998.2	333	2429	101	24.04
1962	1004.1	304	2397	89	26.93
1962/3 South Africa	*101*	*36*	*214*	*3*	*71.33*
1963	302.2	115	614	24	25.58
1964	682.4	218	1564	47	33.27
1965	215	80	534	11	48.54
1966	272.5	90	672	23	29.21
1967	673.3	224	1513	62	24.40
1967/8 Pakistan	*193*	*38*	*505*	*11*	*45.90*
1968	462.5	141	1172	42	27.90
1969	616.2	229	1447	61	23.72
1969/70 West Indies	*59.5*	*11*	*191*	*6*	*31.83*
1970	686	224	1599	60	26.65
1971	567.3	165	1449	39	37.15
1972	392.3	107	1081	29	37.27
TOTAL	**9671.5 †**	**2940**	**23881**	**834**	**28.63**

† *includes 49 eight–ball overs in South Africa in 1956/7 and 1957/8*

He took five wickets in an innings on 25 occasions.
He took ten wickets in a match twice.

His best innings figures were:

34– 14 – 58 – 7	Glamorgan v Middlesex	Lord's	1962

BOWLING IN TEST CRICKET

Year	Overs	Maidens	Runs	Wickets	Average
1960	13	3	34	–	–

BOWLING IN ONE–DAY CRICKET

Years	Overs	Maidens	Runs	Wickets	Average
1964–72	306.4	40	1065	52	20.48

INDEX